D1601570

Writing as Freedom, Writing as Testimony

Judaic Traditions in Literature, Music, and Art
Ken Frieden and Harold Bloom, *Series Editors*

Writing as Freedom, Writing as Testimony

FOUR ITALIAN WRITERS AND JUDAISM

Sergio Parussa

SYRACUSE UNIVERSITY PRESS

First Edition 2008

08 09 10 11 12 13   6 5 4 3 2 1

An earlier version of chapter 1, "The Maternal Borders of the Soul: Identity, Judaism, and Writing in the Works of Umberto Saba," was published in the Italian journal *Psicologie e identità*: "I confini materni dell'anima: note su identità, ebraismo e scrittura nell'opera di Umberto Saba." *Psicologie e identità,* Fall 2005, 113–33. An earlier version of chapter 4, "The Modesty of Starbuck: On Hybrids, Judaism, and Ethics in Primo Levi," was published in the *Journal of Modern Jewish Studies*: "The Shame of the Survivor: Judaism and Textual Memory in Primo Levi, Günther Anders, and Franz Kafka." *Journal of Modern Jewish Studies* 7, no. 1 (2008): 91–106.

For a listing of books published and distributed by Syracuse University Press,
visit https://press.syr.edu.

ISBN: 9780815631989 (hardcover)
         9780815656852 (e-book)

Library of Congress Cataloging-in-Publication Data
Parussa, Sergio, 1964–
Writing as freedom, writing as testimony : four Italian writers and Judaism / Sergio Parussa. — 1st ed.
p. cm. — (Judaic traditions in literature, music, and art)
Includes bibliographical references and index.
ISBN 978-0-8156-3198-9 (hardcover : alk. paper)
1. Italian literature—Jewish authors. 2. Italian literature—20th century—History and criticism.
3. Jewish literature—20th century—History and criticism. 4. Authors, Italian—20th century.
5. Jewish authors—Italy. 6. Judaism in literature. I. Title.
PQ4203.5.J48P37 2008
850.9'38296—dc22
2008038817

To Evan

SERGIO PARUSSA is associate professor of Italian studies at Wellesley College. He is the author of *Eros onnipotente: Erotismo, letteratura e impegno nell'opera di Pier Paolo Pasolini e Jean Genet* (Turin: Tirrenia Stampatori, 2003). He is also cotranslator into English of Ginevra Bompiani's *L'orso maggiore* as *The Great Bear* (New York: Italica Press, 2000) and translator into Italian of L. P. Hartley's *Simonetta Perkins* (Rome: Nottetempo, 2008).

Contents

Acknowledgments

I WOULD FIRST LIKE TO THANK the Oxford Centre for Hebrew and Jewish Studies, where I spent six delightful months as a visiting fellow, starting in the fall of 2004, and where part of this book was written. Many thanks to Piet van Boxel, Joanna Weinberg, and to all the librarians, the fellows, and the staff at the Oxford Centre for their competent and useful advice, as well as for their kindness and generous hospitality.

I would like to thank Wellesley College for granting me a year of sabbatical leave that allowed me to write this book, and to express my gratitude to my colleagues Rachel Jacoff, Fran Malino, Cristina Pausini, and David Ward for their insightful and sensitive comments on my manuscript.

Many thanks to all my friends, both in Italy and the United States, whose criticism has been essential in writing this book. I am especially grateful to Leah Hockman, for her valuable bibliographical suggestions and for being such a good study companion at the Bodleian library in Oxford, and to Valeria Gennero who never shied away from my questions and was always willing to discuss the contents with me.

A very special thank you to Blossom S. Kirschenbaum for being such a good friend and acute reader. Without her friendship and support, I would not have been able to complete this project.

I owe a great deal to Brian Kern, Carol Millen, Tony Oldcorn, and Tony Terrizzi who generously helped me to better my English prose and to translate portions of this book from Italian into English. I'm grateful to Michele Torresani for his help in the final technical aspects of manuscript preparation.

I would also like to extend a special thank you to Glenn Wright, Mary Seldon Evans, Ann Youmans, and all the staff at the Syracuse University Press for their assistance in reviewing my manuscript.

A very special thought goes to my dear friend, the late Anna Jona, with whom I discussed this endeavor from its early stages and whose sense of humor, passion for politics, and love for good books continue to inspire me.

Finally, I want to thank my parents for their encouragement and understanding, and for teaching me how to laugh.

Writing as Freedom,
Writing as Testimony

Introduction

> "He is a Jew," said Reb Tolba. "He is leaning against a wall, watching the clouds go by."
> "The Jew has no use for clouds," replied Reb Jalé. "He is counting the steps between him and his life."
> Edmund Jabès, *The Book of Questions*

DURING THE SUMMER OF 1999, the American artist Mark Dion undertook an original and fascinating artistic enterprise. With the help of a team of volunteers, he combed the foreshores of the Thames River in London and collected a wide variety of objects that the river had left on its banks at low tide: whole and broken glass, precious artifacts and cheap pottery, ancient fossils and plastic bottle caps. All the finds from the Thames digs were carefully cleaned, classified, and arranged in a large wooden cabinet put on display, in the fall of the same year, in the Tate Modern gallery.

The *Tate Thames Dig,* as the installation was finally called, was the result of an artistic process that used principles and methodologies of late-nineteenth-century scientific disciplines. It combined elements of archeology, detection, and taxonomy. It imitated their impulse to collect, classify, and preserve material fragments of the past as tangible proofs of an idea of history as progress. For the nineteenth-century sensibility, the neat and linear organization of fragmentary details—fossils on display in a museum of natural history, primary linguistic roots along the branches of a genealogical tree of languages, or clues in a Sherlock Holmes murder investigation—were proof that history could be interpreted as a linear succession of events leading up to a world of increasing complexity and completeness. In Dion's project, however, all these principles and conventions are inverted to reveal a more personal idea of history as memory. In his cabinet, unlike the nineteenth-century museum showcase, objects are not scientifically classified but are displayed in arbitrary and subjective arrangements. His is an interactive installation that invites viewers to browse and make personal discoveries and free associations. What counts are not just the objects on display, the amount of knowledge and information that they may convey, but the relationship between the objects and the viewers. When the viewers open up one of the cabinet's doors or pull out one of its drawers, they are faced with startling and enigmatic collections of curiosities: shards of precious and cheap pottery, bits of colorful broken glass, scraps of paper, metal and plastic bottle caps, shells, fossils; and while their gaze passes over all these remnants of the past, they may try mentally to reassemble these fragmentary objects, think of the people who handled them, feel surrounded by voices of lost lives, and realize that the large wooden cabinet in front of them is not just a museum showcase but a repository of loss. Now their gaze is no longer the gaze of a nineteenth-century scientist. They are neither archeologists, nor detectives, nor taxonomists, nor historians, whose common goal is to infer from a collection of fragmentary old things a faithful image of the past and to interpret it as a step in the progress of civilization. Their gaze rather resembles the backward gaze of the witness who visits the past to gather and reconnect its remains in the hope that this act will rescue the past from oblivion, change our perception of the present, and build a possibility for the future. What both artist's and viewers' gestures evoke is not so much a nostalgic fusion of past and present or a scientific reconstruction of the past but rather the repetition of an act of remembering in which the past is salvaged from oblivion by means of its reactualization in the present.

From this perspective, Dion's art is more reminiscent of another nineteenth-century discipline, psychoanalysis. In psychoanalytic treatment, the recovery of fragments of one's own personal history is not a nostalgic pilgrimage to the dear places of one's own past nor a faithful reconstruction of the image of one's own childhood but the patient and painful work of unearthing and interpreting lost memories with the final goal of better understanding one's own present. Freud liked to compare the work of the psychoanalyst to that of the archeologist; he said that both ought to uncover layer after layer of the patient's psyche before reaching the deepest and most valuable treasures. In the late 1890s, he became an art collector, and his studio, at 19 Berggasse in Vienna, rapidly filled with statuettes of ancient Egyptian, Greek, and Roman gods. His discipline, though, like Dion's art, was never pure archeology. Unlike the mute and mysterious ancient Egyptian sculptures that crowded his studio, the dreams, traumas, and lost memories that Freud tried to uncover in the subconscious were not mere specimens of the past. Like the debris in Dion's project, they were concrete attempts at rescuing the past from the fury of the waters and bringing it back into the flux of time. They belong at the intersection of past and present. They are past history made alive in the present.

History as active memory is also central to Jewish thought. It has often been noted that Judaism, unlike other ancient civilizations, is characterized by a profound sense of history and by an understanding that institutions evolve within precise historical circumstances.[1] Nonetheless, as Yosif H. Yerushalmi has noted in *Zakhor,* there has been no proper Jewish historiography until very recent times.[2] In fact, Jewish commentators of the Scriptures have often shown a certain indifference toward historical accuracy and have juxtaposed events that happened in remote historical times as if they were contemporary. Unlike the modern conception of history, in which memories of the past are organized in a chronological chain of events linked by strict relations of cause and effect, within the Jewish conception of history, historical events are often translated into models of behavior. Instead of translating memory into history, as Stefano Levi Della Torre notes, Judaism translates history into memory.[3] The Exodus from Egypt into the desert, the destruction of the idols, the establishment of a pact between humans and God are past events retold again and again so that they become paradigms of behavior in the present. During the Passover Seder, the repetition of the words from the Haggadah and the symbolic food assembled on the table, reminders of the biblical story of enslavement and liberation, become vehicles for the transmission of memory from one generation to the next. Here what counts most is the act of remembering the past and its reactualization in the present.

In this act of remembering, history becomes the repetition of an attempt to salvage the past, to rescue its remnants and bring them back into the flow of time in the hope that they get a second chance, another possibility. In psychoanalysis, through interaction between analyst and patient, through the recollection and the interpretation of the patient's dreams, something from the past is salvaged and the present is changed. Similarly, in Dion's art, the process of gathering fragmentary objects from the sand and arranging them in a museum cabinet, as well as the interaction between the objects and the viewer, are more important than the final art work on display. All these gestures, the religious, the scientific, and the artistic—the ritual lifting of a piece of unleavened bread at Passover, the retelling of a fragmentary dream and its interpretation, the gathering of debris from the banks of a river—share a common framework. All, in the encounter between past and present, give a central place to the human subject: not the objective and detached observer of nineteenth-century science, but an involved viewer whose gaze makes this encounter possible.

It may be here, in this meaningful encounter between past and present, in this interaction between a viewer and the remnants of the past, that the notion of history as memory reveals its ethical character as testimony: an act of rectifying and healing the past, which tries to prepare and anticipate the future. Perhaps testimony is nothing but history turned into memory such that we may put right all the injustices of the past. It is an ethical reading of history in which a simple and detached observer becomes an active and involved viewer, a free and responsible subject; and the past becomes the scattered, ungraspable, contradictory mosaic that one cannot refrain from questioning with the hope that it will gain new meanings in the future. And maybe in the end, it is this mosaic of broken and mute fragments, all these drowned remains, as Primo Levi would say, even the people who never returned to tell their story, that are the true act of testimony.

The main working hypothesis of this book is that it is possible to retrace the steps of this idea of history as memory, as individual freedom and responsibility, in twentieth-century Italian literature. I will focus on the works of four Italian writers—Umberto Saba, Natalia Ginzburg, Giorgio Bassani, and Primo Levi—to discuss how this modality defines their relationship with Judaism and to what extent it influences their writing.

When I refer to Jewish culture, it is mostly this modality that I have in mind. Therefore, I will take into account not only specific references to

Jewish history and various Jewish stories or tales, but also the manner in which these stories are told. For the authors I have chosen, the recovering of Judaism and Jewish traditions doesn't consist only in telling stories with Jewish subject matter, but also in the very gesture of memory, in the repetition of an act of remembering in which the past is salvaged by means of its reactualization in the present. Within this gesture, the subject as well as the writer becomes free and responsible: free to affirm difference, of Jewish traditions as integral parts of Italian culture, and responsible to recover those traditions, to bear witness to all that past, to any past, and make them live in the present.

I will discuss too how the freedom of difference may represent an indirect challenge to the limits of tolerance as well as a resistance to totalitarian thought, and I will show how the responsibility to bear witness to the past may put into discussion generally accepted notions of the particular and the universal.

What emerge from this discussion are paradoxical and more complex notions of the particular and the universal. In the end, the recovery of Judaism, of a minority culture, also ends up taking on a universal character. When one tells a Jewish story, it is everybody's story that one tells. Perhaps, for these authors, the recovery of Judaism also meant finding the human within time, his freedom and responsibility, always in balance between past and future, memory and promise, history and eschatology.

ACCORDING TO an age-old legend handed down by Italian Jews, the name *Italy* is a transliteration of the three Hebrew words *I-tal-Jah*: "the island of the divine dew." This etymology was proof that the good fortune they had encountered on Italian soil lay at the very roots of the country's name. Perhaps Italy was the country blessed by the divine benedictions invoked by Isaac on the lands of his son Jacob. Perhaps the history of Israel and that of Italy were profoundly interwoven.[4]

Jewish life in Italy, of course, has not always been peaceful and protective like a providential dew: during the Middle Ages and the Renaissance, Italian Jews experienced different forms of discrimination and persecution.

They were among the first Europeans to be forced to live in ghettos, and, during the 1930s and '40s, like other European Jews, they experienced deportation and extermination in concentration camps at the hands of the Fascists and Nazis. Nonetheless, for more than two thousand years, Jewish life in Italy has been characterized by a degree of continuity and integration that has no equivalent in the rest of the Western world.

The most remarkable features of Jewish life in Italy are antiquity, continuity, and integration. A Jewish presence in Italy is already recorded in the second century B.C.E., when the Jews of Palestine were in revolt against the religious and political oppression of the Seleucid ruler Antiochus Epiphanes. According to the ancient records preserved in the Book of the Maccabees, shortly after the year 161, Judas Maccabaeus, head of the Jewish revolt, sent a diplomatic mission to Rome to ask for help in his fight against the oppressor. The names of the two ambassadors who were sent to Rome to establish diplomatic relations with the Roman power have been preserved: Jason ben Eleazar and Eupolemos ben Johanan. They were the first Jews in Italy, and in Europe, who are known to us by their first names.

Italy is also the only land in the Western hemisphere where Jewish life has been unbroken from ancient times up to the present. Jewish life reached such a deep level of integration in Italian society that it reflects within itself the regional differences that characterize Italian culture. There are Italian Jewish regional identities, as well as Italian Jewish dialects. In the first chapter of *The Periodic Table,* Primo Levi gives a beautiful and detailed description of the mixed language spoken by his Jewish ancestors who peppered their daily conversation in regional dialect with humorous and expressive Hebrew words.[5]

The importance of these three major features in the history of the Jews in Italy—antiquity, continuity, and integration—is confirmed by the fact that the "Jewish-Italian Elegy," a poem on Jewish themes that is also one of the first poems written in Italian, was written in a variety of regional Italian that stands at the very origins of Italian literature. This poem is a *Kinah,* namely a lamentation recited during the fast for Tishah be-Av, the ninth day of the month of Av when observant Jews mourn the destruction of the second Temple in Jerusalem in 70 C.E. The poem begins with a lamentation on the destruction of the temple and the dispersion of Israel, it then narrates an episode of the Diaspora taken from Talmudic and Midrashic literature, and it ends in an invocation to God for the reconstruction of the Temple. According to the most recent philological studies, the elegy dates back to the beginning of the thirteenth century or even to the end of the twelfth century. Therefore, its composition coincides with the beginning of Italian literature. Even though the elegy is composed in a meter that is unusual for Italian literary texts of the twelfth and thirteenth centuries—triplets of lines with the same rhyme and a variable number of syllables—its language is characterized by linguistic and phonetic phenomena specific to the dialects of central Italy, which, together with Sicily and Tuscany, was one of the three places of origin of Italian literature.[6]

In the same period in which the "Jewish-Italian Elegy" was composed, there also lived a Jewish writer who made the first important contribution to the development of Italian literature: Immanuel Romano. Known to his Christian contemporaries as Manuello Giudeo, Immanuel Romano was born around 1261 and died after 1328. He was the author of serious and burlesque poetry in Italian as well as of a volume of twenty-eight compositions in Hebrew entitled *Mahabérot Imanu'el,* a narrative alternating rhymed prose and metrical poetry. The last part of Romano's *Mahabérot,* perhaps composed to commemorate the death of Dante Alighieri in 1321, describes in the form of a vision the author's imaginary journey through hell and paradise. *Mahabérot Imanu'el* was printed in Brescia in 1491 and was among the first books in Hebrew to be printed in Italy. As in his compositions in Italian, Romano employs meters and themes from Hebrew and Arabic poetry of the Spanish school; as in his compositions in Hebrew, he introduces strophic forms and motifs drawn from Italian poetry. In his love poems in Italian, for instance, Romano adopts a vocabulary of his Spanish predecessors characterized by the expression of a physical and sensual eroticism. But among his works in Hebrew, one also finds poems of different intonation that, according to the aesthetic principles of the school of the *dolce stil novo,* idealize love and depict women as angels rather than terrestrial beings. This happens mostly in his sonnets, that is, in the most typical form of the origins of Italian poetry. It is not by chance, then, that the sonnet, which is called *scir zaab* in Hebrew or "golden song," was introduced into Hebrew by Immanuel Romano.[7]

As noted by twentieth-century biblical scholar Umberto Cassuto (1883–1951) in an essay on the relationship between Immanuel Romano and his illustrious contemporary, Dante:

> [Romano's works] provide us with a highly interesting example of a phe-
> nomenon that characterizes the culture of Italian Jews during the late
> Middle Ages and the Renaissance, namely the fact that two different
> elements—on the one hand, Italian culture to which Italian Jews have
> assimilated and with which they have identified, and, on the other hand,
> their ancient Jewish culture to which they have always dedicated them-
> selves with great fervor—flowed together and developed one next to the
> other, without ever mixing, or standing in each other's way, united in a
> unanimous and industrious noble accordance.[8]

Clearly Cassuto is here attempting to interpret the development of Italian Jewish literature throughout the Middle Ages and the Renaissance as a
harmonious and successful synthesis with the Italian literary tradition. By
describing a Jewish cultural heritage and an Italian literary tradition that
meet and intertwine without ever completely overlapping, Cassuto draws
an idealized picture of a coherent cultural and literary juxtaposition that
would mirror the larger peaceful cohabitation of Christians and Jews in
Italy. Cassuto's positive words can be read as part of late-nineteenth- and
early-twentieth-century optimism, which saw Judaism as being in harmony
with Christianity. At the same time, they can also be interpreted as a reference to an aspect that has often been neglected in the bibliography of this
subject, namely acculturation. The relationship between Judaism and writing in twentieth-century Italy is not so much the result of a sharp opposition
between assimilation and difference as the outcome of a historical process
of acculturation, in which a minority has maintained the freedom of fully
participating in the culture of the majority while preserving a cultural difference; it has adopted traits of the culture of the majority while preserving
a sense of cultural differentiation.

In this book, therefore, unlike most of the writing on the subject, I never
refer to Judaism as "other" but as one very important component of Italian
history and its cultural heritage—disproving the myth of Judaism as a culture that remains separated and immutable throughout history, as a set of

fixed religious and cultural traditions that developed in complete isolation from other traditions and remained impermeable to any external influence.

From this perspective, with due regard to all the historical differences between them, Immanuel Romano's experience doesn't seem very far from the experience of some twentieth-century Jewish writers: they too, like Immanuel, try to build a sense of belonging to Judaism within the cultural and literary traditions of their own countries. Perhaps, in a certain way, Romano anticipates their efforts. As Amos Luzzatto has observed in his preface to the Italian translation of *Ha-Tofet-ve-ha-Eden* (Hell and Paradise), Romano was an intellectual who didn't receive a conventional and complete Jewish education. His writings in Hebrew cannot be fully ascribed to the categories that defined the role of the intellectual in medieval society: he was neither a philosopher, nor an exegete, nor a grammarian. Rather, throughout his literary career, he showed a creative attitude toward Judaism and freely resorted to the sacred language to write serious and facetious poetry on secular themes.[9]

And yet, both in his religious and secular texts, whether in Hebrew or in Italian, Immanuel seems to give voice to hopes and expectations that border on a religious sense of waiting. From this perspective, Immanuel's attitude toward Judaism may be comparable to that of Primo Levi, who also showed a creative and free attitude in his approach to Judaism and made use of Jewish religious and cultural themes to write about issues that were pertinent to his time. In his poem "Shemà," for instance, he makes direct reference to the most important prayer in Judaism in order to write about the Shoah. In this sense as well, perhaps Romano is not so far from the experience of modern Jewish intellectuals. Their works speak of a continuity in the Italian Jewish literary tradition inasmuch as they can be interpreted as different and creative answers to similar questions: how to maintain a connection with ancient Jewish traditions while remaining modern, how to preserve a sense of continuity with the past and to be part of an ever-changing world, how to revive in the present the memory of what remains of the past, and how to rescue from the past and save from oblivion the something that remains.

The question of what remains has been posed clearly by Yosif H. Yerushalmi. In his essay on Freud's Moses, he wonders whether a Jewish

collective character can be transmitted independently of direct communication and education by example, whether Jewishness can be transmitted
independently of Judaism. If so, Yerushalmi observes, even if the latter were
to be terminated, the former would be interminable.[10] Without pretending
to exhaust the complexity of the subject, I would here like to advance some
suggestions based on Vladimir Jankélévitch's, Giorgio Agamben's, and Stefano Levi Della Torre's comments on Jewish history and, in particular, on
their notions of the *en-plus* and the *remnant*.[11] As we shall see in the following chapters, the relationship to Judaism of the four writers I discuss in
this book often consists in recovering the past, the remnants of a Jewish
(and not only Jewish) past, and in rediscovering an *en-plus,* a historical,
eschatological depth to meaning—in short, in rediscovering the responsibility to bear witness to the past and a freedom to rebuild a sense of belonging both to Italian culture and Jewish traditions.

Freedom

As the French philosopher Vladimir Jankélévitch writes in his essay *Le
judaisme, problème intérieur* (1957), Jewish history and thought are characterized by a tension between two contradictory aspects: the tendency to
resemble others and adapt to the culture of a majority, and, at the same time,
the desire to preserve a sense of religious or cultural difference. According
to Jankélévitch, in Judaism there is a push to erase difference, to become the
integral part of a group, maybe to the point of blending and disappearing
into it; and, at the same time, there is a desire to maintain that same difference, to preserve it "like a rare flower, like a precious plant that one should
cultivate within oneself."[12]

This contradiction, of course, exists in everyone. We all have felt the
pleasant feeling of anonymity, the need to adapt to our surroundings and
"sweetly disappear"[13] within a larger group; and, at the same time, we
have also felt the desire to resist that feeling and to preserve our own vital
difference. Integration means direct participation in the collective life of
one's society, but it may also mean blending into a group to the point of losing any specificity, any sense of collective or individual distinction. Difference, any difference, tells the individual, "I'm here anyway."[14] Jankélévitch

concludes that this tension represents one of the most profound human freedoms: the freedom to be at once equal and different, oneself and something other than oneself.

In the following chapters, my discussion of the relationship between writing and Judaism is organized in relation to just such a dual freedom. I will discuss Umberto Saba's discomfort with this tension, his being eternally divided between Judaism and Catholicism, between two religions and two cultures that he saw as opposed and incompatible; Natalia Ginzburg's attempt to come closer to this freedom by claiming a double identity, both Jewish and Catholic; and how Giorgio Bassani's and Primo Levi's recovery of Jewish cultural memories, of a secular and cultural sense of belonging to Judaism, also involves the liberty of being Italian and Jewish at the same time. It is precisely this freedom that the narrator of Bassani's *The Gold-Rimmed Spectacles* discusses when, while contemplating the small Jewish cemetery from the top of the walls of Ferrara, he is once more able to find "the motherly face of [his] city."[15] He sees the Jewish cemetery as part of the whole urban topography, and Jewish memory as an integral part of the history of his hometown. Similarly, when Primo Levi, in *Argon,* recalls the humorous Hebrew words that were an integral part of his ancestors' daily conversation in Piedmontese dialect, he is reconstructing a sense of belonging to both Italian and Piedmontese culture, as well as to Jewish traditions. Both Bassani and Levi hint at a freedom that was suspended but never fully erased by Fascism: the freedom of being at once Italian and Jewish without the solution of the vital contradiction that comes with it.

This freedom is one of the main targets of anti-Semitism. According to Jankélévitch, the anti-Semite denies the Jew the possibility not only of being Jewish but also other than Jewish, the freedom of being both equal and different.[16] The anti-Semite compels the Jew to take sides between these two extremes and wants to confine him within the following dilemma: either you stop being different from others, abandon your customs and accept assimilation, or you must be exclusively Jewish and accept the ghetto.[17] As Jankélévitch says, the target of anti-Semitism is not so much the legal condition of Jews, nor a question of appearance or behavior, as the fact that Jews may represent the freedom of being equal and different, oneself and other than oneself.

As a form of uneasiness with this freedom, the anti-Semitism that existed in the nineteenth and twentieth centuries can be compared to other forms of intolerance. In twentieth-century Italian literature, anti-Semitism often occurs linked with misogyny and homophobia. Like women and homosexuals, Jews have often been accused of being *too* different and *too* similar: on the one hand, they have been reproached for not being fully assimilated to the culture of the majority; on the other, for being so integrated within society that they are not recognizable as women/homosexuals/Jews anymore. At times, Jews have been reproached for having a double national identity: for belonging to their country of residence and also to another national or supranational entity, to Israel or to the Diaspora. Similarly, women have been blamed for being the embodiment of the negative qualities that constitute the essence of the *feminine*—weakness, fickleness, sentimentalism—but when they take on roles that are usually reserved for men, when they hold professional jobs, in politics or in the army, they have been accused of the opposite, namely of losing their *femininity*, of imitating men and of having assimilated to the masculine model. Homosexuals are reproached for having an immoral and depraved sexuality that is considered a threat to the survival of the traditional family; but when they set out to create stable families and claim equal rights in matters of cohabitation, inheritance, adoption, they have been accused of being like everyone else, of having become bourgeois, of being, in other words, assimilated. These three attitudes are masks for three forms of hatred toward *difference,* its mobility and imperfection. They are forms of homophobia, misogyny, and anti-Semitism in disguise, three forms of ill-concealed discomfort toward anything that seems indefinite because it escapes the gaze of Medusa and does not agree to fix itself in a final and definite form.

From this perspective, *difference* has represented during the last three hundred years a form of constructive criticism of the principles on which Western societies have built their sense of civil cohabitation, such as tolerance and universalism. The term *tolerance* derives from the Latin word *tolerare,* which means "to endure." In the *Oxford English Dictionary,* it is defined as "the action or practice of tolerating; the disposition to be patient with or indulgent to the opinions or practices of others." The verb *tolerate* is defined as both "to allow [something that one dislikes or disagrees with] to exist or to be done or practiced without . . . interference" and "to endure, sustain (pain or hardship)." Among its synonyms are words like *sympathy, indulgence, forbearance, to bear, to put up with, to allow, to permit*—words that describe states of patience and indulgence, not of acceptance. The very concept of tolerance, and the various meanings of the words that express it, already imply a limitation of one's capability to *really* accept someone who is different. The etymology of the word as well as the different meanings that the word has taken on during the last two hundred years betray the idea that what is expected from others, from those who are tolerated, is that they not go beyond certain limitations, that they respect certain social conventions. Perhaps this means that individual rights are temporary concessions that can be revoked at any moment. As long as the freedom of others is the consequence of an act of tolerance, a gift, and not the result of a real acceptance of difference, this freedom can always be withdrawn.

It goes without saying that, since the age of emancipation, freedom has no longer been conceived as a gift. Instead, freedom has been granted as a natural and inalienable universal right by the egalitarian spirit of the Enlightenment and by the revolutions of the eighteenth and nineteenth centuries. As such, individual freedom should also work to stem against totalitarian drift. Nonetheless, the tragic history of the twentieth century is proof that the natural and inalienable character of human rights is not enough to protect minorities. It took less than two hundred years for the rights of the individual, granted during the Enlightenment, to be overturned and denied by totalitarianism. The principles of tolerance and universal right clashed with people's inability to live in a pluralistic society and to accept its concrete social and cultural differences. It is here that difference becomes a form of indirect and constructive criticism of these principles: it questions what is meant by tolerance and universal rights, it reveals the conceptual frailty that may be inscribed within these concepts, and it suggests ways to give them more substance and soundness.

This frailty may be due to the fact that the Enlightenment, since its very beginnings, was strongly characterized by a sense of collective expectation that the project of regenerating mankind by granting freedom and universal rights would rapidly culminate in an overcoming and an erasure of all the past. As Theodor Adorno and Max Horkheimer have noted in their famous essay on the dialectics of the Enlightenment, individual freedoms were conceded on the presupposition that all individuals, sooner or later, would model themselves on the ideal of the new man of the Enlightenment and that all particularisms, all cultural specificity, would disappear with the passing of time. Paradoxically, the project of the regeneration of man through freedom fed a growing sense of intolerance toward all those who did not abandon the old world of religious rituals and customs, toward all those who did not adapt themselves to what was new and did not embrace the triumph of progress and equality. Thus, when all the differences that were supposed to disappear did not disappear, all freedoms were revoked: progress turned into domination, tolerance into intolerance, Enlightenment into totalitarianism.[18] Perhaps it is in this push to entirely and completely overcome the past, instead of giving it space and significance within the present, in this drive to amnesia, that the frailty of this project lay its roots.

On the other hand, this same frailty may be due to the existence of a discrepancy between what is declared universal in the abstract and what is actually considered so historically. Both the Declaration of Independence in the United States (1776) and the Declarations of the Rights of Man and of Citizen in France (1789) granted natural and inalienable rights to all citizens of the state. Individual rights were universal per definition. They were granted not only to American or French citizens but to all humans by virtue of being human. Religious freedom came with these rights. At the same time, though, the abstract notion of universality implied an idea of humanity that was modeled on an image of the majority. Human rights were conceived as universal, but then historically, since the very moment of their inception or in later interpretations, their universal character has often been denied: the actual citizen that is implied in his historical concreteness has often been the man and not the woman, the Christian and not the Jew, the white and not the black, the heterosexual and not the homosexual. For all the individuals who are excluded from the set of natural and inalienable rights, from the universal, tolerance has been the best option. In fact, the recognition of human rights has coexisted for a very long time, and still coexists, with various forms of injustice: with slavery, with strong limitations to the right to vote, or to the possibility of holding political and social roles because of one's skin color, gender, or religious beliefs. In 1847, Lionel de Rothschild, in spite of having been elected to the British Parliament, could not take a seat there because, as a Jew, he refused to take an oath on the Christian Bible. Only eleven years later, in 1858, after the passing of the so-called Jewish Disabilities Act, did he obtain that right and become the first Jewish member of the British Parliament.

Perhaps the same ambiguity that is at the core of the notion of tolerance—the idea that the freedom of others is a gift and therefore a concession that can always be revoked—seeps through the modern declarations of human rights and weakens them. Or perhaps what is still lacking is the profound belief in the justness of such principles on the part of each individual, where the term *profound* refers to an act of consciousness: acknowledging the emotional uneasiness that each individual feels in accepting what he or she may perceive as different, contradictory, or mobile—in dealing, in other words, with freedom. What is at stake is not only a matter of social, political, or cultural freedom—that is, of negotiating the space of one's own freedom with the freedom of others—but also a question of psychological freedom, of dealing with the fears that may be associated with the very experience of freedom itself.

Finally, at issue is not only the stretching of the boundaries of constitutions to include as many individuals as possible under the umbrella of human rights, but also accepting that individuals may have a contradictory and paradoxical claim to be different, to not fully mirror themselves in that notion. It is a matter of acknowledging a right to difference. For human rights to have a chance of stability, and for them not to easily turn into their opposite, they must be not only natural and inalienable rights of individuals as abstract beings but also inalienable rights of individuals in their concrete historical differences: also, paradoxically, in their desire not to entirely adhere to such a universal model. Perhaps human rights should also include the right to their contradiction.

Over the last three hundred years, Western societies have worked out various ways to resolve this contradiction, to harmonize the principle of the equality of all individuals with humans' claims to maintain some form of religious, historical, or cultural difference. Although these solutions have helped the progress of civil cohabitation, they have not tackled the depth of the problem. In a society that is based on the equality of all its citizens, and whose goal is to create the individual in his essence as a human being, difference may not be completely satisfied with this ideal; it may not want to be limited to one dimension and may wish to be in addition "something else." Difference appeals to an emotional, psychological, historical, or eschatological depth, but at any rate one that always calls into question the human: the desire of the individual to not completely exhaust his subjectivity within the group, of the minority to not entirely blend into the majority, his push to resist something that, perhaps, resembles the human temptation toward the void.[19]

This right to difference, to contradiction, to social and cultural mobility is often neglected in modern Western societies: the freedom to embrace the ideal of the universal man and, at the same time, not to completely adhere to this ideal. If the principle that all men are equal does not include the freedom of being different, then this same principle can easily turn into its opposite, that is, the principle that all men must be the same. Thus right becomes coercion, and the lives that do not perfectly coincide with the human ideal produced by Western society throughout the centuries become *imperfect* lives. Within a Christian, male, heterosexual universe, Jews, women, and homosexuals have been considered imperfect creatures, and, as such, they are individuals who not only occupy a marginal position in society but who are excluded from an idea of universality: the Jew is a non-Christian, the woman is nothing but a complement of the Vitruvian Man, the homosexual is a half-man, a half-citizen who is paradoxically granted inalienable human rights but who, at the same time, is deprived of fundamental civil and political rights. As Joan Acocella has remarked, Jews, women, and homosexuals cannot produce anything universal precisely because they are imperfect: non-Christian, non-male, non-heterosexual.[20] However, an individual's humanity is made up not only of the aspects that transcend his or her historical, physical, or emotional peculiarity, but also of these differences: it is made up not only of abstractions but also of concrete historical contradictions.

From this perspective, difference also represents a resistance to totalitarianism. Totalitarianism is a form of government in which political authority exercises total control over the individual. In a totalitarian system, the state regulates every aspect, both private and public, of the lives of its citizens and the power of the ruler is restricted neither by law, nor by cultural debate, nor by political opposition. Since the mass of individuals that constitute the state is seen as an extension of the body of the ruler— and both are seen as parts of the same homogenous social body—in such a political universe, each reference to difference, contradiction, hesitation, or movement in the social body—in short, each freedom—is seen as a threat to the unity and health of the social body.

Totalitarianism responds to this threat by reducing difference to a fixed image, by turning it into a collective myth, and by assigning it to a definite space at the margins of society. First, it creates various myths of difference (the myths of the wandering Jew, the femme fatale, the pansexual homo- sexual); then, it confines individuals whom it perceives as different to spe- cific locations within the social space: the walls of the ghetto, the invisible contours of the domestic hearth, or the borders of political confinement; finally, it dispossesses them of their civil and political rights. Fascism can also be described in these terms: a political system that turns difference into inequality, that transforms religious or cultural difference, or diversity in gender or sexual orientation, into social inequality. In the face of what is perceived as different, mobile, indefinite, contradictory, totalitarianism responds by creating precise social and political spaces that fix individuals to their difference and deprive them of their individual freedoms. To Jews, women, and homosexuals, totalitarianism assigns specific roles within the social and political organization of the state and, in doing so, it deprives them of their fundamental rights. It does so in the name of what appears to be a disturbing and irreducible difference, that, instead, is only a request for freedom. Ghetto walls, domestic walls, or the waters that surrounded the islands where Fascism confined homosexuals—as well as the laws, the social and linguistic practices that it introduced during the 1930s and '40s to institute inequality—become concrete borders with which Fascism tries to pin difference to the wall of inequality. To the individual who carries a difference that doesn't readily disappear, who does not fully assimilate himself, totalitarianism replies that if he or she wants to maintain a certain margin of difference, it will be *this* difference, and only this one, that defines his or her identity; and this difference will be made visible at the level of the social organization of the state; it will turn into the mad taxonomical logic of the concentration camps that groups humans on the basis of their social condition. Thus, the rich and varied geography of diversity becomes a clear and reassuring map of inequality. The exact location of difference within the social space, its visibility, is nothing but the illusion of the tangible and controllable character of what appears to be different. By pinning difference to the wall of social conformity, totalitarianism tries to free itself from freedom, from freedom's butterfly-like elusiveness, and is thus reassured.

As I will show in the following chapters, the sense of a connection to Judaism and the recovery of Jewish culture are an active response by some of the authors I discuss to this attempt at physical and cultural confinement. In using the language of the oppressor—a move that is typical of persecuted minorities—Giorgio Bassani and Primo Levi assert their freedom by regaining possession of their cultural difference. When Primo Levi polemically states, in a well-known passage from *The Periodic Table* that he, as a Jew, is like a mustard seed, the vital imperfection that is necessary for life to continue, he takes up the thread that he will use over the years to recover a sense of belonging to Judaism. By using this image from a Christian parable about the importance of difference, by using the language of the persecutor, Levi restates his difference, the existence of his culture as well as his individual freedom. A similar example can be found at the end of Bassani's *The Gold-Rimmed Spectacles,* when the young narrator says, "But I would never have returned from my exile. Never again."[21] In the face of his father's decision to accept Fascist discrimination, and in the face of the self-hatred of his homosexual friend Fadigati, who drowns himself in a river, thus internalizing the hatred of the society that surrounds him, he asserts his difference and his exile, and in doing so rejects inequality.

Time

There is a theoretical incompatibility between totalitarianism and Judaism, at least in the way I have approached Judaism in this book, where I focus on the Jewish notion of history as memory. This incompatibility has to do with their different conceptions of time.

Over the centuries, Judaism has developed a conception of time as historical, linear, and open-ended.[22] In Judaism, the notion of time is so flexible and encompassing that reality itself comes to coincide with it. While in Greek Platonism only what is eternal—what is outside of time and its mutability—is real, in Judaism the real is within time. Therefore, reality is not defined as an imperfect entity that needs to be redeemed with respect to eternity, namely an ulterior and perfect reality that represents its model. It rather consists in its becoming, in its coming into being, through the days of creation, in its history. In Judaism, reality is not cosmos, but creation: it is not a stable and ordered entity in which everything infinitely returns but history, a precarious and suspended becoming without stable and definite foundations.

Totalitarianism, on the other hand, as Karl Popper notes in *The Open Society and Its Enemies*, is grounded in the belief that history moves toward an immutable future. In its intolerance toward the unstable and questioning character of contradictions, in its refusal of what is perceived as mobile and indefinite, in its uneasiness toward the vertigo that comes from freedom, totalitarianism manifests a desire for theoretical synthesis of every opposition, for the solution of every contradiction, and for the closing of time. In Judaism, however, time is open and the future is radically uncertain. "There is an infinite perplexity," writes Jankélévitch, "that admits neither end nor solution. I am unable to synthesize contradictory elements within myself, and the Hegelian resolution, for us, is not particularly attractive. Our perplexity will last until the end of times, which are without end."[23] In the face of totalitarianism (with its search for a synthesis of contradictions, for social and political immobility, its belief in a collective redemption that has already taken place, in short, for a closing of time), Judaism has often represented opposite concepts (an ease with open and vital contradictions, with social and political mobility, and an expectation for a collective redemption still to come, in short, for an open time), and, in this role, it has emphasized the importance of individual freedom and responsibility.

Within this opposition between different conceptions of time, there is more than one suggestion for how to compensate for the conceptual frailty of the notion of universal human rights. As Adorno and Horkheimer noted in their theory of the dialectics of the Enlightenment, the project of the regeneration of man through freedom fed a growing sense of intolerance toward all those who did not adapt themselves to what was new and who did not embrace fully and readily the triumph of progress and equality. The entire religious, cultural, political, and psychological past became obsolete and, therefore, dispensable. And the various forms of collective terror that have marked and haunted human history during the last two hundred years—guillotines, genocides, and extermination camps—may have arisen from this.

Expanding on this theory, one might add that the fact that the Enlightenment can turn against itself by becoming totalitarianism also depends on an idea of universalism as the ultimate redemption of humanity. From this perspective, the project of regenerating mankind by granting freedom and universal rights coincides with a collective desire for the closure of time and the end of history, with a rush toward the advent of a collective redemption, and, in the end, with its very opposite: the totalitarian desire to do without individual freedom and responsibility.

Perhaps if the conception of time remains open, if the universality of men is not conceived as a collective redemption but rather as an open and imperfect process that takes into account all the past, if its fulfillment is postponed to the horizon of time, then humans may be able to keep a stronger sense of individual freedom and a responsibility to operate in the present.

Finally, there is a psychological dimension to all this. The haste of running toward the future as well as the need to overcome and erase all the past betray a double fear. They signal anxiety in the face of the radical uncertainty and unpredictability of the future, and dread of looking deeply into the past and dealing with the feeling of loss that may come with it. Totalitarianism may be a response to this double fear.

In 1923, the Italian idealist philosopher Giovanni Gentile, who at the time was minister of education in Mussolini's first government, authored a school reform that prohibited the teaching of psychology in all Italian schools. Gentile feared that the study of human psychology, which found the child within the adult and recalled the past of the individual with all its contradictions, would undermine the integrity of the subject. "The *subject*," wrote Gentile in an indirect reply to Freud, "does not admit the existence of anything prior to itself; there is not even the smallest space that one could assign to this subconscious."[24] Here the idealist and neo-Hegelian notion of synthesis, as well as its distaste for unresolved contradictions and for the past, intertwines with Mussolini's project to create the new Fascist man: a new historical subject that would embody the overcoming of all that preceded it. Psychoanalysis, though, does not replace the adult with the child but finds the child within the adult; it looks for the past to give an ever-new, ever-different definition of a free and responsible adult. "Within the evolution of the future man, within his self-conscious future, there was also a non-self-conscious, or a barely conscious, child. Gentile's pedagogy may try to put him to death once and for all, but Freud's psychology finds the child at every step within the mature man."[25]

Testimony

The tension that Jankélévitch describes between wanting to be equal and different is not only a source of freedom but also a form of responsibility: the duty to bear witness to the past. According to Jankélévitch, this tension depends on an *en-plus,* an additional meaning, something that cannot be precisely defined or ascribed once and for all. This *en-plus* does not depend on religion, which many Jews don't practice, nor on race, whose existence is denied by the authors discussed in this book, nor on nationality, which varies according to the country of residence and which has become richer and more complex since the postwar years and the creation of the state of Israel. Rather, it is a tension that depends on an *arrière-fond,* on a depth, which is both historical and eschatological. On the one hand, the remains of a very ancient history—a huge spatial and temporal dispersion—form the basis of the freedom of choice between being equal and different; on the other, there is the displacement of this contradiction toward infinity, toward the horizon of time.[26]

Echoes of this historical, eschatological depth can be found in the images that Natalia Ginzburg uses in *The Things We Used to Say* to describe the unbreakable bond between the members of her family. To her, their sayings are familiar and recognizable even in a dark cave thanks to their inexplicable depth, to their being like hieroglyphics from an ancient past that still carry significance in the present and whose ultimate meaning can always be postponed and renewed with the passing of time. There is also an echo of this depth in Bassani's definition of Judaism, in *The Garden of the Finzi-Continis,* as "something intimate": an indefinable and almost imperceptible bond between himself and Alberto and Micol Finzi-Contini; or in the imperfection described by Primo Levi in *The Periodic Table*: "the grain of salt or mustard" that "makes the zinc react"—almost an indirect reference to Jankélévitch's description of the *en-plus* as the "additional impurity that prevents the Jew from being a pure man in the chemical sense of the word *pure* (as when I say a pure Frenchman, a pure Russian)."[27]

Perhaps the piece of unleavened bread and all the symbolic foods on the Seder plate at Passover that recall the experience of slavery in Egypt and its liberation, the traces of childhood emotions that the psychoanalyst helps to find in the memory of the adult, the fragments gathered in Mark Dion's cabinet, are also *en-plus.* They represent a historical and eschatological depth that never fully disappears, that never completely annihilates itself and whose ultimate meaning is always postponed to the end of time: the remains of a past that asks not to be forgotten—that asks to be made alive in the present—and whose ultimate signification is always postponed. This is our past, say the remains, the history of our liberation from slavery in Egypt, but it is also the living memory of our present, of every slavery and every liberation, both individual and collective, in the present. This is the child; these are his thoughts and emotions that are made present and alive within the adult through analysis. These are the fragments of a lost past that, through the work of art, seem for a moment to regain a gaze and a voice in our gaze and voice of today and to have a chance in the future.

The *en-plus,* then, is not only the foundation of a freedom turned toward the future but also the foundation of a responsibility toward the past. Not only the freedom of choice that depends on it but also the duty to bring testimony to something that never fully assimilates itself, that cannot be forgotten and that remains. This is the place where historical, scientific, and artistic freedom and responsibility intertwine, where religion, history, psychology, or art are not only technical activities but also human disciplines inasmuch as they embrace the *en-plus,* the imperfection, the voice, the something, the *remnant* that is the human.

In *The Time That Remains,* a commentary on the concept of messianic time, Giorgio Agamben has advanced a suggestive interpretation of the notion of the remnant. As Agamben notes, Isaiah and other biblical prophets often address Israel as a whole and yet announce that only a remnant will be saved: "For though thy people Israel be as the sand of the sea," says the prophet Isaiah, "[yet] a *remnant* of them shall return" (Isaiah 10:22; emphasis added). Theologians have often interpreted *remnant* in this passage, as well as in other passages from the Bible, as a quantitative numerical portion: either as the portion of Jews who survived the biblical catastrophes or as the whole of Israel that survives the final destruction of all peoples.

The notion of the remnant, though, implicitly refers not only to the part or the whole of what survives, but also to what doesn't survive. The remnant is not only what remains but what does not remain. It recalls not only what will be there but also what will not be there. The presence of survivors, writes Primo Levi in a famous passage of *The Drowned and the Saved,* reminds us of the absence of those who did not survive. The saved remind us of the drowned. And since those who survived are not necessarily the best ones— but just those who did not drown by means of prevarication, skill, or simple good luck—then perhaps, Levi concludes, survivors are not the true witnesses of the past; if this is so, then who are we who remain? The remnant recalls what has been lost and is missing; it is the tangible memory of that loss and that absence, and, as such, it recalls the impossibility of a full identity.

Thus, notes Agamben, the biblical notion of the remnant must be reinterpreted. From his point of view, the remnant coincides neither with the portion of Jews who survived the biblical catastrophes nor is it simply identical with Israel itself, as the chosen people who survive the final destruction of peoples; it is neither the part nor the whole. Rather, it represents the impossibility, for both the whole and the part, to fully coincide with itself. Since there is always a loss that has to be taken into account and remembered, since there must be a memory of the past, there is always a remnant between every people and itself, between every identity and itself. "At a decisive instant," writes Agamben, "the elected people, every people, will necessarily situate itself as a *remnant,* as not-all."[28] In the face of the unstoppable passing of time—a time that appears to be open and without end—the answer to the question "Who are we?" is ceaselessly postponed. In the meantime, one could say that humans are also the part that is lacking. As long as there is memory, the notion of identity as fullness and completion—as purity, lack of contradiction, synthesis, or appeasement—is postponed to the end of time.

Agamben applies a similar interpretation to Paul's *Letter to the Romans*—the text on which the Catholic Church has founded its doctrine of universalism. In contrary to the common interpretation, Paul's letter does not eliminate the distinction between Jews and Gentiles. It does not introduce Christianity as the completion and the overcoming of Judaism; rather, it represents an intellectual operation that leaves a remnant: a non-Jew or a non-Gentile, who neither fully coincides with the part nor with the whole, who is neither entirely a Jew nor a Gentile. From this perspective, Paul is not the apostle of universalism. His distinction does not represent the overcoming of Jewish particularism and the affirmation of Christian universalism; rather, it represents the impossibility for both Jews and Gentiles to fully coincide with themselves. Perhaps here, as in the biblical prophets, the remnant hints at loss and absence, but unlike in the prophets, this hint does not imply a remembrance of the past but rather a fault of memory: a desire that all the past be overcome and repressed in a new Christian man, in a new and noncontradictory identity. It hints at the desire for a closure of time. Yet here, too, there is a remnant.

Though with different emphasis, both Agamben's notion of the remnant and Jankélévitch's concept of the *en-plus* focus on the existence of a vital and contradictory tension between past and future, memory and hope, the particular and the universal. They are both able to see in the concrete, historical, minority experiences of Jews living in the Diaspora aspects of human existence that lead them to theoretical formulations of great interest for us today. In Agamben, this tension takes on an unmistakably twentieth-century flavor. It becomes a discrepancy, an absence, a fracture that is mostly the result of the historical conditions of Jews living as a minority, as well as of the experience of the Shoah. His interpretation is turned toward the past. In Jankélévitch, however, the same tension becomes an opportunity and a choice for the future: the freedom to choose between being the same and different, oneself and other than oneself.

At the same time, though, both interpretations hint at similar contradictions. As long as time remains open, as long as there is past and future, memory and hope, as long as there is a remnant or an *en-plus,* namely a historical and eschatological depth, there will be lively contradictions, a vital *impurity* and *imperfection* of identity. Both interpretations hint at the need to rethink our common understanding of the particular and the universal.

If Paul is not the apostle of universality and of the overcoming of Jewish particularism, then the universal is not, as has often been stated, the overcoming of all particulars but rather the impossibility of the fullness of identity. In Agamben's interpretation, the universal is not a search for a transcendent principle—such as the humanity of man—that would erase all differences and beyond which there are no possible distinctions. It is not a search for the human essence in the depth of man but a discrepancy between individuals, people, and their sense of identity. Within the Jew or the Greek, one does not find the Christian, the universal human being, but just the impossibility of the Jew or the Greek to fully coincide with himself.

Similarly, in Jankélévitch's terms, if the freedom to choose between the particular and the universal exists, then the universal cannot coincide with the overcoming of the particular but with a tension between the particular and the universal, with a remnant, or an *en-plus*. Within the modern individual, then, one finds neither the Nietzschean Übermensch, nor the New Man conceived by Fascist and Communist ideologies, nor any of the nineteenth- and twentieth-century embodiments of the ideal man who, either by means of a spiritual connection with a mythic, pure, and undivided origin or by means of an ontological revolution, would overcome the past limitations of the historical human being. Nor does one find the Christian, the Vitruvian man, the citizen of the Enlightenment, meant here as the overcoming of all human cultural limitations, differences, and particularisms; rather, one finds an individual who can never fully coincide with himself, who is never fully particular nor fully universal, never completely different, never completely the same, but who happens to be, or aspires to be, both.

In this contradiction there is a form of paradoxical universality. As mentioned before, the traditional concept of the universal—meant here as the overcoming and erasure of all past differences in a new, better person—has limitations. No overcoming is ever complete. There is always a fragment of the past that by chance survives, or stubbornly resists the passing of time, and that may question us with its mute presence; and paradoxically this remnant, this *en-plus* that remains, this desire to be one and the other, this difficult freedom and responsibility, is typical of everybody's experience and, as such, is the human.

The universal, then, should be redefined. It is not the overcoming of all particularisms of the past by means of a palingenesis of all people into a new better human but rather the road that one has to travel between past and future so that the remnant, the *en-plus* that remains, will find its place, its meaning, its voice in the present, and will set humans free to build their future by choosing, day by day, between being the same and being different.

Finally, halfway between Jankélévitch's and Agamben's interpretations I would like to mention a third interpretation by Stefano Levi Della Torre, in which the remnant is not only the vehicle of a possible freedom or the sign of an imperfection, but also the responsibility to bear witness to the past. In *Mosaico*, Levi Della Torre writes that *remnant,* as it is formulated in Isaiah, refers not so much to those who have been saved through their goodness as to those who have had the privilege of surviving and who therefore have the responsibility of bearing witness and putting history back into motion.

As Primo Levi writes in a famous passage of *The Drowned and the Saved*:

> We, the survivors, are not the true witnesses . . . We survivors are not only an exiguous but also an anomalous minority: we are those who by their prevarications or abilities or good luck did not touch bottom. Those who did so . . . have not returned to tell about it or have returned mute, but they are . . . the complete witnesses, the ones whose deposition would have a general significance . . . We who were favored by fate tried, with more or less wisdom, to recount not only our fate but also that of the others, indeed of the drowned; but this was a discourse "on behalf of third parties" . . . We speak in their stead, by proxy.[29]

Those who have been saved and have survived the catastrophe are neither the best nor those predestined by a providential design to be the bearers of a message. They are just the remains of a catastrophe. They do not carry any particular quality save that of having the possibility, and the responsibility, of recounting their fate and the fate of those who did not survive. It is in this act of remembering, in this bearing witness to the past existence of what is irremediably lost but that still questions us with all its remains—the photographs, the piles of shoes, the very presence of survivors among us—that Jewish history takes on its peculiar character of active memory. Here, history takes on the form of a repeated act of remembering: the repetition of an attempt to salvage the past from oblivion and rescue life from extinction, to rescue its remnants and to bring them back into the flow of time in the hope that they get a second chance, another possibility.

And time is really the place where all the contradictions that I have mentioned, all the tensions between the particular and the universal, past and future, loss and hope, find a momentary resolution. "There is a solution to this contradiction," writes Jankélévitch, "and this solution is time."[30] It's in an infinite and joyous work to recover all of the past, to not to let anything get lost, that the conciliation of the two opposite needs is realized and that the contradiction is solved.[31] The work is infinite because the solution to this contradiction is turned toward the end of time—it happens here and now, in every moment—but its ultimate solution is unceasingly postponed to the end of time. And it is joyous because, in living this contradiction, the Jew shakes off the tragic condition that is often ascribed to him, that of the victim, and rather rejoices at both his normality and his difference, at his being both Israel and Diaspora.

Thus from this temporal perspective, in this infinite and joyous work of recovery of all the past, the *en-plus* that remains represents both a freedom to choose in the present and a responsibility to bear witness to the past. It is at once future and promise as well as past and testimony.

Of course, this suspension between past and future, this radical uncertainty between memory and promise, this joyous and compassionate gaze that looks at the remnants of the past to prepare a future recall Walter Benjamin's famous image of the angel of history:

> There is a painting by Klee called *Angelus Novus*. It shows an angel who seems about to move away from something he stares at. His eyes are wide, his mouth is open, his wings are spread. This is how the angel of history must look. His face is turned toward the past. Where a chain of events appears before *us, he* sees one single catastrophe, which keeps

piling wreckage upon wreckage and hurls it at his feet. The angel would like to stay, awaken the dead, and make whole what has been smashed. But a storm is blowing from Paradise and has got caught in his wings; it is so strong that the angel can no longer close them. This storm drives him irresistibly into the future to which his back is turned, while the pile of debris before him grows toward the sky. What we call progress is *this* storm.[32]

Where we see a chain of events, the angel of history sees one single catastrophe whose ruins keep piling up at his feet. The angel's piteous and dismayed glance rests on this broken and scattered past and tries to gather and reconnect its remnants in the hope that this will change our perception of the present and build a possibility for the future.

It is this wreckage and this gaze—the broken, incomplete, displaced character of the remnants, and the possibility of rescuing and redeeming them in the present, like small pieces in an always different and unfinished mosaic—that will provide the theoretical framework for our discussion of the relationship between Judaism and writing in contemporary Italian literature. The interpretations of Jankélévitch, Agamben, and Levi Della Torre will help us to see how, for the four Italian writers discussed in this book, the sense of belonging to Judaism often coincides with the feeling one has when standing before the remnants.

Agamben's interpretation of the remnant as a discrepancy, as a lack of full coincidence with oneself, will help us to describe these authors' various and contrasting sentiments toward Judaism. Their attempts to define their sense of Jewish identity hint both at the failure of the idea of universality and at the impossibility, in modern times, of providing a definition of identity as completeness and fullness. Rather, what emerges from their writings is an idea of identity as exile from those parts of one's self that haven't survived the past or that have survived only as elements of a fragmentary, imperfect, and therefore vital and open, condition.

Levi Della Torre's interpretation of the remnants as the fragments of history that should be rescued by memory and brought back to life in the present, as the possibility of a *new attempt* at putting history into motion, namely as responsibility, will enable us to discuss how these authors' sense of Jewish identity is also animated by a profound sense of dismay and piety toward what has not survived the past and, therefore, by the ethical duty to remember and to construct a hope in the future.

This theoretical framework highlights how these authors' attitude toward Judaism changes over the span of a century: how it shifts from a perception of Judaism as a constraint on freedom, a limit to one's own ability to make an individual life, to a conception of Jewish identity as a tool for intellectual emancipation that can enable one's sense of individuality. Two good examples of how this change occurs are Umberto Saba's *The Jews* and Primo Levi's "Argon," one prose piece written at the beginning of the twentieth century and the other toward the end.

In 1953, while rummaging among old papers, Umberto Saba came across some early pieces that he had written between 1910 and 1912. He sent the recovered writings to his friend Carlo Levi who persuaded Saba to publish the portion of the manuscript entitled *The Jews*. They were five recollections in narrative form of Jewish life in Trieste's old ghetto toward the end of the nineteenth century. Some were memories of Saba's Jewish ancestors, and one in particular was a memory of his maternal uncle Samuel David Luzzatto, the celebrated biblical scholar Shadal. These five stories, as Saba explains in the preface to the book, were written when anti-Semitism seemed like a joke and the author was able, without remorse, to write in a light and ironic tone about his Jewish past. The fracture that the Shoah introduced between past and present seemed so deep that he would have been unable to write these stories after World War II. Saba felt the need to conclude his preface in a similar light vein by saying that much of what looked different in Jewish life at the time was in its customs and settings: it was more a matter of style than of substance, it was nothing more than a splash of color added to a world of wonders.

In 1975, Primo Levi dedicated the first chapter of *The Periodic Table*, entitled "Argon," to his Jewish ancestors. Like Saba, Levi portrays his own ancestors with an ironic and affectionate touch. They appear as noble, inert, and rare individuals: people of whom little was known, who were voluntarily or forcefully relegated to the margins of life, and who tried to reproduce the epic and biblical situation of the people of Israel on a provincial scale. In spite of their similarities, however, Saba's and Levi's narratives are constructed around a different use of memories and a different attitude toward the Jewish past.

Unlike Saba's ancestors, who seem to look at us from a remote and unreachable distance, Levi's are near and familiar. The place that they inhabit resembles the eternal present of family memories where the mere mention of one's ancestors' personal traits—their humorous language, peculiar habits, or quirky attitudes—seems to be enough to bring them back to life. One can also detect differences at the level of style. The tone of Saba's stories is realistic. His tales are recollections in narrative form of "people and things he knew and saw, or as was even more often the case, of whom he had heard talk during his childhood."[33] His five recollections unfold in front of the reader as small decorative paintings depicting Jewish life in Trieste toward the end of the nineteenth century. They are memories that have already begun to partake of the light and comforting touch of forgetfulness. Levi's "Argon," on the other hand, has the sharp and disquieting quality of memories that are still alive and do not want to be forgotten. They are juxtaposed in the casual and unpredictable order that is characteristic of involuntary memory; sometimes they are prompted by oral memory, by humorous sayings and witticisms; sometimes they have the evocative quality of visual memories, like those black and white photographs that seem to sum up an entire life in one pose or expression. In Levi's memories, his ancestors often appear "figés dans une attitude,"[34] as if their lives had been stopped and rescued just an instant before they fell into oblivion.

One memory, which appears at the very end of "Argon," is particularly significant. When *Nonna* Màlia, Levi's paternal grandmother, dies, a landslide of old things falls out of her carved walnut closet: an army of bedbugs, linen sheets that have never been used, stuffed hummingbirds that crumble into dust as soon as they are touched, and hundreds of bottles of precious wine that have turned to vinegar. Here the hyperbolic list, more typical of magic realism than of Levi's clear and sober style, is not only meant as an ironic reference to his grandmother's obsessive impulse to accumulate objects, but also as a reference to the whirling passing of time. Like a storm that takes everything away with it, time does not make distinctions between exquisite objects and garbage, and it is in sharp contrast to all that Levi is trying to build by writing "Argon": a barrier against oblivion. "I remember almost nothing about [my grandmother],"[35] he writes a few lines later. But significantly he adds a last and important memory. When Levi was a child, during his customary Sunday morning visits to his grandmother's house, the old Màlia would dig out of some recess a box of old chocolates and offer one to the child. The chocolate would be worm-eaten, and the child, with great embarrassment, would quickly hide it away in his pocket. So ends "Argon." It closes abruptly on a poignant and powerful image—and on a gesture that hints at the troubling complexity of generational memories and at the need for these memories, no matter how old, frail, and unpleasant, to be passed on, held tight and not forgotten.

There is a discrepancy between the elusive and comforting character of Saba's "splash of color" and the concrete and troubling image of the old stale chocolate. The reassuring and colorful tones of Saba's harmless recollections contrast with the troubling and bittersweet flavor of Levi's memories that cannot be easily swallowed and forgotten. Unlike Saba's *The Jews*, Levi's "Argon" is not just a collection of anecdotal memories, amusing stories that lie safely behind and can be visited from time to time at one's own discretion. Rather, "Argon" is peopled with characters, objects, and memories that may be on the verge of being forgotten but still demand to be remembered. It is not an oleograph of memory but an attempt at translating its lively, mutable, and elusive character into words. These two different approaches, these two different ways in which memories can operate, also reflect two different attitudes toward Judaism and the Jewish past. While reading Saba's recollections, one has the impression that the Jewish past is pushed back to a remote, safe distance. While reading Levi, one has the impression that writing about the Jewish past is a way to recover a connection with it and regain a sense of belonging to its history and traditions.

It is not surprising then that a few pages later in *The Periodic Table*, in the chapter entitled "Zinc," Primo Levi draws a comparison between his sense of Jewish identity and a mustard seed.[36] As a Jew, he writes, I'm the impurity, the mustard seed that is necessary for the soil to be fertile, the wheel to turn, life to be lived. Here, Levi's ties with Judaism take on a polemical concreteness: by making a direct reference to the Christian parable of the seed of mustard, to the Christian discourse on the importance of difference, Levi states the importance of Jewish difference within Christian culture. By referring to a Christian sacred text, by interpreting it, by using the image of something tangible and concrete like a seed, Levi regains possession of his sense of belonging to Judaism that would otherwise be imposed only by the external gaze of the persecutor.

In between Saba's and Levi's contrasting images, in between their opposite attitudes toward the Jewish past, there are intermediary steps. There is, for example, Natalia Ginzburg's reluctance to consider herself part of a collective—a wavering that she explains as a double form of belonging both to Judaism and Catholicism, and that she describes as a recollection of ancient words and phrases pronounced by familiar voices heard "in the darkness of a cave." And there is also Giorgio Bassani's "intimate" feeling that the Jewish past coincides with a notion of history as collective memory and a sense of individual identity as the choosing of life. In passing from the splash of color to the voices heard in the darkness of a cave, to an indefinite feeling of intimacy, to the chocolate and the seed of mustard, there is a shift toward images that express a more and more concrete and subjective sense of belonging. These writers' relationship with Judaism is no longer defined by a distant and external gaze, by a subject that casts a careless glance at a colorful splash of color on the canvas of time; rather, it is reconstructed by a subject who first listens to familiar voices, collects their words and phrases from the past, finds the feelings that link to a group, a history, and a past, and then "holds tight" to the objects that may represent her sense of belonging to a Jewish heritage. Finally that sense of belonging is reclaimed by means of a polemical reference to a Christian parable. From a glance to a voice, to a feeling, to a concrete historical condition, the external look is reabsorbed in an emancipatory perspective that regains a sense of belonging to Judaism.

Writing

Finally, the last, but by no means the least important, of our hypotheses deals specifically with writing. When the notion of history as memory becomes an integral part of a literary text, the act of writing changes. When faced with memories, writing opens up to a historical and eschatological depth, to the various meanings that past events may acquire at the horizon of time, to all the vital tensions that appear when the door of time is opened—the tension between history and imagination, between individual and collective voice, between coded literary genres and expressive freedom.

In the first place, when memories become an integral part of writing, a vital tension is generated between the rights of imagination and the rights of history. In the face of historical memories, the writer is confronted with a difficult choice between imagination and truth, fiction and reality, or, to quote Natalia Ginzburg, between "playing with domestic kittens" and "taking wild tigers out for a walk."[37] On the one hand, there are the restrictions, the limitations, and the clichés that may characterize fictional writing and on the other, the burden of history, the traps of memory, and the complexity of truth. What is at stake is how to take reality into account—how to remain faithful to the truth of historical facts while going beyond the objective and detached language of history—and, at the same time, go beyond the mere historical document without falling into the many traps of writing—trite expressions, conventional images, stale clichés, and all those embalmed forms of language that are falsifications of the truth—and, in the end, reach that moment of questioning and healing of the past where the human memory resides.

When it comes to Jewish memories in the twentieth century, of course, the Shoah is central; for example, in the recovery of a sense of belonging to Judaism that is reflected in the works of the writers I discuss. As James E. Young remarks in *Writing and Rewriting the Holocaust,* since the war years, European and American Jews often identify themselves as Jews only in relation to the Shoah. The Austrian writer and survivor Jean Améry, the son of a Christian mother and a Jewish father, for example, thought of himself as Christian until the Nazis declared that he was Jewish and persecuted him as such. As a consequence, he came to consider himself a "Catastrophe Jew," and described his sense of Jewish identity as a condition strictly linked to persecution.[38] When Primo Levi was asked about his relationship to Judaism, he also said that his sense of Jewish identity was mostly the result of the promulgation of the 1938 Fascist racial laws and of his deportation to Auschwitz. When he was asked about the source of his writing, he traced it back to the experience of the concentration camps and said that, without Auschwitz, he would never have become a writer. Primo Levi's entire work is deeply informed by the experience of the Shoah. Umberto Saba too, with the publication of *Shortcuts,* attempted to rethink his notions of Judaism and Jewish identity in the light of the Shoah: *Shortcuts* was published between March and July 1945 and, as Saba says, the book is born out of Majdaneck—the first Nazi concentration camp to be freed by the Soviet Army in July 1944. Natalia Ginzburg, on more than one occasion, said that she became aware of herself as a Jew from the moment the Jews began to be persecuted. For her, Jewish identity consisted mostly in a feeling of closeness to Jews as a persecuted minority. Giorgio Bassani dedicated most of his literary work to narrating the history of the Jewish community of Ferrara under Fascism and during the war years. It may not be entirely by chance that the publication of Bassani's *The Garden of the Finzi-Continis* (1962) and of Ginzburg's *The Things We Used to Say* (1963) occurred shortly after the Eichmann trial, when, through the attention dedicated by the media to the event, the Shoah had just started to enter the collective historical consciousness in Italy.

However, these writers' recovery of a sense of belonging to Judaism is not just a passive consequence of persecution and the Shoah. It is, rather, an active response to these events. By reconnecting with the centuries of religious and cultural Jewish life that preceded and followed the Shoah, by establishing continuity between past and future, they revive an idea of Judaism as history and culture that includes the Shoah but is not exclusively identified with it. By making the past live in the present, by the practice of history as active memory, they avoid the idea of Judaism as a series of museums, monuments, and memorials to the Jewish past. In this light, their recovery of a sense of belonging to Judaism opposes Hitler's design to annihilate Judaism as a living religion and culture and transform it into a monument to a past civilization. "By eradicating the Jewish *type* of memory," Young writes, "the Nazis would also have destroyed the possibility of regeneration through memory that has marked Jewish existence."[39] The survival of the practice of memory is also the survival of Judaism.

When an enormity like the Shoah becomes part of literary texts, however, issues of objectivity, accuracy, or truthfulness in the representation of historical facts may arise. Debate has gone as far as questioning whether or not it is appropriate to make the Shoah a subject of artistic representation, whether its events should ever be described with the tools of imagination. In this debate, emphasis often falls on the sharp opposition between history and imagination, objective and subjective narration. As preoccupied as he was with preserving memories of Auschwitz and combating the propaganda spread by deniers of the Shoah, Primo Levi remarked that, in order not to misrepresent the truth, one should write in a clear, understandable, and approachable style—a claim that was also the result of his scientific and positivistic background. Nonetheless, in spite of his attention to the objectivity of historical facts, Levi's works on the Shoah include not only narratives of historical events but also personal memoirs, literary essays, poems, and novels, in which, while being attentive to the truth of historical facts, he felt free to incorporate fictional accounts, literary references, rhetorical and figurative devices born out of subjective imagination.

According to Roland Barthes, the claim to absolute objectivity on the part of historians is an illusion. "This illusion," he writes, "is not confined to historical discourse: novelists galore, in the days of realism, considered themselves 'objective' because they had suppressed all traces of the *I* in their text."[40] Not only the historical discourse but also the literary one can be characterized by the illusion of objectivity and, therefore, by the tendency to eliminate every trace of subjectivity within the text. The Shoah, of course, is a unique historical event, a collective tragedy that affects people who are still living, and whose existence is routinely denied by self-styled historians and revisionists of all kinds. Therefore, the attention that survivors, historians, or simple readers devote to the objectivity of historical facts is more than justified. However, as Young notes, to remove the Shoah from the realm of imagination, to place it in a distant and untouchable sanctuary of the past, is to risk excluding it altogether from public consciousness.

To make room for subjectivity within the text, allowing traces of the *I* does not necessarily mean undermining the authenticity of history. On the contrary, a narration based on imagination may have its own authenticity that can contribute to a different type of knowledge of the facts, a knowledge that is more than historical. Paraphrasing Young, one could say that the wisdom of fictional narrations is not less credible because it stems from imagined, rather than actual, events.[41] The point is not to concentrate on the threat that imagination may pose to the integrity of historical narratives but to move from historical events to the explanations and knowledge that are created through the narration of events—and, at the same time, to move to a kind of narrative that incorporates historical facts without denying the existence and the importance of the subjective gaze. A writing that takes reality into account without sacrificing, in the name of objectivity and realism, other subjective aspects, such as the emotional and the ethical dimensions of writing: the acknowledgment of past sorrows and joys as well as the exercise of judgment.

From this perspective, one no longer needs to draw a sharp distinction between historical facts and their literary representations, objectivity and subjectivity, history and imagination. What exists between them is, rather, a tension. As Young writes:

> The purely literary and the purely historical worlds were never really pure of each other, but were often all too tragically interdependent. Contrary to those who see the world and its representations operating independently of one another, "life" and "life-in-writing"—catastrophe and our response to it—have always interpenetrated; in this way, literature remembers past destructions even as it shapes our practical responses to current crisis.[42]

Language and reality are never sharply opposed since it is language that makes our knowledge of reality possible. Thus history and literature, facts and their interpretations, past and present are profoundly intertwined, and the place where they are most closely interdependent is memory: the place where we remember the historical past in order to shape possible responses to our present. History as memory, the historical fact, which through memory becomes a paradigm for behavior in the present, changes the opposition between history and memory into a vital tension. Thus what results is not an undermining of the credibility of historical facts. It is rather a matter of comprehending how history is known, told, and understood in narratives, and what the consequences are of these narratives, which may serve as both "inspiration to and paradigm for resistance."[43] What counts, as Young has rightly remarked, is the capacity of a narrative to sustain and enable life itself.[44]

As Aharon Appelfeld has written in *Beyond Despair,* when remembering the recent Jewish past, when writing about the Shoah, historical research must meet up with artistic writing. In the fifty years following the end of World War II, survivors have produced an impressive body of memories of their experiences in the extermination camps; historians have gathered and interpreted a vast number of facts that provide us with an exhaustive political, social, and psychological background of the period. Now, notes Appelfeld, we must transfer the atrocious experience of the Shoah from the field of history to that of art, since it is only art that has the power to take sufferance out of the abyss, to put it back within the circle of life.[45] The works of the writers discussed in this book develop precisely in this delicate passage between history and art. They are on the ridge where truth and historical facts can no longer be eluded, and imagination and creative writing become precious tools to give voice to the past: not only a factual and documentary voice but a voice of questioning and healing. The act of writing becomes a difficult but vital exercise of mediation between history and imagination: an act of ethical responsibility toward the historical past as well as an act of free imagination and preparation of the future that lies ahead.[46]

From a strictly literary point of view, this mediation implies a series of changes in traditional narrative structures. Writing about historical memories is no longer just a question of including past historical events within the narrative plot or a matter of depicting historical figures as fictional characters, as it would be, for instance, in a traditional historical novel. It is rather a question of recovering memories of the past within the present as a possible preparation and anticipation of the future. Both Ginzburg's *The Things We Used to Say* and Bassani's *The Garden of the Finzi-Continis* are literary works whose structures and narrative styles are informed by the recollection of past events and by their questioning in the present, so that a future may still be possible. Consequently, in both Ginzburg's memoir and Bassani's novel, the plot is not organized in a rigid chronological order; rather, it seems to adjust itself to the flux of memories, to their random and fragmentary nature, as if the narrating voice were in constant mediation between past and future, between history and imagination, between a past that asks to be remembered and the various possibilities of giving it a voice and meaning in the present. Similarly, historical events are never structured as an organized and coherent fresco meant as a historical background for the actions of the fictional characters. History, in these novels, appears as a storm of random and fleeting events, a chaos of words, faces, details, fragments that are questioned in their seeming absence of significance and for the meaning that they may gain in the present.

Secondly, the inclusion of living memories within the literary text generates a tension between individual and collective history: between the narrating voice of the individual who wants to tell a story, which is larger and older than him, and the many narrative techniques at his disposal to tell that story. In the literary texts discussed in the following chapters, the transmission of Jewish memories often coincides with a dilution of the experience of the individual within a collective experience, and with a translation of the narrating "I" into a narrating "We." To be capable of telling his or her own story, the subject has to take into account the larger and more ancient history of those who came before. Writing about oneself becomes a way to bear witness to their past lives in the present.

A third consequence of this tension is the emancipation of writing from highly coded literary genres. When historical memories become part of a narrative, writing is emancipated from the strict hierarchy of genres that has characterized the Italian literary tradition for centuries. From this perspective, the act of testimony also becomes an act of literary freedom.

The Italian literary tradition is founded upon the norms of imitation of Greek and Latin classical authors that were established at the end of the Middle Ages by Humanist intellectuals. This notion of writing implies the existence of a universal, immutable, and undifferentiated language of artistic expression on which authors have to draw to compose their literary works. This idea of language also builds a thin but robust wall between reality and writing that nurtures a self-referential notion of writing as a creative work that feeds mostly on itself and that, ultimately, contradicts pluralism of expression.[47] What does not approach the ideal and immutable model of literary expression cannot be considered "true literature." That is what occurs with some of the works written by the authors under discussion in this book. As all hybrid works that do not fit easily within the defined boundaries of traditional literary genres, these invite us to question commonly accepted criteria of authentic literary writing used to determine what falls into the realm of Literature and what does not. In particular, these writers set themselves free from traditional literary genres and create hybrid forms of literary communication that are in between autobiography and fiction, historical essay and literary work, moral meditation and aphoristic poetry. Saba's *Shortcuts,* Ginzburg's *The Things We Used to Say,* and Levi's *The Periodic Table,* to name just a few of the works I discuss, are literary works that are born out of a need to take into account Jewish memories, to bear witness to a distant and recent, tragic and comic Jewish past. In order to fulfill this task, their authors push the boundaries of traditional literary genres and create new modes of writing that represent innovations in the Italian literary tradition and may change consolidated notions of Literature and writing. These works take us back to the moment in which writing becomes literature, to the place where one begins to wonder why we write and how we write, to that peculiar literary practice where reality peeks in and the mechanism of fiction is laid bare. Of course, these works are not conceived by their authors as normative examples of how to write; they are not prescriptive invitations to abandon fiction in favor of purely documentary writing—as a matter of fact, their authors wrote books inspired both by reality and imagination. Rather, these works stand before their readers as question marks without definite and secure answers. Or, to resume the leading metaphor of our discourse, as unlabeled vessels in which one may be able to find remnants of a broken past, the tiles of an incomplete and unfinished mosaic that always subtracts itself from any final classification and in which what counts is not so much the overall picture but the meanings of the individual parts and the relations among them. What counts is the provisional and incomplete picture that one succeeds in putting together with the remnants from the past, the fragments of reality that fall at one's feet, and the life that one is able to infuse in them.

When asked about the presence of Jewish motifs in her writing, Clara Sereni—author of *Keeping House*—referred to this fragmented, nonhomogenous and nonsystematic character of Jewish culture:

I think that there is . . . an aspect of my writing . . . that gives to my literary works a profoundly Jewish character: it's the giving up of the fresco,
of the overall picture, in favor of the mosaic, namely the composition
characterized by a particular care for the meaning of the individual tiles,
and for the links between them, more than by the claim to provide the
readers with unambiguous and exhaustive answers. It is a way of writing
that may have something to do with the type of speculation typical of the
Midrash and is different from the Christian and Catholic traditions, both
inclined more towards the parable than the questioning, more towards the
use of edifying words than dialectical words.[48]

By means of a definition of Jewish culture based on the double meaning of the word *mosaic*—which may refer to the art form as well as to
Mosaic law—Clara Sereni compares the survival of Jewish elements in her
literary works to an act of recovery and a combination of "tiles" that have
meaning in their incomplete, nonsystematic, relational character. An echo
of this view of reality may be found at the beginning of a letter that Kafka
wrote to his friend Milena on June 23, 1920: "It's difficult to tell the truth,
since there is only one truth, but that truth is alive and therefore has a
lively, changing face."[49] Jankélévitch concludes in his essay on the tension
between resemblance and difference, "It is not the Jew who is undecided
and contradictory, it is the very truth that presents itself as lacerated and
undone . . . It is truths that are sporadic and incompatible and that cannot
be honored all together."[50] Here, as in Kafka and in Clara Sereni, the unity
of meaning—that may descend from monotheistic faith—and its elusiveness—that comes from history—seem to be preserved in the existence of
a lively and fragmented truth and in the possibility of catching a glimpse
of it in its various facets, by gathering and assembling the fragments of a
stormy history in a new picture that, in its new form, may find again its
ancient familiar face. "What is old," wrote Vittorio Foa, "finds itself again
by becoming different."[51]

1

The Maternal Borders of the Soul

IDENTITY, JUDAISM, AND WRITING

IN THE WORKS OF UMBERTO SABA

IN MARCH 1945, before an audience of members of the Roman cultural circle *Ritrovo*, whose president was Princess Marguerite Caetani, Umberto Saba read a selection of the poems he had composed between 1935 and 1943. The occasion, as we learn from an article by Giacomo Debenedetti, was a solemn one: Saba was seated near the fireplace in a large room draped with tapestries and read his poems to a refined and elegant audience that was ready to see in him one of the greatest living Italian poets.[1] The war, however, was not yet over; though Rome had been liberated in June 1944, a large part of northern Italy was still occupied by the Fascists. As Saba read his poems, massacres and deportations were still taking place.

On that occasion, Saba also read a short poem dedicated to Federico Almansi, the *celeste scolaro,* the "heavenly pupil" the poet had met fifteen years earlier, who had become his friend and the dedicatee of several of his poems.

> You used to run about your father's house
> silent as a cat. Pain you knew by name
> alone, and not for what it really is.
> Far from your companions, the roses
> on your bony cheeks began to fade.
> Dear young friend, flower of life,
> reborn within my soul. It's yours,
> this final, yet remaining tear
> of mine, which you can't see.

The poem, published in 1944 in *Lost Things* (1935–43) under the title "For a Sick Boy," was read to the *Ritrovo* with the title "For a Jewish Boy." On March 16 of the same year, Saba wrote in a letter, "The poem for him [Federico], called 'For a Sick Boy,' which I read with the title, 'For a Jewish Boy,' after I read it, met with something like a murmur of approval in that elegant room."[2] Perhaps that period of horrors and ambiguities that was coming to a close cast a dark shadow over Saba's decision to change the title of Almansi's poem, over the pairing of illness and Judaism, and over the murmur of approval that ran through the audience of *Ritrovo*. Perhaps something of the ancient and durable myth of Judaism as disease subsists in the poet's desire to change the title, for in his youth he had been a passionate reader of Weininger.[3] And perhaps in the murmur of the audience, faced with the popular nineteenth-century image of the sick Jew, one can already see signs of the attitude toward the Shoah that would come to the fore after the war: the sentimentalism that Cynthia Ozick discusses in her essay on Anne Frank's diary, in which grief for the fate of an abstract victim is merely the obverse of indifference to the extinction of a real life.[4]

True, from the end of the 1930s, Federico Almansi was afflicted with a serious mental illness that would lead to his premature death, and, as the son of a Jewish father, from 1938 on he would face the discrimination and persecution of the Fascist regime, but in the poems that Saba dedicates to him, the poet goes beyond the events of the young man's life and seems, with a touch of nineteenth-century melodrama, to want to weave together illness, psychology, and the Fascist racial laws: "Far from your companions, the roses / on your bony cheeks began to fade."[5] Flowers, pallor, and nineteenth-century languor draw a veil of sentimentalism over the tragic events that befell the persecuted young man and bring his illness back into the reassuring fold of other literary illnesses: they relegate it to the mythic domain where illness becomes the reflection of a defect in sentiment, a blemish in psychology, or a foundering in history. Perhaps Saba is flattering his elegant *Ritrovo* audience because he knows that sentimentality is but a form of forgetting.

Three years later, in 1948, in a brief essay—the preface to the single volume of poetry that the young Almansi published—in which he reconstructs the stages of their friendship, Saba connects the appearance of

Almansi's illness to the promulgation of Italy's anti-Semitic laws: "In the meantime came 1938 with its cortège of troubles. The eternally ominous year brought with it, among other absurdities, the absurdity of the racial campaign in Italy. In addition, it brought to the young Federico Almansi a grave illness, from which it was feared he would die."[6] Moreover, in the same preface, referring to the young Almansi's education in medicine, Saba insists on the existence of a close relationship between illness and morality: "On yet another evening, I led him on a walk along the pleasant banks of the Bacchiglione. I told him some of my ideas about medicine. Above all else, I told him about the close relationship between the physical and the moral and that a good doctor could not ignore this relationship, especially after the many strange things which had been discovered on the subject in recent years."[7] Thus, in the golden glow of a walk along the banks of an urban river, the terrible myth that illness has an emotional cause springs up, and the specters that haunt the age seep into the somber landscape that is the background of Almansi's education for life.

For Saba, Judaism too takes on the traits of a psychological illness, an emotional disturbance that manifests itself in excessive pessimism. As consumptives in the nineteenth century seemed to be laden with feelings that needed to be attenuated, and cancer patients in the twentieth seem bereft of feelings that should be encouraged, so it seemed to Saba that he had inherited from his Jewish ancestors a heavy emotional burden that needed to be tempered.[8] The change in the title of the poem for Almansi can perhaps best be explained as the projection of the poet's ego onto the sick young Jew since Saba himself, as the son of a Jewish mother and a Catholic father, thought he had been afflicted from birth with a spiritual illness, a sort of difference, a divided heart: "Oh my heart split into two from birth, / how many pains I endured to make it into one! / How many roses to conceal an abyss!"[9]

Some people have seen unequivocal signs of Jewish anti-Semitism in the way that Saba relates to Judaism; others have looked at this relationship for evidence of the survival of a Jewish soul.[10] What interests me, in the context of a book dedicated to the relationship between Judaism and writing, is how—through his friendship with Almansi, his conflicted relationship to Judaism, and his discovery of psychoanalysis—Umberto Saba's life and works help us better understand the uneasiness that appears in European culture with regard to Judaism and Jewish identity in the late nineteenth and early twentieth centuries. They also help us to see how Saba's choice of literary genres at a later stage in his career—in particular, his ultimate privileging of prose over poetry—mirrors his ambivalence toward Judaism as well as reflecting his attempts to overcome it.[11]

Umberto Saba was born in Trieste in 1883 to an unhappy union between a Jewish mother and a Catholic father. In a letter to his friend, Nora Baldi, Saba describes the conflicts that flared up between his parents immediately after their wedding. His mother, Felicita Rachele Coen, who the poet claims "didn't know how to live, nor how to let others live,"[12] was of a serious nature that did not complement the volubility of his father, Ugo Edoardo Poli, a man who was "light and cheerful."[13] Saba's father had been arrested by the Austro-Hungarian police for Italian nationalist activities (Trieste was not yet a part of Italy) and was actually in prison on the day of his son's birth. He abandoned his family only one year after his wedding, abjuring the Jewish faith to which he had converted in order to marry. Saba thus spent his childhood divided between the attentions of a Catholic wet nurse, into whose care he had been placed after his father's flight, and the affection of a maternal aunt and other members of his mother's family.

All of Saba's work can be read in light of the complex family geography that the poet later interpreted as a breach—between two lives, two home-lands, and two religions—that could not be healed. "My triple misfortune," he wrote, "was to be born Italian, Triestine, and of a Jewish mother. These three misfortunes together made the *Songbook*,"[14] as if writing and inspiration were situated precisely in an incurable breach of identity.

It is into this literary and psychological context that Saba's friendship with Federico Almansi is etched. The aspiring young writer appears to the older poet as another version of himself, in whose youth he finds perhaps that last precious opportunity to give meaning to this breach in identity. Through his friendship with Almansi, Saba has the impression of being able to retrace his steps through time, to be able to recover once more the joys of his own youth and his hopes for the future. "But what I've lost," he wrote in a poem dedicated to the boy, "you give me back, nightingale / alighting on my branch."[15] Elsewhere, he wrote, "Young starling in whom I placed / some hope for the future."[16] In his conversations with Almansi, Saba tried to focus on as complete an image of himself as he could, turning his triple misfortune into a form of identity: "'This is an odd city,' the young writer Federico Almansi replied to me promptly, as he accompanied me this summer along Viale XX Settembre. And, with a surviving gratitude or tenderness in his eyes for his oh so very old teacher, added, 'Like you.'"[17] Like the city of Trieste, on the border between the Austro-Hungarian empire and the kingdom of Italy, between central European and Mediterranean culture, and between Communism and capitalism, Saba remained an eccentric when viewing himself through Almansi's eyes, and he made this eccentricity the hinge upon which the fortunes and misfortunes of his identity as man and writer turned.

Saba was introduced to Federico Almansi in 1930. The poet had met Federico's father, Emanuele Almansi, an antiquarian book dealer, in Padua, where he had gone on a business trip for his own *Libreria Antiquaria*. The book dealer invited him to his home, where Saba met his six-year-old son. "A shy boy," Saba would say of him many years later, when recalling that first meeting.[18] On other occasions, he called him "wild cat," "young starling," "nightingale," and "canary," including him in the affective zoo in which he liked to group people who were dear to him. At the invitation of the boy's mother, during one of his sporadic visits to the Almansi house Saba read Almansi some of his poems, thus initiating him into writing poetry, a literary education that would culminate in 1948 with the publication of the latter's first and only volume of poems.

After the war, Saba was a periodic guest in the Almansi apartment in via Andrea Doria in Milan from the fall of 1945 until May 1948. The poems of those years, by both Almansi and Saba, give us an image of domestic life in which the friendship between the old and the young man takes on the traits of an exceptional spiritual experience: the teacher is compared to a god, the disciple to a "heavenly schoolboy," and their relationship develops according to a pattern that recalls the classical forms of Socratic pedagogy, whose potentially erotic implications are sublimated in the young man's initiation into the spiritual language of poetry. "A god, teacher, I saw you on earth. / Good voice you corrected me with love. / You taught hopes and rare good things. / My fresh age bloomed before yours / tired, in decline," Almansi wrote in a poem dedicated to Saba and significantly entitled "Teacher."[19]

But pedagogy was merely the external form of this loving friendship. Its substance is the frisson of self-knowledge or, rather, the feeling of discomfort a subject has when faced with that part of himself that has not yet been identified. In a recent inquiry into the concept of genius, Giorgio Agamben states that when we feel emotion, we enter into contact with that which precedes the definition of subjectivity. Emotion therefore would be nothing but "the presence within us of a part that is forever immature, infinitely adolescent, and hesitant to cross the threshold of any individuation."[20] Even the strong emotional correspondence between the old Saba and the young Almansi, the very reason for their intimacy, presents itself as a hesitation on the threshold of identity, as the result of a tension between the ego and genius, between the necessity to give a name to one's own individual consciousness and the need to conserve what has not yet been identified in us. It is precisely by virtue of this tension that, for the older poet, the young man's presence possesses the generative capacity to call back to life what no longer exists. "Dear friends revive in you / and the dead seasons. That you exist / is a wonder," Saba wrote in a poem from *Late Things* dedicated to Almansi.[21]

Such exceptionality, however, implies another exceptionality founded on the specular nature of their relationship: "But another [wonder] surpassed it: that in you I refound my own time that was."[22] Like Narcissus at the spring, the poet sees himself in the young man and finds in the other a period of his own life; he sees himself as an adolescent again who can still move between identity and indefiniteness, comprehension and ignorance. He once again finds the hope of understanding the incomprehensible feeling that he has in the presence of what has not been identified, and that remains unknown: "It is this elusive young boy, this *puer,* who stubbornly pushes us toward others, in whom we seek precisely the emotion that remains incomprehensible in ourselves, hoping that by some miracle it will be clarified and elucidated in the mirror of the other."[23]

Moreover, the picture of Almansi's life that can be gleaned from his poems and from Saba's writing is a reflection, almost a reverse image, of the life of the young Umberto. Almansi too was the son of an oppressive mother and an absent father. "I have seen a mother / kill her son with too greedy a kiss . . . I have seen hate in her pale blue eyes,"[24] writes Almansi in a poem that is almost a reverse paraphrase—that is, transferred from father to mother—of the famous verse of *Autobiography* that Saba had written twenty years earlier: "My father was for me 'the murderer.'"[25] Several of Almansi's poems take their inspiration from his father's distance and from the feeling of incomprehension the son has when faced with his father's aging and his loss of authority:

> You moved away in the darkness of night,
> at a bend in the road I lose you.
> The sound of your steps is lost
> in the wind that raises dead things.
> Now it is silent between the dull houses.
> Everything is inert again, without life.[26]

Saba himself located the kernel of his poetic inspiration in this feeling of longing for an absent father. Almansi too was born to a marriage of parents of different religions, but in his case, his father was Jewish and his mother Catholic. And, like Saba, he too would refuse Catholic baptism as a means of avoiding the racial discrimination and persecution of the Fascist years.

But if specularity is what makes the relationship between the old man and the young man possible, it also sets a limit. The mirror image conceals the coldness and giddiness of self-love, of the narcissistic cult of one's own image. Saba and Almansi shared the same bedroom, they watched and listened to each other, but, in the silence of sleep, the reversed symmetry of the image reflected in the mirror cracks. "Sleep has descended invisibly," Almansi wrote, "your / face in repose abandons itself to dreams. / No shadow obscures your peace."[27] Indirectly Saba replies, "At night, when awake, I hear the young boy / groaning in his sleep; when asleep, I hear / the gasps of souls in torment."[28] The young man's troubled sleep contrasts with the peaceful sleep of the poet; one man's peacefulness and dreams and the other's sobs and stirrings, almost a foreboding of the terrible mental illness that would afflict the boy in a few years. If the old man finds himself in the young man, perhaps the boy is beginning to lose himself in the fixity of an image of himself that is modeled on the other's desires.

One day in April 1946, Almansi found among his papers the draft of a poem that Saba had sent him from Trieste. The poem's last lines are inspired by Rubens's *Rape of Ganymede*: "But the boy was of the sky already / and sprinkled the earth for the last time."[29] Nestled in the image of the last line, as in the choice of the poem's subject, is a certain cruelty, a slight sadism. Along with the composition "Narcissus at the Pool," the poem forms the diptych "Two Ancient Fables," as if to suggest that rapaciousness is the other side of a relationship based on specularity, and that the image that corresponds to a reflection on the water's surface is the flight of a dark eagle into the cloudless blue, into which all of Saba's heavenly friends disappear.

"I'd invested such hope in the game! But then, / once they were laid on the table, / *all the cards were against me,*"[30] Saba wrote in the poem "Card Game." "I loved you for listening to me," he would add in his famous poem "I loved," "and my good card, turned in at the game's end."[31] In a game in which he has the impression of having received all the wrong cards, Saba remains uncertain until the end about how to close out the hand. But he holds on to his one good card. The friendship between Saba and Almansi belongs to that moment when Prospero hesitates over whether to abandon Ariel. And by hesitating, he loses him.[32]

Occasionally, when reading Saba's poems, one has the impression of walking the streets of a city where everything has changed: streets have become unrecognizable, certain corners no longer provide comfort, squares and courtyards are not the same as before. This city is a series of places whose change reflects a transformation in the soul: it is the end of a happy youth that has been shaken by a noisy and hostile adult life, as if the poet, by naming these places, were trying to trace before the reader's eyes a vast map of loss.[33] They are real places, like the streets and neighborhoods of Trieste, but they are also abstract and imaginary places that need to be cut out and preserved in the map of the soul for life to be more tolerable. For then one can find a happy space, the sweetness of a warm corner, the propitious oasis in which one's heart is still reflected in one's words; or, beyond urban topography, the Dalmatian coasts that the young Ulysses sailed in a sonnet by Saba, or the little port on the edge of the Adriatic that becomes, lyrically, a door that opens onto dreams. They become all the places in the world, as the poet would write in the poem "I had," where "I was safe."[34]

Even the friendship between Saba and Federico Almansi is inscribed within a geography in which external space and its changes reflect changes of feeling. The room that Saba shared with Almansi during his stay in Milan thus becomes the reflection of a painful passage from adolescence to adulthood, as well as of the possibility of healing the breach that the poet sees in his own identity. More particularly, an interior space opens up in his friendship with Almansi that changes with their respective identities. The relationship between the two takes on a different hue from that of a simple friendship between an old man and a young one, or between a teacher and his student, and turns into a family relation between parent and child. In this relation, however, Saba is not the father but the mother. "I look at him / breathing close to me," he writes in the poem "Friend" dedicated to Almansi, "like tender mother / would look at a son / born beyond hope."[35] Only in this way, only through this transformation of a lover's friendship into maternity, is Saba able to find his own past again and, with it, the hope of a second possibility, of a life that is finally complete.

Take, for example, the poem "Metamorphosis," published in *Mediterranea* in 1946. The inspiration for its composition was a short conversation between Saba and Almansi on love of one's country. Almansi asked the poet what country he would like to belong to if he were not Italian, and Saba answered by asking the boy the same question. Of Almansi's reply, which is intentionally not given in the text, Saba records only the image of his mouth that "form[s] / a name like a kiss," and of his great big eyes that "in their sweetness touch the soul's / maternal borders."[36] Once again, in place of an ability to relate, in place of a poetic dialogue between a subject and an interlocutor, Saba prefers specularity, the projection of an "I" onto a "you"; he prefers a dialogue of glances to one of words. But Saba's silence provokes Almansi; the boy's softness turns to anger, his looks become stern, he is filled with hate, and the poem closes, significantly, with the word "enemy." In Saba's poetic universe, the mere mention of a homeland causes a breach. To Almansi's questions about the ideal homeland, Saba's silence and thoughts on the borders of the soul form a contrast. Against the paternal borders of nations, Saba offers the maternal borders of the soul as a counterpoint; against those of a definite space, an indefinite space; against paternal love, maternal love; and against a place of conflict between father and son, a place of harmony expanding like a womb to accommodate a son. "Reborn within my soul," Saba had written of Almansi in the poem that he read to his *Ritrovo* audience, "flower of life."[37] Similarly, in "The Sapling," the poet's pity for a little tree that reminds him of a boy who is too tall for his green age widens in a maternal embrace: "Vast in its grief / is your motherhood."[38]

Obviously, in this contrast, more than one echo from the poet's own life can be heard: his birth in a homeland like Trieste, divided in its allegiance between Austria and Italy, to an absent father who was arrested by the Austro-Hungarian police for Italian nationalist activities on the day of his son's birth. In Saba's writing, homeland and paternity are difficult paths fraught with hardship. Not coincidentally, "Metamorphosis" is the second in a group of three poems dedicated to Telemachus, a young man who, like Almansi and the young Saba reflected in him, awaits with his mother the return of a distant father. Motherhood seems to be the only path possible. It is within the maternal borders, in a womb that is both real and metaphorical—significantly located in the middle of the three stanzas that make up the poem "Metamorphosis"—that words like *sweetness* and *kiss* are paired. In the last stanza, however, there is room only for words such as *harsh, hatred,* and *enemy,* and Almansi's soft eyes become fiery. "A boy fights with his father," Saba writes in a brief prose piece from the collection *Shortcuts,* which shows a clear Freudian influence, "afterwards, he can feel freer, even happy. But if he fights with his mother, the gloom accompanies him for several days. Patricide is in man's nature, one of the conditions of his progress. Matricide is a different thing. And he is pursued by the Furies of Orestes."[39]

In order to better understand the meaning of this opposition between fatherhood and motherhood, one must follow the path indicated by Saba himself in this prose piece, the path of Freudian psychoanalysis. Saba was a firm believer—at least from the beginning of his analysis with Dr. Weiss in the late 1920s—in the Freudian interpretation of the work of art as a sublimation of socially unacceptable impulses. Saba often applies this analysis and interpretation of literary texts to his own works as well as to those of others. In a letter from August 1953 to Pierantonio Quarantotti Gambini, a young writer from Istria, Saba congratulates the young man on the beauty of a passage from his novel, *The Wave of the Cruiser (L'onda dell'incrociatore),* that describes two boys falling into the water: "The most beautiful moment of your novel is . . . when the two boys, fighting, lose their balance and fall into the water—for your and the reader's unconscious take refuge in the mother's womb: sea (mare) = mother (ma[d]re). It goes without saying that, in writing it, you were unaware of it (indeed, you didn't have to) and the reader doesn't know it either, but he notices it."[40]

For Saba, who proposes a psychoanalytical reading of this literary text, the fall of the novel's protagonists, Ario and Berto, into the water is clearly the expression of a desire to regress into the maternal womb that has been mediated through writing. The magic of the relationship between the two boys, the fact that the moment described above is both an embrace and a struggle, love and hate, is providentially preserved by the fall into the water, that is, by regression into a space that precedes birth, where the subject can still be conceived of as whole: "The mixed sensations of eroticism of the two youths, who tussle with each other in the boat and while they seem—and are—animated by hate, are dazed by each other's power and enjoy it, until, providentially, they lose their balance and both fall into the water—their sensations are shown with a grace and a care that make them appear new."[41] That the two boys fall into the water is also providential because it frees them from having to become aware of the desire they feel for one another. In psychoanalytic terms, this is a metaphor for the return to the womb, namely for the desire to regress to a state of unconsciousness in which the subject believes he can find his own innocence and wholeness again. The womb excludes consciousness.

Not surprisingly, then, in another letter to Quarantotti Gambini, Saba comments negatively on the development of the novel's plot, in which he glimpses the presence of a sense of guilt. At the end of the novel, the young protagonist is unwittingly responsible for the death of an innocent character. The novel ends with the image of a floating hat that belonged to an old Alpine climber, who, because of a clumsy joke played by Ario and Berto, sinks under water along with a heavy *maona,* an old barge used for unloading goods, and drowns. Saba did not like this ending because he thought it grew out of an unconscious need on the part of the author to find among the characters of the novel someone to punish for his own sins. It is no coincidence that the provisional title of the novel was *The Heavy Barge (La greve maona),* a choice that places at the novel's center the situation in which a character who symbolizes guilt is found dead. The novel's final title, *The Wave of the Cruiser,* was based on a suggestion by Saba, who preferred the lightness of the wave's foam to the weightiness of the *maona*.[42] Here, Saba contrasts the search for happiness without consciousness with the idea of combining joy and consciousness.

More relevant still, for the purposes of my inquiry, is the fact that Saba, commenting on the novel's conclusion, connects the weight of a sense of guilt to Judaism: "And why," he writes in a letter to Quarantotti Gambini, "inside of you, have you made an assassin of the sweet Ario? The image that comes to mind—the first—is that of the 'chosen people' who loaded their sins onto a goat. But I don't know how valid this could be. Of course, it's not about facts, but about tendencies more or less repressed and buried in the subconscious, which are then brought to light through art."[43] Even in his reading of Quarantotti Gambini's novel, Saba finds his own existential breach once again, that clear separation between the heaviness of guilt and the lightness of life, thereby establishing a link between the former and Jewish morality, and between the latter and an abstract concept of innocence.

Ernesto, the novel that Saba worked on in the last years of his life, also relates the story of a metaphorical regression to the womb that helps resolve a conflict between sexuality and chastity. After a homoerotic encounter with an adult, Ernesto confesses his "guilt" to his mother and receives her pardon. In the novel, Saba's artistic and moral sensibility touches on the homoerotic subject; he describes homoeroticism as a longing and a search for an absent father only to push it away and situate it outside of consciousness. After his homoerotic experience, his confession to his mother, and her pardon, Ernesto meets Ilio, a young man who not only appears so perfect to Ernesto that the latter wishes to be him but who also seems innocent, free of the "guilt" with which he is tainted. One only has to see him to understand that Ilio has never given himself over "to that, neither with women nor men."[44] Outside the womb, Ernesto finds Ilio, an alter ego who is whole because undivided by the guilt of sexual desire. Perhaps Ilio and Ernesto, joined in the womb like Ario and Berto in Quarantotti Gambini's novel, are an attempt to heal the breach in identity, to resolve the contrast between sexuality and guilt, between "the two races in ancient strife."[45] But the novel is unfinished, and Ernesto's story is left hanging. Ilio does not become a real character; he remains only the projection of his friend's desire for completion—as Almansi, perhaps, was for Saba.

So the breach in Ernesto's identity is not healed in the world of the novel. For Saba's readers, there remains on the one hand lightness as represented by Ernesto, strolling along Trieste's streets in search of a father and finding homoerotic love, and on the other, a sense of the heaviness of guilt and the boy's metaphorical flight into the womb. Because of this breach, as Mario Lavagetto has remarked, the novel is enveloped in "a premeditated atmosphere of 'ancient Greece,' of a world apparently free of Jewish heritage."[46] "I am not an anti-Semite," Saba wrote in a letter in 1953, "I am so only when I read the Greek poets. Because it's the Jews who have spread through the world 'the sense of guilt' (compare the Greeks and the Bible), who have, above all, cast the evil eye on love."[47] As is well-known, however, this clear distinction between Semitism and Hellenism, between the idea of a divided historical present and the phantasm of a mythical past of wholeness, was not simply the personal mythology of a few poets; it was also a collective fantasy, an invention of the culture of the mid-nineteenth century, which was ill at ease with modernity. And it was Freud who pointed to the psychological and individual root of this collective unease called identity.

In Turin, at number 6 via Carlo Alberto, there is a marble plaque dedicated to Friedrich Nietzsche's brief stay in the city. The house is not far from the equestrian statue of the king who conceded the Albertine Statutes, one of the first Italian constitutional documents, and from the palazzo that welcomed the first parliament of United Italy. On the plaque, which was placed on the house to celebrate the centenary of the German philosopher's birth, are these words: "In this house, Friedrich Nietzsche knew the fullness of the spirit which attempts the unknown, the will to power that gives rise to the hero. Here, to testify to great destiny and genius, he wrote *Ecce Homo,* the book of his life."[48] The date on the plaque is one of the darkest imaginable: October 15, 1944, the twenty-second year of the Fascist era. Almost one year had passed since the day on which 1,259 Roman Jews had been deported to Auschwitz.[49] Only a few months had passed since the massacre at the Ardeatine Caves and the departure of the first convoys of deportees from the transit camp at Fossoli. And only a few days had passed since the slaughter of innocent civilians at Sant'Anna di Stazzema and Marzabotto. A good part of northern Italy was still occupied by the Fascists, and in Turin, in the same places that had celebrated the ideals of equality and unity of the Risorgimento, people were trying to resuscitate a half-dead idea of homeland and fatherhood in Nietzsche's name, to impose an intellectual genealogy that did not stem from unity and equality but from division, singularity, and domination—the domination of heroes over peoples, of teachers over disciples, and of fathers over sons.

Saba's writing reflects the ambivalence that permeated European culture from the middle of the nineteenth to the middle of the twentieth century with regard to themes of belonging and identity, homelands and literary fathers. His poems feel the effects of this climate of clear opposition between the grayness of the present and the splendor of a mythical past, between the seriousness of the Jewish and Christian traditions and the lightness of the Dionysian spirit of ancient Greece. In Florence, where he had taken refuge to escape deportation and anti-Semitic persecution after September 18, 1943, Saba began work on a first draft of *History and Chronicle of the Songbook,* the study in which he attempted a critical organization of his literary work, by looking once again at the intellectual paternity of some of his poems. In the pages where he comments on the poems he had written between 1913 and 1915, he discusses at some length the subject of the poem "The Patriarch" and its inspiration. In an old farmer at work on a hill in front of his house, Saba sees a biblical figure: an old patriarch who "after fecundating a whole world with himself, thinks, 'Happy are the unborn.'"[50] To Saba, this negative vision of life seemed to confirm his "innate pessimism (essentially Semitic)." At the same time, however, the poet adds that his poems were never laden with the incurable melancholy and sadness that can derive from this vision of life. On the contrary, he claims to have always been sensitive "to those few drops of gold that fall upon our tongues from time to time, and which led Nietzsche to despise those who either don't notice them or pretend not to notice them." "Almost all of Saba's later poetry," he then adds, "is made up of those rare drops of gold."[51]

Once again, Saba places himself and his literary work between two positions that he deems antithetical: on one side are the seriousness and existential pessimism that he perceives as deriving from Jewish culture, and on the other, the lightness and joy of artistic creation that he affiliates with Nietzsche's thought.[52] Hovering on these pages are personal ghosts and collective fantasies—not only the biographical phantasm of his Jewish mother's seriousness and his Catholic father's lightness, but also the collective myth of a clear opposition between a Judaism laden with a sense of guilt in contrast to a light, free, and vital Hellenism. "Precisely the tragedy is proof that the Greeks were not pessimists: Schopenhauer was in error here, as he was in error everywhere," Nietzsche wrote in *Ecce Homo.*[53] Not coincidentally, the subtitle of Nietzsche's essay on the birth of Greek tragedy is *Hellenism and Pessimism,* which defines the relationship that the Greeks had with pessimism and its subsequent surpassing in the tragic sense of the Dionysian: "'Hellenism and Pessimism': that would have been an unambiguous title: namely as the first lecture on how the Greeks managed their pessimism—how they *overcame* it."[54]

Beginning in the middle of the nineteenth century, German culture—and to some degree also Italian culture—began to develop a myth of a vital, whole Hellenism as a response to its growing discomfort and disorientation with respect to modernity and a need to redefine a sense of collective identity.[55] In the idea of serenity and harmony of Winckelmann's Apollonian Greece, as well as in that of the drunkenness and darkness of Nietzsche's Dionysian Greece, German culture developed a myth of an imaginary and ideal homeland to set against a threatening modernity, a present that was abstractly identified with Christianity and Judaism. Even the Semitic patriarch of Saba's poem of that name is only a product of poetic imagination, an image from a "mind loaded with ghosts" inspired by the figure of an old farmer whom the poet sees from the window of his house.

Nevertheless, despite the contradictions opened up by history, and even though he was well aware of the influence of Nietzschean thought on the formation of totalitarian ideologies, Saba never wanted to renounce his Nietzsche: "He understood many things, and anticipated others, that man. 'But what if he was one of those responsible for Nazism?' I don't know. I know that the proximity of Doctor Rosenberg would have been enough to make him vomit his soul out of disgust. But before that he would have strangled, with his own hand, his despicable sister."[56] Thus, on more than one occasion, Saba felt the need to clarify that his Nietzsche, "his good

Nietzsche," was not the theorist of the superman that D'Annunzio loved, nor the philosopher used by the Nazis to justify totalitarian ideology, but an explorer of the soul, almost a psychoanalyst before his time:

> But my brief D'Annunzian digression was over. What could I have said to him? Besides, I had recently discovered Nietzsche, although the Nietzsche I admired was different from D'Annunzio's, in fact, the perfect anthithesis.[57]
>
> My Nietzsche, my good Nietzsche (not that Nietzsche of others) is so fascinating because he speaks to one's soul and about the soul.[58]

In these last two lines, as in many others, one notes the indirect influence of someone who was one of Saba's good "teachers of life," namely Nietzsche—not the Nietzsche of the Superman, who fascinated D'Annunzio and too many others with him, but Nietzsche the psychologist, who intuited many truths about the human soul, and whose work, for this reason, can be considered as a vast foreshadowing of the discoveries of Freud.[59]

On numerous occasions, beginning in the spring of 1945, Saba evinced a desire to reinterpret Nietzschean thought and to turn the German philosopher into a precursor of Freud. The whole of the prose work *Shortcuts and Very Short Stories* must be read in the light of these two authors. In the last *Shortcut,* placed as the epigraph to the volume of prose pieces, Saba writes, "Genealogy of Shortcuts: Nietzsche—Freud."[60] "In these prose writings," he writes again in *History and Chronicle of the Songbook,* "he [the author] relies, without concealment (with his customary 'defenseless clumsiness') on the two thinkers from whom he learned most: Nietzsche and Freud."[61] And again, in a passage from *The Splinters of the Wondrous World (Le schegge del mondo meraviglioso),* he refers to the prose work as a "short book written in collaboration with Nietzsche and Freud."[62] If it is permissible to interpret the dash that separates and unites the names of Nietzsche and Freud as an arrow pointing to the right, or as the descending branch of an intellectual genealogy, then Saba is not only proposing an interpretative path for a single prose work; he is also suggesting a possible reading of his intellectual paternity. He is pointing to a critical path that would clearly establish a continuum between Nietzsche and Freud, between two writers who in the spring of 1945 must have seemed irreconcilable. Perhaps not only in his life but in the reconstruction of his own intellectual genealogy, in his search for his literary progenitors, Saba noticed a breach that, beginning at least with World War II, he would try to heal by establishing a continuum between Nietzsche and Freud and turning the former into a precursor of the latter. In this way, he tied his own desire for "lightness," which he thought of as Nietzschean, to a sense of introspection and to a pessimism that he thought Jewish.

Saba's stylistic itinerary, too, his complex coming and going between poetry and prose, mirrors a need to heal this breach. Often, in his theoretical writings, Saba entertained the notion of a substantial opposition between poetry and prose as two different means of literary expression corresponding to two different stages of consciousness: poetry as the art of youth and sensual expression, prose as the art of maturity and moral meditation. "To create," Saba wrote, echoing Pascoli, "just as to understand art, one thing is necessary above all: that somewhere in us our childhood be preserved. But this is something the very process of living tends to destroy. The poet is a child who, having reached adulthood, marvels at the things that happened to him."[63] Poetry "dies within, with the extinguishing of sensuality," he wrote to his friend Nora Baldi in 1953, a few months before dying, "but prose yes. I have at least twenty or so *Ricordi-Racconti* that wait for nothing else than to be written."[64] In another letter of the same year to his friend Piero Quarantotti Gambini, he adds, "A poem is an erection, a novel is a birth."[65]

From World War II until the end of his life, Saba's literary production was characterized by a renewed interest in prose. He published old stories that he had written several years before, put together anthologies of short stories and personal recollections, and experimented with new modes of prose writing. Starting in the mid-1940s, Saba's collections of poems alternated more and more frequently with autobiographical memoirs, aphoristic meditations, and brief moral tales in which his individual history is diluted in the larger contexts of collective memory and an ethical meditation on history. Such stylistic changes were connected with the poet's theoretical and practical dealings with psychoanalysis. They also coincided with the emergence of a new awareness of history, in particular of Jewish history, as a consequence of the Shoah and of the months that the poet himself had spent in hiding in order to escape Nazi-Fascist persecution. Both these experiences translated into hybrid forms of literary communication that, by privileging memory over imagination and meditation over expression, can be interpreted as stylistic attempts to bridge the gap opened up by the war in personal and collective history. In other words, in Saba's transition from poetry to prose, his giving precedence to the one over the other, one may also hear an echo of his "ancient strife": another attempt to bridge his existential gap in order to reach a desirable, as well as impossible, integrity of the subject.

This complex intertwining of psychoanalysis, awareness of Jewish history, and change of literary genre can be seen in the subsequent stages of the publication of Saba's prose works. In 1956, Saba published *Other Stories–Other Memories,* a volume of prose works composed between 1910 and 1947 in which an openly autobiographical subject becomes a fictional one and reality, as suggested by the title, mixes with imagination. The volume also included five brief tales entitled *Jews (Trieste, 1910–1912).* Written at the beginning of the century when, in Saba's words, anti-Semitism seemed like a joke and the author had the freedom to use a light touch when describing his Jewish family background, *Jews* is a collection of five sketches of the Jewish environment of Trieste at the turn of the century whose ironic and tender tone reminds one of Primo Levi's "Argon"—the first chapter of *The Periodic Table* dedicated to the memory of the author's Jewish ancestors. Unlike in Levi, though, Saba's recollections arose from two contrasting impulses: a reaction to his Jewish mother's lifestyle and nostalgia for his absent father. Saba kept these tales in a drawer for more than forty years and only after World War II, in the 1950s, on Carlo Levi's advice, decided to publish them. Therefore the first collection of prose works published by Saba begins with five tales about Jewish subjects. His debut as a prose writer coincides with a recollection of his family's Jewish past, as if the search for new modes of writing also implied the emergence of past memories and of a new historical consciousness.

But *Jews* is only one step in Saba's complex shift from poetry to prose. In Rome between February and June 1945, he assembled a volume of aphorisms and brief prose compositions that would be published in 1946 as *Shortcuts and Very Short Stories,* another mixed title that hints at the hybrid and almost experimental character of Saba's prose works, balanced between autobiography and fiction, memory and imagination. The book's title was a suggestion of the literary critic Giacomo Debenedetti who, during a conversation with Saba, noted the composite and uncertain character of these texts and their partaking of different literary genres: aphorism, moral tale, fable, apologue, and other modes of writing characterized by precision and brevity as well as by a tendency to cast an ethical eye on reality. A cumbersome and ineffable reality knocks at the poet's door—perhaps still partially sheltered in the ivory tower of a Romantic and Decadent sensibility, with their insistence that a poet's glance be turned inward. Now, the writer is assigned the tasks of preserving memory and being a witness to history. *Shortcuts* is also born out of a response to Majdanek—the first Nazi concentration camp discovered in Germany by the Allies: the prose pieces in the collection "were born from ten or more experiences of life, art and sorrow," wrote Saba. "They are, among other things, in a way, like *survivors* from Majdanek." As new literary modes, they may also work as antidotes against the Nazi poison: "From his blaring loudspeaker, Doctor Goebbels poisoned the world with his propaganda. Within the limits of my meager capabilities, I am trying in the columns of *Nuova Europa* to detoxify it with *Shortcuts*."[66] Thus Saba's new literary season consists of a collection of ethical meditations on history that are also responses to the tragic history of twentieth-century Jews.

At the same time, as noted above, these pieces are the result of Saba's interest in psychoanalysis. The idea to write *Shortcuts* began to take shape around 1934–35. A few years earlier, in September 1929, Saba had begun his first analysis with Edoardo Weiss, a brief but fruitful experience that was interrupted in 1931 when Doctor Weiss had to move to Rome. *Shortcuts* can be seen primarily as the result of Saba's colloquia with Doctor Weiss: "*Shortcuts* then," he wrote in a letter to his analyst on March 29, 1949, "are almost all yours; on my part I have added the 'style.'"[67] In *History and Chronicle of the Songbook,* he added, "His [Saba's] psychoanalytic education, dearly acquired at considerable cost, he put, if anywhere, into what to this day is still his only book of prose, *Shortcuts and Very Short Stories*."[68]

At this intersection between psychoanalysis and historical awareness, one may also place Saba's last prose work, *Ernesto,* inasmuch as this book too is the result of a psychological and spiritual development in the shape of a literary experiment—almost a psychoanalytic journal whose subject presents itself to the writer with the strength and the inevitability of a liberation from trauma. From this perspective—if one may see a predecessor of *Ernesto* in the "miscarried" book mentioned by Saba in a 1948 letter to the poet Vittorio Sereni—Saba's last narrative enterprise goes one step further than *Shortcuts*: he wrote that he wanted to write a book that would be "a step even beyond *Shortcuts,* with something even freer, and more detailed, and more—at least in appearance—detached from the discipline out of which *Shortcuts* was born."[69]

In *Ernesto,* unlike in Saba's poetry, readers no longer encounter the lyrical expression of the subject's emotions but, rather, their development in a historical context larger than the individual. In *Ernesto,* the still image of the young and beautiful adolescent, the heavenly figure of the *celeste scolaro,* is set in motion and, by its immersion in the dynamism of a collective history, gains psychological and cultural depth. The result is also the fictionalized memory of the author's Jewish adolescence in Trieste at the turn of the century, of "a boy who was sixteen in Trieste in 1898."[70] *Ernesto* is a partial attempt to bring to consciousness the author's youth as well as to express and free the tension between moral sense and homoeroticism that characterized his life. I use qualifiers like "partial" and "almost" because, as mentioned earlier, Saba was not able to conclude his novel. Nevertheless, in his incomplete attempt to emancipate his narrative subject from this tension, from the author's mythological notion of an unbridgeable gap between maternal Judaism and paternal Christianity, and by making of the history of an Italian Jewish boy everybody's story, Saba gave to Italian literature one of its first examples of a novel with a homoerotic theme.

In giving birth to Ernesto, to a heavenly flesh and blood adolescent, to a full-fledged character with a first name, a psychology, and a social context, Saba made his strongest attempt to bridge the gap he felt between morality and sensuality that was at the root of his ambivalence toward Judaism. Of course the events of the war and the realization of what had been done to Jews by the Nazi-Fascists played an important role in tempering Saba's hostility toward Judaism. It was a change that would never be expressed in terms of belonging but in a series of indirect attempts at reconciliation with a Jewish past. The poet's dealings with psychoanalysis, his shifting from poetry to prose, his reconstruction of an intellectual genealogy that established a connection between Nietzsche and Freud, as well as his writing of *Ernesto,* may also be read as scattered and random attempts at reconciling his long-lasting ambivalence toward Judaism with a new historical awareness. Perhaps it was in Rome, in March 1945, while reading the poem dedicated to Federico Almansi at the *Ritrovo,* that Saba began reconsidering his attitude toward his Jewish past. Perhaps his decision to change the title of his poem was a way to remind himself and his audience, helped by the distance created by sentimental language, that Almansi was a persecuted Jewish boy. Ten years later, another boy, Ernesto, seems to stretch out his hand toward Federico in a last attempt to confront and release the ghosts and mythologies that poisoned the age, as well as to keep together those aspects of life that must have seemed irreconcilable to the poet and to a good part of the culture of his time: responsibility and joy.

2

I Knew That There Was a House

BELONGING AND NONBELONGING
IN THE WORKS OF NATALIA GINZBURG

ON THE COVER of the first edition of Natalia Ginzburg's *The Family*, published by Einaudi in 1977, is a detail from a painting by David Hockney, *Le parc des sources*. The painting shows two young men sitting before a peaceful and harmonious urban garden: the grass is well-kept, the benches form a row, there are orderly lines of trees that stretch to the horizon. There is an empty chair next to the two young men who are sitting with their backs to the viewer. The tranquility of the bourgeois park, the two young men sitting with their backs turned, and the empty chair—reserved perhaps for a father or a mother, a son or daughter who will come; or perhaps destined to remain empty—announce the main theme of the two novellas of *The Family*, and of so many of Ginzburg's other works: the crisis and disintegration of the traditional family.[1]

There is in addition a formal link between Hockney's painting and Ginzburg's prose. Looking carefully, one notices that what the young men in the painting are admiring is not a real garden but the image of a garden reproduced on a canvas. It is not reality but a representation of reality. And as Hockney in his painting plays at exploring the flexible border between reality and the image that represents it, Ginzburg in her prose describes the crisis of the bourgeois family oscillating between reality and imagination, between memory and fiction. All of Ginzburg's work seems to be characterized by this uncertainty on the part of the narrative voice, which hesitates between the need to tell of a painful reality, glancing at it with a gaze of pity and dismay, and the desire to turn that same reality into an image that is very close to, but not quite, the truth, in the manner of a trompe l'oeil. Thus at times the interiors of the bourgeois households that Ginzburg describes are circles that allow entry, landscapes that may be traversed, worlds that seem to be right there at one's fingertips; they remain, however, at one remove from us, closed and inviolable. And it is precisely in this hesitation between reality and image, between memory and fiction, that Ginzburg narrates the difficulty of belonging.

NATALIA GINZBURG was born in 1916 in Palermo. Her father, Giuseppe Levi, was a renowned biologist from Trieste who taught comparative anatomy at the University of Palermo. Her mother, Lidia Tanzi, came from a Lombard family of old socialist traditions. Her father was Jewish and her mother Catholic, but neither was practicing. In the upbringing of the family's five children, the ideals of socialism and anti-Fascism carried greater weight than religion: "Neither the one nor the other ever entered a church or temple. They liked to call themselves materialists or atheists: my father with greater conviction, my mother less resolutely and certainly."[2]

Three years after Natalia's birth, the family moved to Turin where the writer spent her childhood and youth and where she would later come into contact with the intellectual circles of the Piedmontese city. The famous names of the resistance to Fascism and several prominent figures in the political and cultural life of Italy between the 1920s and '30s gathered in the sitting room of her house: the Rosselli brothers and Adriano Olivetti, Carlo Levi and Cesare Pavese, Filippo Turati and Felice Balbo. The cosmopolitanism, the openness and the variety of this world, of this bourgeois family that was neither rich nor poor, that lacked a precise regional, social, and religious identity, left in Ginzburg the sensation of having grown up in an indefinite, rarefied circle in which it was difficult to find her own space. As she herself relates in a short essay titled "Childhood," the first years of her life were permeated by a feeling of not belonging and by resentment toward a family that seemed to her not to have roots: "We didn't go to church or, like some of my father's relations, to synagogue: we were 'nothing,' my brothers had told me;

we were 'mixed,' that is, half Jewish and half Catholic, but in fact neither one thing nor the other: nothing."[3] In the eyes of the young Ginzburg, as in the eyes of the young Saba, the hybrid character of her family was disorienting: belonging to two religions and to two cultures is like not belonging to any; to be "mixed" is like being "nothing."

Similarly, the social conditions of her family, their being neither rich nor poor, spurred in the young Ginzburg the sensation that she was prevented from participating in collective rituals practiced by the majority, like going to church, attending public school, or speaking in dialect. Since her father thought that one would catch illnesses in public school, Ginzburg was educated at home by a private tutor. And when, at the end of the school year, she was taken to a public school for her final exams, she felt growing inside her the sensation of being excluded from the life of others, the haughty and humiliating feeling of being different and, therefore, alone:

> The children crowded round me, curious and timid . . . They spoke in Piedmontese, a language I understood very little, and loved and envied because it seemed to me the chosen, blessed language of the poor, of those who could go to school and to church, of those who had the immense luck of being all the things I wasn't. I felt growing in me, like a mushroom, the proud, humiliating conviction that I was different and therefore alone.[4]

This sense of being different and alone translates into nostalgia for the undifferentiated and undivided life of everybody else and for the elevated and blessed language of the dispossessed. So, at times, even her lifelong anti-Fascism, the political education that she had received from a family of solid socialist and liberal traditions, was silently contrasted with a feeling of uneasiness for not being allowed to wear the Fascist badge and the uniform of the Little Italian during gym lessons: "All my life I had hoped to fight fascism, to run through the city waving a red flag, to sing on barricades, covered in blood. The odd thing is that I didn't give up those dreams, but the thought of finding myself there in the gym, without a badge, before the gym mistress with her cross face under the big hat, seemed to me a dreadful humiliation."[5] Here, the desire to be different and free is contrasted with the opposite desire to be like everyone else, to disappear within the majority while losing any sign of religious, cultural, or social distinction.

Ginzburg's adult life too was characterized by the double belonging that had characterized her childhood. In 1938 she married Leone Ginzburg, a Jewish intellectual of Russian origin; in 1950, a few years after the death of Leone, who was tortured and murdered in 1944 at the hands of the Fascists, she married Gabriele Baldini, a Catholic musicologist and professor of English literature. "They married in a church in Turin in the spring of 1950," writes Maja Pflug in her biography of Natalia Ginzburg. "In the meantime, Natalia's dearest friend and colleague, Felice Balbo, who some time before her marriage had persuaded her to take baptism, had moved to Rome with his wife."[6]

Unlike Saba, for whom the tension between Judaism and Catholicism remained an incurable fracture, Ginzburg sought to transform her childhood feeling of disorientation and foreignness into a dual nationality, into a feeling of being at once Jewish and Catholic. In the text of a radio conversation from 1990 that she held with Marino Sinibaldi, one finds this exchange:

> SINIBALDI: Perhaps we can complete the picture of Balbo by saying that he was one of those figures—not so rare at the time—who was a Communist Catholic. How is it that you, neither Catholic nor Communist, came to be attracted to this double "belonging," you who came from a total "non-belonging"?
>
> GINZBURG: I became a Communist and . . . well, now I feel Jewish and Catholic, both.
>
> SINIBALDI: You turned your childhood non-belonging into a dual citizenship.
>
> GINZBURG: Yes, into a dual citizenship . . . yes.[7]

In this same conversation, Ginzburg makes clear that her sense of being Jewish also includes a feeling of empathy for the Jews as a persecuted and exterminated people: "I feel profoundly Jewish because Jews have been exterminated. I felt at that time just how much Jewishness there was in me. I also felt Catholic. I couldn't explain."[8] As in Saba's poem "The Goat,"[9] the Jewish condition becomes a symbol for universal suffering, and belonging to Judaism coincides with a feeling of identification with the Jews as victims of history. In an interview with Peg Boyers, published in 1992 in the journal *Salmagundi,* Ginzburg returns to the subject of Jewish identity and restates how her sense of belonging to Judaism does not depend on having received a formal religious education; rather, it consists in an identification with a people in diaspora, a feeling of closeness with Jews as a persecuted minority and in an awareness of what being Jewish may entail:

> My Jewish identity became very important to me from the moment the Jews began to be persecuted. At that point I became aware of myself as a Jew . . . So, while I did not have any sort of formal Jewish upbringing, I nevertheless felt my Jewishness very acutely during the war years (my first husband, Leone Ginzburg, was a Jew) and after the war, when it became known what had been done to the Jews in the camps by the Nazis. Suddenly my Jewishness became very important to me.[10]

It may be due to this absence of a formal religious upbringing that in Ginzburg's works there is sometimes a lack of direct knowledge of Jewish history and culture. Some critics, for instance, have noted that Ginzburg, in a passage of *The Things We Used to Say* (1963), confuses Ashkenazi with Sephardic Jews. Others have remarked that there are only a few Jewish characters in Ginzburg's fiction—the character of Franz in *All Our Yesterdays* (1952) and the Polish doctor Chaim Wesser and his brother Jozek in *Sagittarius* (1957)—noting that all are marginal characters and seem to be modeled, in a conventional way, on the idea of the Jew as the citizen without a homeland.[11]

But all these characters are in line with the idea of Judaism that interests Ginzburg, that is, Judaism as Diaspora and the Jew as the persecuted, wandering victim of the injustices of history. Franz, Chaim Wesser, and his brother Jozek are refugees from Eastern Europe who fled Nazi persecution in their countries of origin and found safety in Italy. The other characters are indifferent toward a tragic past that, to them, appears as vague and distant as the black and white pictures of Chaim's and Jozek's relatives, all murdered by Nazis, that the Polish doctor keeps showing to them from the pages of his family album. The three Jewish characters are mirrors of the crisis of the Italian bourgeoisie. Franz reflects the bourgeoisie's confusion and indecisiveness, its incapability to comprehend the imminence of war and the grave reality that awaits. Chaim and Jozek reflect the vanity and inconsistency of the bourgeoisie's aspirations during the postwar years.

In this light, the character of Chaim Wesser in *Sagittarius* becomes the personification of the Diaspora Jew as victim, the embodiment of the fears of others, the scapegoat for their inability to understand the nature of their own unhappiness. Throughout the novel, Chaim is seen through the eyes of the character of the mother who perceives him as the biggest threat to the realization of her bourgeois dreams of happiness and success: the opening of an art gallery in a big city and the marriage of her daughter Giulia to a wealthy, blond youth whose professional aspiration is to become a judge. Ironically, in spite of Chaim's warnings, the mother will lose all her savings by entrusting them to a group of strangers whom she chooses as friends and partners in business, and her daughter will marry Chaim who is "neither handsome, nor rich, nor young."[12] When the mother learns that her daughter is engaged to Chaim, the narrating voice registers the great void that she feels in the depth of her soul: all the beautiful dreams she had stored up had all of a sudden come to nothing.[13] As the embodiment of the mother's fears of social failure, the Polish doctor ends up carrying the physical and psychological traits of marginality, of what, in the mother's eyes, are unequivocal signs of social awkwardness and failure. Unlike the young man to whom she would like to marry her daughter off, Chaim is thin, shy, poor, and socially awkward. He is described either as sunk into an armchair while chewing his nails with a meek smile and a quivering shoulder or as making boring speeches to Giulia and reading German poems to her that he translated. Although at the end of the novel the plot reveals the vacuity of her dreams, the mother still holds among the possible causes for her unhappiness the Polish doctor, his lack of money, and his marriage to Giulia.

In a later text, written in 1970 and entitled *The Child Who Saw Bears,* a brief description of a journey to New England to visit one of her sons and his family, Ginzburg once again proposes to her readers her cherished idea of the Diaspora Jew. As she watches her grandchild cross the road holding his father's hand, Ginzburg sees in her grandson, in his gait, in his long, delicate, proud head, in his dark, profound expression, something Jewish that she has never seen before. She sees a human being who knows that the world is dangerous and fleeting, that nothing belongs to him and that he must be self-sufficient: "a little landless Jew, he crossed the street with his bag."[14] Perhaps one can conclude that the part of herself that Ginzburg understood as Jewish was mostly the vulnerable, the persecuted, and the Diaspora self.

If the Diaspora Jew is the image of Judaism that is mostly dear to Ginzburg, then it is no surprise that she expressed on several occasions her ambivalent feelings toward Israel. In 1972, nearly twenty years before the radio interview quoted above and in response to a survey by an association of Catholic journalists about the murder of the Israeli athletes at the Munich Olympics, Ginzburg wrote *Jews*, an essay that gathered her opinions on the tragic events at Munich and reflected on the theme of Jewish identity. In this essay, Ginzburg describes Judaism as a heavy and cumbersome inheritance but also as a spontaneous feeling of secret complicity that recalls the intimacy that Giorgio Bassani speaks of in *The Garden of the Finzi-Continis*:

> I am Jewish. Everything that has to do with the Jews always seems to relate to me directly. . . . I am Jewish only from my father's side, but I have always thought that my Jewish side must have been heavier and more cumbersome than the other side. If I happen to meet someone somewhere whom I discover to be Jewish, instinctively I have the sensation that I have something in common with the person. A moment later I may find them repellent, but a feeling of secret complicity lingers on.[15]

Unlike Bassani, for whom, as we shall see in chapter 3, this feeling of complicity translates into a sense of collective belonging, for Ginzburg it remains something anomalous, dark, and irrational: "when I meet a Jew, I'm unable to repress a certain strange and dark feeling of connivance."[16] This mixed feeling of spontaneous affinity and dark complicity characterizes the remainder of the essay. At first, Ginzburg refuses any theory of racial or biological difference. The idea that the Jews of Israel, inasmuch as they were survivors of genocide, have rights and privileges above those of others seems erroneous to her. And when she discusses Zionism and the state of Israel, Ginzburg pauses to reflect on her own feeling of ambivalence: on the one hand, she feels an impulse to defend Israel when the Jewish state is attacked, a sense of revolt and obscure offense almost as if her own family were being attacked; on the other, she feels an impulse to switch to the other side when someone speaks of Israel with admiration and extreme devotion. The essay ends in an impasse, on the idea that today, even if our instinct pushes us to take sides, it is impossible to choose: "The only choice that is open to us is to be on the side of those who die or who suffer unjustly."[17] Thus the essay ends on a suspension of judgment and on the expression of a generic need to belong to the world of those who suffer.

When Ginzburg's essay was published in "La Stampa" in 1972, the writer received hostile, threatening letters from readers who accused her of being both pro-Zionist and anti-Semitic:

> SINIBALDI: These harsh and certainly complex comments on Jews came out at a dramatic moment for the state of Israel . . . Your comment met with harsh reactions.
>
> GINZBURG: Yes. I got so many indignant letters—some agreing, but most indignant—from Jews, and also indignant ones from anti-Semitic non-Jews. So, I got a lot of letters.
>
> SINIBALDI: And you haven't changed your mind?
>
> GINZBURG: No.
>
> SINIBALDI: Not at all, over these last twenty years, and with everything that has transpired?
>
> GINZBURG: No, I haven't changed my mind. The conflict between Israel and the Palestinians is simply one more hardship that has befallen us. It seems to be one of the most painful lacerations from which we suffer.[18]

And when Peg Boyers, in the interview quoted above, questions her about her involuntary identification with the Jews, which seems to contradict the anti-Zionist position she developed in her essay on the Munich massacre, Ginzburg again states the she places herself equally distant from both extremes in the Middle Eastern conflict and, yet, still identifies with the Jews: "My criticism extends to the terrorists and fanatics on both sides. It's a terrible world we live in. But of course one can say that without being able to do anything about the sort of involuntary identification you mention."[19]

At the same time, in her public positions, in her editorial work at Einaudi, and as a member of the Italian House of Representatives, elected by the party of the Independent Left, Ginzburg put her political and cultural engagement at the service of the struggle against anti-Semitism. On May 27, 1990, for example, in response to the desecration of the Jewish cemetery of Carpentras, in France, by a group of neo-Nazis, Ginzburg gave an interview to the monthly magazine *Rinascita* in which she mentioned several possible therapies against the resurgence of anti-Semitism in Europe: reading, being informed, and remembering.[20]

> SINIBALDI: Among the few possible therapies you suggested this: get people to read Anne Frank's *Diary*, get people to read Primo Levi's books, get people to see films, to make them remember.
>
> GINZBURG: Yes. Get them to remember, it's so important, essential.
>
> SINIBALDI: And do you think it will be enough?
>
> GINZBURG: No, but it is something that should be done to ensure that in schools children are aware of what happened to Jews in those years, what genocide was.
>
> SINIBALDI: Because your impression is that people forget, that there is a tendency to forget?
>
> GINZBURG: People claimed that Anne Frank's *Diary* was a fake, that it was written as part of pro-Jewish propaganda. They said awful things.[21]

In 1954 Ginzburg, who had read Anne Frank's diary in its French translation while she was in Turin in the late 1940s and early 1950s, had the book translated and published by Einaudi. And in 1990, she translated into Italian *When Memory Comes*, a childhood memoir by Israeli historian and Holocaust survivor Saul Friedlander. The book was published by Einaudi as *A poco, a poco, il ricordo*. Yet it was she who, in 1947, rejected the manuscript of *Survival in Auschwitz*, which Primo Levi had sent Einaudi for consideration and whose content, it seems, Ginzburg found too Jewish for publication.[22]

Ginzburg's whole life seems to have been marked by a difficulty with respect to belonging, a difficulty that, throughout the years and through her writing, she appears to have resolved into a dual nationality in which the weight and difficulty of difference are transformed into a common, widespread lightness. In a reflection on her years in high school, she likens Judaism to a melancholy inclination, to a heaviness that leads her to write sad poems:

> One day I heard my mother say to my brother: "This little girl is developing such a Jewish pathos." To me these words, as all of my mother's words, seemed totally inadequate, but they filled me with relief. My mother's voice had always had an irritating, yet reassuring power over me . . . In the words "Jewish pathos" I immediately recognized my sadness, and I thought that if my mother could easily talk about this out loud, it meant that what had stricken my soul was perhaps not a strange disease but a relatively light, widespread, common thing.[23]

Ginzburg gives a Jewish connotation to her youthful sadness, to that which made her different from her schoolmates and which at times inspired her poems. But fundamentally, once it has been expressed out loud by her mother, that sadness is no longer a strange illness but a simple, commonplace melancholy with which one can learn to live.

As I will show in the following pages, writing, and in particular the composition of *The Things We Used to Say,* is the domain in which she partially resolves her tensions relative to belonging and the domain in which her uneasiness about not having a house, about being neither wealthy, nor poor, nor Jewish, nor Catholic, about not being anything becomes a voice.

It is perhaps because of this sense of belonging that the home is at the center of Ginzburg's narrative imagery. In her stories there are small and big houses, simple and elegant ones, comfortable and less fortunate ones, but above all there are homes that seem to be forever on the point of crumbling: "And I saw all of us sitting one morning in the ruins of our house," she writes in *Childhood,* "which had crumbled in the night through sheer poverty, and was filled with stinging nettles and submerged in a cloud of dust."[24]

To begin with, the image of the house in ruins translates the child Ginzburg's fear of sudden poverty and mirrors her haughty and humiliating feeling of living in a different home and, therefore, of being condemned to be friendless and alone. From her childhood, the home appeared to her in the ambivalent, contrasting image of a place that was both beloved and detestable, a safe haven and, at the same time, the cause of her difference: a sort of den where she could hide but to which she could never truly belong. "The image of my home, which was both hateful and dear to me, now appeared as a refuge in which I would soon be hiding but where I would find no consolation, because the sorrow of being friendless would pursue me forever, and everywhere."[25]

Nevertheless, the house in ruins is also an expressive image of the disintegration of the family tribe, of the crisis of the modern family and the tragedy of the history that batters it. In the mass of weak men, strong-willed fathers, irresponsible children, and sick babies that inhabits her books, Ginzburg describes with a mixture of nostalgia and relief, of irony and worry the end of the traditional family and of patriarchy, and the emptiness that their end has left behind. In *Dear Michael* (1973), the novel that more than any other work by Ginzburg details the disintegration of the traditional family, the main character Michele paints pictures of vultures and owls that flutter over houses in ruins.[26] Moreover, his father, whose absence, illness, and premature death are clear symbols of the crisis of the patriarchal family, leaves his son and daughters an old tower in ruins as their inheritance.[27] "Never sell bricks and mortar, never," is the contrasting philosophy of the character of Ada in the novel *The City and the House* (1984). "You have to hang on to bricks and mortar for dear life."[28] The house is an anchor, a den, but it is also a place that is difficult to belong to, since men have abandoned it—either by choice, or destiny, or simply because the world never stops changing.

The image of the house in shambles may also represent the loss of the traditional Jewish family: "[My parents] were totally unobservant. You might say that a Hebrew spirit dominated the household in the sense that my father had a very strong, very authoritarian character."[29] Within the image of the house, Ginzburg also inscribes her idea of Judaism as the solid, authoritarian spirit of the father that dominates over the household. The crumbling of the paternal house, then, is also the crumbling of that spirit, and its ruins are the image of the impossibility of fully embracing it.

Similar accents can be found in Ginzburg's description of the house she shared with her first husband, Leone. After his death, Ginzburg wrote,

"That house had become very dear to me, but I did not feel as if I had the right to live there, because it did not belong to me, because I had shared it with a man who had died without a word for me."[30] When Natalia Ginzburg returned to Turin, after her dear friend and intellectual father Cesare Pavese had committed suicide, the city appeared to her like a house that is not there anymore.[31]

It is no surprise, then, that if next to these real and metaphorical houses in shambles, next to these houses in ruins after the disappearance of the male figures that inhabited them, and the vanishing of the religious, ethical, and cultural worlds that they may have represented, there is a house of women, which is also on the verge of falling apart due to the absence of men. In an article from 1973, Ginzburg expressed her dislike for certain aspects of feminist ideology and described feminism as a fragile and unstable house that is not destined to last:

> Feminism bases itself on the antagonism between men and women; it justifies this antagonism by pointing to the humiliations that women have been subjected to. These humiliations in turn give rise to a desire for compensation and vindication. Thus feminism is born of an age-old inferiority complex. But we cannot build a vision of the world on inferiority complexes. Thought is clear when it has come to terms with this inferiority and can walk away from it. We cannot build anything stable on inferiority complexes. It is like building a house with cheap, second-rate material.[32]

Whether the house in shambles is a real house threatened by the end of patriarchal values, by the vanishing of the ethical spirit of Judaism, by poverty or by wealth, by being "nothing," or whether it is a metaphorical house, deprived of its intellectual teachers or undermined by a sharp ideological opposition between women and men—what counts for Ginzburg is the fact that, from its ruins, from their recovery through the act of memory, writing is born.

In 1940, while in confinement in the little Abruzzi town of Pizzoli with her husband Leone and their children, Ginzburg worked on her Italian translation of Proust's *Swann's Way*. Leone was a gifted translator and advised her to look up every single word, even those she thought she knew, in order to produce the best possible translation. "I took his advice very literally," Ginzburg said in her interview with Boyers, "and looked up every single word, even *maison*."[33] It is significant that, from among all the words she could have chosen to exemplify what is familiar, basic, well-known, Ginzburg mentions the word "house." To be sure, if one wishes to do a proper translation, one has to go back over and over to the words, places, and things that one thinks one knows best. For Ginzburg, the house is the starting point because it is the place that is closest to her childhood, her father, her husband, Judaism, and, metaphorically, also to culture, gender, and art. Years later, when Ginzburg and her second husband were looking for a house to buy in Rome, they chose, significantly, not the most comfortable one nor the one that was best adapted to their needs, but the one that was closest to her childhood dreams, to her memories of the past, a house that was near "a part of the city that I recognized as a friendly place, a place where I had once dug myself a lair."[34] Another time and place are inscribed within her choice of a new house: a past emotion and a past choice are reborn in the present, and life is renewed.

It is in these houses and in their ruins, symbols both of the desire to belong and of the difficulty of belonging, that Ginzburg finds her inspiration by questioning the truth that lies hidden in that burning rubble: "Truth sometimes brings memories that make him [the writer] suffer. He has grown used to writing in the midst of ruins and rubble; yet he is afraid that if he touches all these memories, they will burn his hands and his eyes."[35] Despite the pain and fear that one experiences when approaching the truth of this rubble, the writer knows that in it is hidden the possibility of a story, that from this rubble "the edifice of memory," as Proust says,[36] may rise again. And so to the interviewer who asked her what the inspiration for the character of *Valentino* (1957) and the events of that novel were, Ginzburg replied simply, "When I began the story, I didn't know how it would end; I knew that there was a house."[37] Before beginning to write, Ginzburg knew little or nothing about the story she was to write, of the circles and characters that it was to describe, except that there was a house, a space to find again, to remember and to belong to.

It has rightly been observed by critics that Natalia Ginzburg's writing evinces a certain expressive indecision that lies between memory and imagination; it hesitates between truth and fiction. Works such as *All Our Yesterdays, Voices in the Evening* (1961), and *The Things We Used to Say* are difficult to classify precisely because they stand somewhere between autobiography, historical memory, and novelistic fiction. Ginzburg herself frequently pauses to discuss the difficulty that a writer encounters when the choice must be made between truth and fantasy. In "Portrait of a Writer," a short essay on writing that is almost a declaration of her poetics, Ginzburg describes this tension between invention and memory in terms of a choice between playing with domestic kittens and taking wild tigers out for a walk:

> Compared with telling the truth, invention seems to him like playing with a basket of kittens, whereas telling the truth is like being involved with tigers. Sometimes he tells himself that a writer can do anything in the cause of writing; he may even free the tigers and take them out for a walk. But really he doesn't feel that writers have rights that are different from other people's. So he finds himself faced with a problem he cannot solve. He doesn't want to be a shepherd of tigers.[38]

In the quotation above, truth appears like a feline impulse that must be kept at bay, while narrative fiction is an innocuous, domesticated instinct. The one appears as a fascinating but dangerous duty, while the other as an enjoyable, but fundamentally futile activity. Ginzburg's narratives occur within this unresolved tension.

In the same essay she also touches on the subject of the ages of life and of writing: between the love for narrative invention that filled her youth and the love of truth that dominates her old age. In Ginzburg's words, the writer's life moves through the years from invention to memory, from imagination to truth: at first, writing seems to be the mad race of a young boy who has just stolen some grapes; then the slow, patient work of a cook or a pharmacist who mixes the ingredients of truth with those of invention; finally, the calling of someone who contemplates truth and almost cannot write because he is blinded by violence and by the immensity of the painful memories that life has thrown at his feet.

At bottom, the tension in Ginzburg's writing is similar to the tension I discussed in the preceding chapter with regard to Saba's passage from poetry to prose, from a lyrical poetry inspired by subjective emotivity to a hybrid prose inspired by the events of contemporary history, by ethical reflections and by Jewish memories. The urgency of history, with its element of tragedy, weighs on both writers and changes their relationship to writing. For both of them, writing, at a certain point in their lives, becomes linked to the need to tell a collective story to which they belong, to the need to preserve the memory of that history; it is linked to the question of how to tell this story so that a memory of it remains. For both Saba and Ginzburg, writing is therefore linked to a notion of belonging, in particular to the notion of the difficulty of belonging to Jewish history.

At the same time, Ginzburg's oscillation between invention and memory seems also to be tied to a deeper uneasiness, to a difficulty in saying "I," that is, to relate in the first person events that really happened. Already during her adolescence, when she began writing her first stories, Ginzburg had resolved to avoid autobiography at all costs as she considered the genre to be negatively characteristic of female writing. Accordingly, she wrote her first stories, such as *An Absence* (1933) and *The Mother* (1948), in the third person; in narrative experiments such as *My Husband* (1948), she employs the fiction of a male first-person narrator. In *The Road to the City* (1942), the narrating voice is a woman, but she belongs to a social class different from the author's. These stories were also written with the intention of avoiding the transformation of personal events into sentimental, novelistic form.

It has more than once been remarked that the female narrator of *The Things We Used to Say* says little about herself and that she tends to disappear behind her characters, to dissolve in the myriad of family voices. Ginzburg herself says in the interview already cited, "I didn't want to write about my own experience of childhood. I wanted to write about my family and talk more about them than about myself."[39] Similarly, when asked by the literary critic Giulio Nascimbeni why she chose to understate the most important moments in Manzoni's life in *The Manzoni Family* (1983), she answered, "I wanted to write about the Manzoni family, not about Manzoni."[40] In *The Things We Used to Say,* the result of this approach is an indirect self-portrait of the author who, by talking about the members of her own family, about their habits and their ways of speaking, indirectly talks about herself. It is of course not a coincidence that the title of the collection of radio interviews published in 1990 is *It's Hard to Talk about Yourself*. Similarly, the title of her first collection of essays, *Never Must You Ask Me* (1970), is a verse from Wagner's *Lohengrin* in which the hero says to his beloved Elsa not to ask him to reveal his name. In order for narration to be possible, the name of the narrator, his or her identity, must remain hidden. For Ginzburg, the adoption of first-person narrative was a gradual process.

But perhaps both the hesitation between truth and fiction and the shame of saying "I," that is, the uneasiness about narrating real historical events in the first person, are part of a larger uneasiness, a difficulty in telling stories about Jews. In the radio interview from May 1990 with Mario Sinibaldi, Ginzburg said:

> I had never dared use surnames, for a very simple and personal reason: all the surnames that came into my head were Jewish ones, and at the time I did not want them all to be Jewish. I wanted to be mixed in with everyone. . . . And finally, in *The Things We Used To Say*, I used Jewish surnames, real ones.[41]

Ginzburg's inability to give real last names to her characters, that is, her inability to tell a family memory in the first person without the veil of fiction, is also linked to an uneasiness with regard to difference. As I discussed in the preceding chapter, Saba's uneasiness with regard to Judaism takes on the form of open hostility; in Ginzburg, it is shaded with a desire for universality and perhaps for assimilation. In order to be able to write and speak about everyone, the author suggests, one must mingle with everyone, one must assimilate into the world. In order to find a universal narrative voice, one that is able to tell stories in which everyone can recognize him or herself, one must dilute a specific memory, a Jewish memory, in a universal history, as if one's own minimal, marginal story of a Jewish family from Turin were not enough to interest every reader, as if the particular could not contain the universal.[42]

But Jewish history reveals an opposite paradigm. In the biblical stories, and in the Jewish manner of reading the Bible, the universal cannot be

grasped in an abstract, ahistorical totality but only in the historical concreteness of the lives of its characters. As Auerbach has remarked in *Mimesis,* biblical stories present the imperfection and openness of historical time
in contrast to the perfect, concluded time that characterizes the Homeric
epic.[43] The psychological mobility of biblical characters is in opposition to
the fixed, defined, abstract nature of the characters of the Homeric legends.
The passions of Achilles and Odysseus do not develop at all, they remain
the same from the beginning to the end of their lives. But between the young
Jacob, who snatches the benediction of primogeniture, and the old Jacob,
whose beloved son is torn to pieces by a wild animal, there is a trajectory
and a mutability that are foreign to the Homeric heroes. In this regard, the
biblical stories do not seem like far-off paradigms of human behavior but
like events belonging to the present, narratives of ancient events in which
we are even now immersed.

Thus in biblical stories, an event, a character, a particular gesture, even
an anonymous one, can reverberate throughout time, can be close to us
and assume a universal meaning precisely because of its particularity and
historical concreteness: for its representation preserves the multiplicity of
internal and external events that one finds in the confusion and contradictoriness of history. This narrative modality cannot be played out in space,
in multitude, quantity, in a coincidence with everything, but rather in time,
in quality, in the way in which that particularity, that part of the whole,
that remnant presents itself again in the whirlwind of time and through its
presence proposes once again the possibility of awakening forgetfulness, of
a revitalization, of a challenge of life to death.

> O meek Rebecca whom I have never met!
> Just a handful of centuries divides us,
> a blink of the eye for him who understands your lesson.
> Only the divine is total in the sip
> and the crumb. Only death triumphs if
> you ask for the whole portion.[44]

Montale wrote these lines in a poem from *Satura* titled "Rebecca," after the
Biblical character. The unity and universality of meaning cannot be grasped

in the whole but rather in the particular gesture of the docile Rebecca, who managed to drink with only a little water and still gave water to strangers and their camels. Thus the writer grasps the meaning of Rebecca's gesture, reverberating throughout time, and "with little wood to burn" in his kitchen, "attend[s] to the pen and the soup plate / for himself and for others."[45] Paradoxically, the detail of a minute, concrete, and contradictory story allows the possibility for a story of universal proportions.[46]

Until the publication of *The Things We Used to Say,* Ginzburg tried to get around this paradox by seeking the universality of her stories in narratives of abstract, generic, and indefinite character. One need only glance at the titles of her first stories to realize how she tries to elude her own particular history, to dilute her own family memory in the account of general aspects of life: *An Absence, House by the Sea, The Mother.* "I want detachment," she said in an interview, "I have never managed to climb up mountains and see everything from above. And yet this is what I aspired to: but I couldn't do it."[47] To an interviewer who asked her about her characteristic avoidance of the third person, Ginzburg replied: "The third person I simply can't seem to make it work for me. When I tried, it just hasn't come out right. I've attempted here and there. I do use it occasionally, referring to 'him' or 'he' or 'she' but only with a single passing gesture. What I can't get is the *panoramic view of things*" (emphasis is mine).[48]

Perhaps the oscillation of Ginzburg's writing between memory and invention is a reflection of this search for detachment from the particulars of her own life in order to cast a panoramic glance onto a world in which one does not see the details or ruggedness of the terrain but rather the uniform, completed colors of a map. Perhaps in her desire to mingle with others in order to tell stories of a universal nature, in the indefiniteness and generic nature of her narrative subjects, in the distance and in the expressive dryness that characterize her writing, Ginzburg finds a suspension of the sense of nonbelonging. As she says at the end of an essay on the hesitation between memory and imagination, writing is like "belonging to the earth,"[49] as if there were an intrinsic naturalness in writing that coincides with belonging to the totality of things. But this desire to belong to everything, to embrace the totality of life with a single glance from above takes one further from reality and leads to abstraction; it brings the writer closer to sadness and to the tragedy of existence, but it brings him further from the pain and tragedy of each life, from the particularity of each person's story, from the contradictions and fragmentariness of memory:

> For many years I had the title *Vicenda* [Event] in my head, and I can't tell how many different stories I began to write with that title, only to destroy them because they did not seem worthy to me of such an indistinct, wonderful word. And when I would walk along the streets and was happy for some reason, I would say: "And now I'm going to write that story *Vicenda*," and I perked up at the thought of the happy seasons that the future held in store for me.[50]

Enclosed in the "indistinct" and "wonderful" title of this story that was never written is the desire to put the greatest distance possible between oneself and the particularity of the world. The quest for universality, the quest to become part of the whole, gets stranded in the emptiness of an abstract title for a story never written, as if mixing with everyone did not mean belonging but rather losing oneself. Until, with *The Things We Used to Say,* memory imposes itself with its contradictoriness, its fragments, its ordinary, distinct character.

In *Voices in the Evening,* a text that precedes *The Things We Used to Say* by but a few years, truth has already become such a pressing necessity that it pushes the narrator to abandon certain conventions of narrative, such as giving fictional names to the places that one is talking about: "I didn't even think of disguising them: this time they wouldn't have put up with it. And from the places of my childhood sprang up the figures of my childhood, and they conversed, among themselves and with me. I experienced a great joy. From this joy all I did was to start a new paragraph; I started a new paragraph with each sentence."[51]

Nevertheless, the story of the Olivetti family, who provide the inspiration for a part of the events that the story narrates, is transformed, masked, and changed in the story of the De Francisci family: "Yes, it isn't their story, and it isn't that they are really these characters. But I imagined a family rather like the Olivettis as I knew them. I think that Vincenzino, who is the dead brother of Tommasino, was based a little on Adriano."[52]

In *Voices in the Evening,* like a cook or a chemist, Ginzburg mixes various ingredients taken from reality in order to recount a novelized version of the truth. But in *The Things We Used to Say,* the writer definitively delves into her memory, she adopts real last names, and her writing becomes a form of liberation and testimony. This is to say, first of all, the liberation of Jewish history, and then the emancipation of an expressive form that is no longer constrained by the imperatives of imagination. Paradoxically it is only when Ginzburg tells a particular story, only when she tells the story of her family, that she is able to tell a universal story and thus dissolve the creative impasse between memory and invention. Only when the narrator is able to utter real last names, only when she is able to recount a story from the particular point of view of an Italian Jewish family, only then will she find the courage to say "I" and to tell universal stories that really happened. Only when she becomes part of the collective history of a family will she find her individual voice as a writer.[53] The narrative subject can take shape only in relation to a collectivity, to its memory and its history:

> I don't know if it is my best book, but it is certainly the only book I wrote in a state of absolute freedom . . . For one thing, I was using Jewish surnames. I was doing dialogue or not doing dialogue, it didn't matter: I didn't have the constrictions of imagination . . . I was throwing away everything that could have been invented, I would think of something and say, "No, I'm making that up." I was looking for the truth, what I remembered. It is a book that comes straight from memory.[54]

By making itself a form of testimony, Ginzburg's writing frees itself from the closed form of literary genres and from all the constraints of imagination. Her awareness of her own belonging to Judaism and the possibility itself of talking about it are to be found here. Clearly this discussion goes beyond *The Things We Used to Say* and informs, with all of its novelty, the history of contemporary Italian literature. The liberation of a Jewish history, that is, its literary expression, signifies as well the liberation of a new form of writing: new for Ginzburg, as she narrates in the first person events that really happened, but new for Italian literature as well inasmuch as it is an expressive form that frees the writer from the constraints of imagination and literary genres and turns a literary history into not the history of rigid genres nor the history of Literature, but the history of writing. The emancipation of writing from the rigid classification into genres that has characterized the history of Italian literature corresponds to the liberation of a Jewish narrative subject, to the testimony of a family memory.

Thus in *The Things We Used to Say,* language becomes a form of belonging. As in Primo Levi's "Argon," a story that Ginzburg particularly liked and for which she wrote a glowing review, roots have the suppleness and mobility of words.[55] One need only read what is perhaps the most frequently anthologized excerpt from *The Things We Used to Say* to see how, in Ginzburg, the home, even when it dissolves into the darkness of a cave, continues to stand thanks to its walls made of words:

> There are five of us brothers and sisters. We live in different cities, some of us abroad, and we don't write to each other very often. When we meet we can be indifferent or distrait. But among us a single phrase is enough. A single word, a single phrase is all that it takes, one of those old sayings that we heard repeated endlessly during our childhood. We only need to say, "We haven't come to Bergamo to take a summer break," or "What does hydrogen sulphide stink like?" to rediscover at a stroke our ancient bonds and our childhood and youth, linked indissolubly to those words and sayings. One of those words or sayings would be enough to make us recognize each other in the darkness of a cave or among a million people. Those sayings are our Latin, the lexicon of our bygone days, they are like the hieroglyphics of the Egyptians or the Sumerians, the evidence of a vital nucleus which has ceased to exist but which still survives in its texts, preserved from the fury of the waters and from the corrosions of time. Those sayings are the basis of our family solidarity, which will exist for as long as we remain on this earth, reviving and recreating itself at the opposite sides of the globe whenever one of us says, "My dear Signor Lipmann," and at once my father's impatient voice rings in our ears. "Enough of this story! I've already heard it more times than I can say!"[56]

These family sayings are not only a nostalgic anthology of old phrases that permit the members of the family to regain their childhood and youth each time that they are uttered, but they are also a way in which the subject recognizes her own belonging to a group and finds a place in a history that is older and vaster than she. Thus words become the foundations of a family unity that is re-created and resuscitated in the most varied points of the world and of time whenever they are uttered—even when the house, now in shambles, will have become as dark as a cave. Reflected in this small Jewish family from Turin and in its sayings are the story of the Jewish Diaspora, the abstraction of a people without a home, the recent assimilation into Italian culture, the coming into being of a civilization whose vital nucleus seems to have ceased existing, but that survives in the memory of its words, in its texts, salvaged from the fury of the flood of time.

Of course this could be said of every civilization. Ginzburg herself compares her family's sayings with the hieroglyphics of the ancient Egyptians and the Assyrians and Babylonians. But those hieroglyphics are practically a dead letter for us. The Egyptians, the Assyrians, and the Babylonians no longer exist. Their hieroglyphics speak to us in their absence. Jewish texts such as the Ginzburg family sayings, however, speak to us of the past in the presence of their authors. They do not speak to us of the nostalgia for an archeological past, but of the active memory of a past that makes its presence felt and of the survival of civilization.

In Western history, the Jewish Diaspora has often represented such a modality. Both in its religious rituals, as in the celebration of the exodus from slavery in Egypt during Pesach, and in its historical and cultural position as a minority, Judaism has staged this drama of the dispersion of civilization and of its continuing survival in what remains after centuries of migration: a way of cooking, laughing, or, of course, speaking. In his 1934 preface to the Hebrew translation of *Totem and Taboo,* Freud wrote, "If the question were put to him [the author]: 'Since you have abandoned all these common characteristics of your countrymen, what is there left to you that is Jewish?' he would reply: 'A very great deal, and probably its very essence.'"[57]

It is not easy to establish direct connections between Judaism and writers who, like Freud and Ginzburg, were not religious, did not know Hebrew, or were not engaged in the Zionist cause. But perhaps one can perceive certain resonances between a Jewish cultural inheritance, the historical condition of the Jews in the Diaspora, and the gaze that these contemporary intellectuals and writers turn toward the past. What one perceives is therefore not an essence but historical relations; not an immutable, ahistorical entity but a modality of memory, a way of looking at the past, of saving it from oblivion and giving it a second possibility of life in the present, an attempt to construct an incontestable hope in an uncertain future, and thus to affirm life through a memory that is not nostalgic but active.

Perhaps one of the strongest resonances between Natalia Ginzburg and Judaism can be found in this sense of history as active memory and in her notion of storytelling as a piteous, almost religious glance at the past—as dismay for what has happened and as an effort to put back together, piece by piece, a house in shambles. In Ginzburg, as Judith Pastore rightly remarks, the act of remembering resembles a religious experience inasmuch as it helps her characters to maintain a relationship with their loved ones even in death. Like Proust's madeleines, all the memories of words and objects from the past that readers encounter in Ginzburg's works are capable of triggering the remembrance of a loved one and transcending the limitations of materiality and time.[58] In Ginzburg, though, unlike in Proust, the emphasis is not so much on the sensory and involuntary character of memories as on their being an active and voluntary recovery of the past in the present. "We are deeply and painfully rooted in every being and thing in the world," Ginzburg writes in *The Little Virtues* (1962), "the world which has become filled with echoes, and trembling, and shadows, to which we are bound by a devout and passionate piety."[59] Through writing, the narrator's gaze settles upon every being and every thing in the world, every echo, every shiver and shadow of what once was there and seems not to be there anymore, upon the catastrophes and the ruins of history, preparing a second chance at life for them. Memories, then, have a religious character inasmuch as they are attempts at answering the most religious question of all: "why catastrophes, ruins, evil?" In Ginzburg's writing, words, and the memory of words are the bricks of a house that is no longer there—as the words of the Torah, those that are written, and those that are missing in the blank spaces between letters, are the foundation and the abstract walls of Judaism as Diaspora. In Ginzburg—and, as I will show in the following chapters, also in Giorgio Bassani and Primo Levi—writing often fits between memory of the past and the anticipation of the future, between the biblical imperative to remember the past and the motivation to build a hope for the future. Thus the narrative gaze rests on a past that is no longer there in order to give it a second chance, in order to build a paradoxical hope for the future and to attempt to assemble, using the worn, scattered tiles of the past, a mosaic for a future, which is there to become.

At the beginning is a desire to preserve everything: "Even as a child I wanted to become a writer and I was sorry that minutes would get lost. I would have liked them to remain in some way, that there were a big book to keep them in . . . I was sorry that people's lives would get lost, and had the feeling that everything had to be preserved in some book."[60]

It is no surprise, then, that Ginzburg's books are crowded with memories of words of all kinds, turns of phrase, little poems, puns, and nursery rhymes, and that they are full of curious and ordinary objects that stand like colorful flags of the past in a mixture of melancholy and irony: a dress with buttons in the shape of fir trees and a cup of instant coffee, a nightgown the color of tobacco and a tattered shirt, a tunic with dragons and a red scarf.

This emotional urge to save everything from the past and to preserve everything in a book may explain why Ginzburg, at times, leaves her readers with the impression that she is only one step away from striking a sentimental key, from starting to sing a melancholic hymn to the good old days—as if, behind her sober and controlled voice, there were another weaker, slightly melodramatic one, almost on the verge of tears, that keeps repeating "Do you remember?" As Ginzburg remarked in her essay "My Craft," ("Il mio mestiere," 1949), when one writes, one is continually beset by the danger of "suddenly starting to tease or perform an aria."[61]

As a matter of fact, Ginzburg tried to avoid sentimentality at all costs and maintained a sober, detached, and often ironic narrative style throughout her literary career. In the preface to her 1964 collection of short stories *Cinque romanzi brevi,* she writes of her early feelings of "horror" and "terror" at the thought of becoming a sentimental, "sticky," "sickeningly sweet" female writer.[62] Here, too, in her aversion toward sentimental prose, one may detect a hesitation between a desire to abandon oneself to the memories of the past, to pure melancholic nostalgia, and the understanding that memories, in their concrete and factual character, in their actualization, may be the key to giving meaning to the past in the present. "Later," Ginzburg added in her interview with Walter Mauro, "I understood that one doesn't preserve everything, but that one filters and preserves what is needed."[63] In order to preserve something from the past, Ginzburg seems to say, the aim should be not to save the whole but the rest, not the universal but the particular, not just facts in themselves but the paradigmatic value that those facts acquire in the present. "The rest," wrote Ginzburg, "is despised as useless. Within the rest, though, there is a world of things . . . Among them, there are individual moral judgment and responsibility, as well as individual moral behavior. All that constitutes the life of the individual."[64] What remains of the past may have both an emotional and an ethical value. Its preservation may be a response to the feeling of loss, and its actualization may be the understanding that ethics have their roots in individual freedom and responsibility. Thus all the words and objects that one encounters in Ginzburg's books are not just metaphors for the past, relics of a time gone by that one has to preserve carefully and visit religiously. They are not vehicles of a nostalgic journey to the past. Rather, all of these words and objects are remnants of a real and concrete past in which life is still beating—as if the liveliness, the little idiosyncrasies of the people who pronounced them and owned them were still fluttering around. As Cesare Garboli has rightly remarked, in the voices of *The Things We Used to Say* one can hear the voices of those who are no longer able to speak and ask not to be forgotten;[65] as such, they are fragments torn from the indistinct, they are the fruits of an effort to carve a sense into the senseless. In 1961, in his review of Ginzburg's novel *Voices in the Evening* (1961), Italo Calvino noted how Ginzburg's stylistic key, her aversion to sentimentality and her passion for concreteness, had translated precisely into emphasizing distinct and isolated objects rather than the stories of individual characters.[66] Ginzburg tells her stories not only through traditional elements of storytelling—such as plot, setting, or character psychology—but also through the emphasis she gives to her characters' words, to their turns of phrase, their linguistic tics and little habits, or simply to the objects that they own, as possible concrete vehicles of memory. In this light, writing means remembering. And remembering means freeing a voice that can no longer speak, bearing witness to its existence. It means rereading an infinite number of times all of those mute hieroglyphics, reawakening them, putting them back into the flow of life so that they have a second chance. Learning to write, then, is like learning to live under the weight of this past: "like a man who has learnt to breathe when crushed by a heap of rubble."[67]

However, between the publication of *The Things We Used to Say* in 1963 and *Dear Michael* in 1973, Ginzburg seems to change her attitude toward memory and lose faith in its power. As Cesare Garboli has said, in her so-called Roman novels, *Dear Michael, Family, Bourgeoisie,* and *The City and the House,* Ginzburg destroys the idea of family she had built in her novels up to *The Things We Used to Say. Dear Michael,* like *The Things We Used to Say,* tells the story of a bourgeois Italian family. Here, however, the action takes place in the early 1970s, and the book is not a memoir but an epistolary novel whose letters are for the most part addressed to a young boy named Michele. Instead of being enlivened and burdened by the cumbersome though beneficial presence of a patriarch, *Dear Michael* is haunted by his absence. The novel records a world in which the old order of traditional beliefs and patriarchal values has vanished to be replaced by a meaningless universe in which both men and women live marginal and lonely lives. The story revolves around the members of a scattered, dysfunctional family who, at first, have to deal with the absence of their irresponsible, artistic father, then with his illness and subsequent death. Through dialogues and letters, the novel details their sad and pointless existence, their lack of clarity and sense of direction. Uncertainty hangs over everything: Is Michele really involved in politics? Was his friend Oswald, who was married to Ada, once also his lover? Is he the father of Mara's illegitimate, unwanted child? The book ends with Michele's mysterious and anonymous death in Bruges, perhaps due to his involvement in political activities.

As reviewers and literary critics have remarked, in *Dear Michael,* as in *The Things We Used to Say,* Ginzburg pays careful attention to the trivial and the minute aspects of daily life. Her narrative voice "exhumes" expressions from the past, "unearths" fragments of the universe of memory, and gathers all the "debris of domestic life" that may help to give meaning to the present.[68] Nonetheless, while in *The Things We Used to Say* every small expression, every little object is a door that opens onto the past, in *Dear Michael* those same words and objects are no longer agents of memory but silent remains that do not bear witness to anything but the inaccessibility of the past and the absence of meaning. In *Dear Michael*, objects lie abandoned under the cold and detached gaze of the characters, and words float around without establishing any meaningful connections among them. Unlike the words and phrases gathered in *The Things We Used to Say*, the letters exchanged by the characters in *Dear Michael* do not form a family lexicon but a surrogate of meaningful and authentic relationships. They no longer have a shared past and words instilled with personal inflections that can evoke that past.

Where there was a family, now there is a scattered group of lonely and bewildered individuals; where there was a home, now there are many houses that no one seems to inhabit. Where there was anti-Fascism, now there is just an old Spanish anti-Fascist song whose lines nostalgically recall the time of high ideals and political struggle; or there is Michele's distant and seemingly aimless political activity abroad, where he will find his death. In the end, there is no longer a young Michele to represent the future but only his green chamois hat, striped cashmere scarf, and woolen undershirt that his friend and former lover Oswald gathers and puts away with the devotion due to relics. Through these empty words and bare objects Ginzburg is perhaps describing the impossibility to bear witness to the past and therefore of the power of memory: "Young people today," says Oswald at the end of the novel, "don't remember anything. They have no sense of the past and above all they make no effort to remember."[69]

Dear Michael is at the other end of the narrative parabola that has its vertex in *The Things We Used to Say*. As sunny and humorous are the words and phrases of *The Things We Used to Say*, so shadowy and somber is the air that enshrouds the letters of *Dear Michael*. In *Dear Michael*, all that remains is a sterile nostalgia for the past. "Nostalgia is a wonderful thing," Vittorio Foa once said to Ginzburg, "as long as it is nostalgia for the future."[70] Here, Foa succinctly defines memory as an encounter between past and future, as the place in time where nostalgia for the past is paradoxically turned into an anticipation of the future, where history and hope meet. It is this idea that Ginzburg seems to doubt in *Dear Michael*—as if words had lost their power to evoke the past and construct the future and the act of remembering had become nothing but a nostalgic song in which the past is totally lost and the future is no longer an option, as if the act of testimony, the act of writing, were reduced to gathering meaningless words and to lining up old objects that tell their story only through their silence.

"In old age," Ginzburg writes in *Fantasy Life* (1974), "we realize . . . that we are no longer inventing for the future but for the past. . . . We amend our past, we plunge abruptly into a fantasy life devoid of hope."[71] Memory and hope, the historical and theoretical hinges of Jewish experience, at this point in Ginzburg's writing career, seem no longer to exist. The future is no longer in sight since there is no hope. The past can no longer be revived through memories, only amended; and writing is neither testimony nor imaginative craft but merely the pedantic and silent work of emendation.

"A roasted chicken" are Michele's last words: the absence of meaning now borders on silence. It is therefore unsurprising that Ginzburg dedicated a marvelous short essay to the theme of silence. Published in 1951 in the journal *Cultura* and again in 1961 as part of the collection *The Little Virtues,* the essay's point of departure is the staging of Claude Debussy's opera *Pelléas et Mélisande* (1902). In comparing the words to *Pelléas* with those of older opera libretti, Ginzburg asks whether these elusive and impressionistic words do not foreshadow the silence that is poisoning the modern era. Perhaps, Ginzburg remarks, the small, light, lifeless words of Debussy's opera, which seem to sink so easily into silence, are born in response to a disgust for the large, heavy, bloody words of old operas, a disgust for the weighty, magniloquent words uttered by fathers and mothers. And the children of these parents, thinking that the old words are no longer useful, store up secret new ones, confident of being able to use them later with people who will understand them. But when they do finally free themselves from the old words, which have now become like money that has been pulled from circulation, they find themselves burdened with sterile words that seem like a prelude to silence. Ginzburg says they are cold, slippery, "watery," as if they were being uttered by someone who cannot be heard because he lies below the surface of the water: they are mute, smothered, and indistinct sounds that are unable to vanquish silence.

Thus in the modern world silence has become a mortal illness. It is an inexplicable, indelible illness that inhabits our earth and concerns all human beings. It is something from which everyone seeks to free himself but into which we all fall again—as the created world continually risks falling into the empty, deserted space from which it emerged at the beginning of time. For Ginzburg, silence is also a vice of the soul that must be contemplated and judged from a moral perspective. It is not up to human beings to choose whether they be happy or unhappy, but it is up to them to choose between good and evil, justice and injustice, truth and lies. "It is not given to us to choose whether we are happy or unhappy. But we *must* choose not to be *demonically* unhappy."[72] Faced with silence, Ginzburg therefore raises a religious question and a moral one: "Why does it exist?" and "What to do about it?" Between instincts and consciousness, there is not much space for human beings save the freedom to choose words over silence.

One of the writer's tasks is therefore just that of coming to the aid of all those words that have sunk in silence: "signals of castaways, beacons lit on the most distant hills, weak, desperate summonses that are swallowed up in space."[73] From this standpoint too, all of the words of a family's sayings are signals, fires, echoes in opposition to silence; they are a weak but persistent "yes" that is set off by the "no" of the silent void.

Books that issue from reality, Ginzburg writes in the preface to *The Things We Used to Say*, are often nothing but "feeble glimpses and fragments of the things we have seen and heard"; they are only a *part* of a history of "gaps and omissions"[74] because memory is slight. And it is precisely because of memory, however slight, that writing gathers the splinters, the remains of the past; it snatches them from the sea of silence and tries to give them a voice, to fill the void that looms over them and swallows them up. Even in the last pages of the book, when it seems that the narrator is trying to prolong her parents' chattering as long as possible—as if to continue their dialogue even after death—even here it seems that the sound of their chattering, of that familiar language that continues like a sweet melody, is life itself.

Reading those pages, one imagines that the narrator has already been reduced to a little point, to a figure sitting at the end of an empty theater on whose barely lit stage one makes out the silhouettes of the mother and father who are still chattering, whose voices repeat this infinite story made up of sayings, proverbs, neologisms, remains of an infinity of long-gone conversations that did not escape the shipwreck of time but that still resist and take up life the moment they are uttered, in the darkness of a cave or at the backlit ending of this novel.

The religious and moral nature of this treatment of silence and the reference to the ethical function of writing bring one back to Judaism. Jewish religion and culture—whether in the theological tradition or in the lay one—reserves a great space for the subject of silence as negativity.[75] In Genesis, of course, there is the silence that enshrouds the chaos—the empty, deserted universe that precedes the emergence of the divine, creative word. Similarly, in the prophets, there is a silence that precedes the advent of the Messiah. André Neher writes in *The Exile of the Word*:

> The Word, in the Bible, is neither at the beginning nor at the end, but it lies at both extremities, overflowed by silence, since silence is at the beginning of the Bible, in the chaotic prologue where no word has yet been known and whose essential points of reference are night and death, and there is silence also at the end, beyond the Bible, in the zone where the prophetic dialogue was abruptly broken off, and whose night envelops us still.[76]

The Bible, Neher concludes, could be described as an extraordinary theological document plunged between those two infinite silences.

Additionally, the theme of silence as negativity has taken on an important role in the lay tradition of contemporary Judaism. For Freud, death is silent, in dreams as in myths.[77] The aggressive, destructive instinct operates silently.[78] And the unconscious is also mute, speaking only through slips, maxims, symptoms, signs—the remains, indeed, of a forgotten past that, through this detritus, demands to be questioned.

In Benjamin too nature is silent, and its silence is a sign of the fracture between God and the world. In *On Language as Such and on the Language of Man* (1916), he writes that after the Fall, when God's word curses the earth, nature is stricken with a deep sadness that renders it mute. Abandoned by God, nature becomes silent because "in all mourning there is the deepest inclination to speechlessness."[79] But if nature could speak, it would begin to lament, and it would lament first its inability to speak. "Speechlessness: that is the great sorrow of nature. . . . Because she is mute nature mourns."[80] Even in its imperceptible wailing, in the most undifferentiated and impotent expression of language, even when this barely contains a breath, like a breeze that passes through the trees, one can hear the deep sadness of nature, which has been forced into silence.

Then of course there is the unredeemable silence of Auschwitz: God's incomprehensible silence and man's pained silence in the face of the horror of history. This is the silence that is perhaps foreshadowed by the cold, slippery, watery words of *Pelléas et Mélisande*. In *The Drowned and the Saved,* Primo Levi notes how the first days passed in the Lager remain fixed like a silent film in the minds of all concentration camp survivors: "a hubbub of people without names or faces drowned in a continuous, deafening background noise from which, however, the human word did not surface. A black and white film, with sound but not a talkie."[81] Here is a universe in which the human word drowns in a background noise, in feeble, sterile, and watery words that presage silence.

All the same, the negativity of silence is dialectical, for it is silence itself that sets off words. As the world is generated from nothingness through a creative act, so the first step after Auschwitz is the one that puts us at the point in which nothing more exists but in which everything may once again exist. As André Neher has remarked, "It is from within the void, from the depths of absence, from the heart of 'no' that there arises a 'yes.'"[82] It is from the silence of the void of the universe, from the mute horror of Auschwitz, from the shame for the existence of the void and of evil, shame for the absence of justice that human consciousness and the witness's word are born. "It is in the moment of Silence which once, at the beginning of the world, held back the Word while also being its womb, of that Silence which at Auschwitz but a short while ago was identified with the history of the world."[83]

The incomprehensible words of Paul Celan's poems, reduced to pure sound, to shouts, to insignificant background noise, are but the artistic equivalent of the triumph of silence and death. It is the job of the witness, the writer, of humans, to redeem things from silence. "For the sake of [nature's] redemption the life and the language of *man*—not only, as is supposed, of the poet—are in nature."[84]

Thus, from the void, from the scattering of her tribe, Natalia Ginzburg draws a voice, gathering the remains of their broken, scattered language and reassembling for the reader the disparate mosaic of all those lost stories that were and are no more, and that question us with their silence.

3

From Myth to History

THE CONSTRUCTION OF THE NARRATIVE
JEWISH SUBJECT IN GIORGIO BASSANI

GIORGIO BASSANI dedicated a considerable part of his literary work to narrating the life of the Jewish community of Ferrara during the Fascist period and World War II. While reading the cycle of his stories that begins with *A Prospect of Ferrara* (1956) and ends with *The Smell of Hay* (1972), readers encounter the same characters and the same settings, find the same streets and squares, hear the same voices, and become part of a contained literary world filled with internal references and echoes; at the same time, they find themselves in front of a microcosm that takes on meanings that extend beyond the small northern Italian city and its Jewish community. Bassani gathered five of his novels and five of his short stories in a collective volume entitled *Il romanzo di Ferrara*: the tale of a particular small city written in a literary form, the novel, that was conceived for a large, general readership.

In a brief review article written in 1974 for the magazine *Il Tempo*, Pier Paolo Pasolini wrote that Bassani's literary works, as well as his inspiration to write, were the result of the author's nostalgia for the world of the middle class.[1] Since he was Jewish, Fascism banned him from a world to which he was deeply connected. Deprived of the freedom of being bourgeois, the bourgeoisie appeared to Bassani in a nostalgic light, as a lost condition and a world to regret. According to Pasolini, Bassani's writing is a nostalgic *nostos* to the heavenly places from which he was exiled.

Although I agree with Pasolini's interpretation that Bassani's writing is characterized by a profoundly nostalgic tone, in this chapter, I contend that Bassani's nostalgia pertains to something larger that the bourgeoisie inasmuch as Ferrara, its middle class, and its Jewish community also represent the general passing of time, the past, and what is lost of the past. Similarly, Bassani's detailed accounts of the life of the Jewish community of Ferrara, as well as his narrator's recovery of a historical and cultural sense of Jewish identity, are not so much consequences of persecution and exile as an active response to it, not so much a nostalgic pilgrimage to the dear, lost places of one's past as a sentimental journey that, through narrative, tries to bring the past back to life.

In *The Gold-Rimmed Spectacles* (1958) and *The Garden of the Finzi-Continis* (1962), the two novels that are the second and third part of *Il romanzo di Ferrara,* Bassani comes to the construction of a narrative Jewish subject and, indirectly, to the deconstruction of old literary myths. My examination will unfold in three parts. In the first part, after comparing Shakespeare's Shylock and the young Jewish narrator of *The Gold-Rimmed Spectacles,* as well as analyzing the novel's intertextual references, I will discuss the construction of the narrator's Jewish identity as a response to Fascism and anti-Semitism, as a choice of life in response to a collective death drive. Second, through an analysis of *The Garden of the Finzi-Continis,* and in particular of its main character Micòl, I will discuss how belonging to Judaism takes on the form of a feeling of memory, the emotion of being part of the history of a group. Finally, I will show how, in Bassani's works, the preservation of Jewish memories does not simply consist of narrating Jewish stories but rather of sharing a way of remembering the past that is central to Jewish history and thought: the idea of history as memory, as an attempt at salvaging the past and changing the present.[2]

IN SHAKESPEARE'S *Merchant of Venice,* the curtain rises on Antonio's sadness. "In sooth I know not why I am so sad," says the merchant to his friends (I.1.1).[3] Salanio and Salarino think that Antonio is sad because he is in love or because his thoughts run across the ocean after the goods that fill his beautiful ships. Gratiano, on the other hand, believes that his sadness is little more than a "melancholy bait" (I.1.101) that the merchant employs in order to gain a useless reputation as a wise and serious man. But Antonio's spirit is not like those of the other rich Venetian lords and merchants who are puffed up like the imposing sails of their ships. The root of his sadness is deep, its composition mysterious. "How I caught it, found it, or came by it, / what stuff 'tis made of, whereof it is born," Antonio says, "I am to learn" (I.1.3). However, the effect of this sadness is clear: the merchant is lost and no longer seems at all like himself. "And such a want-wit sadness makes of me / that I have much ado to know myself" (I.1.6). Antonio's personality has become so somber that, by the second scene of the play, the merchant is ready to negate himself and his goods in his friend Bassanio's desires and give him three thousand ducats so that he may conquer the young and beautiful Portia. "Be assured [Bassanio] / My purse, my person, my extremest means / lie all unlocked to your occasions" (I.1.136). It is not only his goods but his very person that Antonio puts at his friend Bassanio's complete disposal, to such an extent that it "lie[s] . . . unlocked to [his] occasions," as a room that no longer guards a secret, and that lies open and ready to be pillaged.

"Fie, fie!" (I.1.47) says Antonio when Gratiano suggests that the cause of his sadness may be love. Antonio denies his friend's suggestion with an exclamation that expresses disgust, annoyance, or reproach maybe at the thought that he, a mature, wealthy Venetian merchant, might still be caught and entangled in a love web like an inexperienced youth. Critics have wondered whether Antonio's affection for Bassanio is friendship, platonic love, or sexual desire. However one decides to label Antonio's feelings, the merchant's entire emotional life is turned toward his friend and depends on him. As W. H. Auden has remarked in *Brothers and Others,* Antonio is "a man whose emotional life, though his conduct may be chaste, is concentrated upon a member of his own sex."[4]

Thus, at the root of Antonio's sadness, there may be a perception of love's asymmetry. Maybe, unconsciously, the merchant knows that there is a difference between his condition and Bassanio's, a lack of balance that will be even greater once his friend goes on a pilgrimage to Belmont to conquer the beautiful Portia: the difference between old and young, wealthy and needy, unmarried and married. For Antonio, this is the moment to realize that Bassanio cannot fully requite what Antonio feels for him. So, to compensate for this asymmetry, Antonio sets himself up to love his friend and care about his life more than he loves himself and cares about his own life. "If equal affection cannot be, / let the more loving one be me," as goes the famous couplet by Auden.

In this play, though, as in the sick, pale light of Belmont where its action ends, everything seems to happen as if in a semiconscious state. Antonio does not know, does not understand the reason for his sadness; he just feels it. His is not awareness but perception. It is a feeling that hides and, at the same time, hints at the repression of a sense of loss: the loss of the symmetry that love always expects. In Antonio's inexplicable sadness, there may hide a loss that hasn't reached consciousness yet. In this light, Antonio's sadness recalls Freud's description of melancholia in his 1917 essay "Mourning and Melancholia": a state in which the subject belittles and despises himself for the loss of a loved object. Since, as Freud contends, the melancholic is incapable of expressing resentment toward the beloved, he represses his hostile feelings by transferring them onto himself. And by denigrating himself, he subtracts love from its dissolution.

Like Freud's melancholic, Antonio fails to acknowledge the root of his sadness: *"I don't know"; "I am to learn"; "I have much ado to know myself"; "No, believe me, no"; "Fie, fie!"*—says he while hesitating to find an explanation for his mood. "Not sick, my lord, unless it be in mind, / Nor well, unless in mind" (III.2.233), says Salanio of Antonio's state, making a pun that hints at the elusive and vague character of Antonio's illness. Freud too writes of the elusive character of melancholia when he observes that, in melancholia, it is sometimes difficult to clearly see what has been lost. Unlike mourning, a state in which the loss of a loved object is fully conscious, melancholia is connected to a loss that somehow is removed from consciousness.

Like the melancholic, Antonio is incapable of blaming the beloved for his sense of loss, and ends up blaming himself instead. He commemorates the loss of the loved one by devaluing himself. He disregards his needs and desires, and represents his own self as negative and worthless:

I am a tainted wether of the flock,
Meetest for death; the weakest kind of fruit
Drops earliest to the ground, and so let me.
You cannot better be employed, Bassanio,
Than to live still and write mine epitaph.
(IV.1.114–18)

What use is the life of the wether of the flock and of the weakest fruit if not to perish and nurture the life of Bassanio, who will mournfully survive Antonio in order to write his epitaph? The shadow of the beloved stretches across the lover's ego and folds it in a melancholy embrace, in a semblance of mutual affection that in reality masks a process of gradual emptying and negating of the lover's ego. Antonio's sadness may be the symptom of this transfer of feelings. It is the joy of love that shrouds itself in the melancholy of mourning.

Like the melancholic, Antonio repudiates his own being to the point of taking on the beloved's personality. The beloved's body and soul, needs and desires, become his own to the point that he is ready to be vilified, "cast out and punished."[5] His devaluation of the self culminates in a delusional expectation of punishment. Antonio doesn't mind dying as long as Bassanio is present at his sacrifice: "Well, jailer, on. Pray God, Bassanio come / To see me pay his debt, and then I care not." (III.3.35).

As a result, the vital instincts of the melancholic, his attachment to life, are overpowered: "I think he only loves the world for him," says Salanio to Salarino, "I pray thee let us go and find him out / And quicken his embraced heaviness / With some delight or other" (II.8.56). Antonio's love of life exclusively depends on his love for Bassanio and on his friend's happiness. All the doors to his body and soul are open; the beloved may enter and take what he wishes, his goods and his person, including that pound of flesh, which he is ready to put on the platter of Shylock's scales in the name of a goodness and of a happiness that are not his.

In this light, perhaps, Antonio's sadness echoes another, larger sadness. It is linked to the malaise that seems to entirely permeate *The Merchant of Venice* and that has made the play's readers question its classification among Shakespeare's comedies. "I think *The Merchant of Venice*," writes Auden, "must be classed among the 'Unpleasant Plays.'"[6] And unpleasant and disquieting is the sensation that the play leaves in its audience: the impression that what is portrayed on stage is not just a traditional comedy, whose amours, frauds, and intrigues are all resolved in a final happy ending, but a false comedy that seems to depict the triumph of love, wealth, and happiness and represents instead its opposite. Unlike a traditional comedy, in which the moral order of a society is transgressed so that it can be reestablished at the end even stronger and more stable than before, in *The Merchant of Venice* moral transgressions translate into a new social order, represented by Belmont, that validates those very transgressions. Belmont validates a society in which justice is administered by a fake judge, fidelity is put to the test with a low trick, the rights of parenthood are canceled by the use of force and deceit, and those who stand outside the normal bounds of society are not welcome: "Mislike me not for my complexion, / The shadowed livery of the burnished sun, / To whom I am a neighbour and near bred," (II.1.1) says Morocco, the first of Portia's suitors, when he arrives at Belmont. And when he chooses the wrong casket, and is forced to leave empty-handed, Portia dismisses him with a phrase that groups and expels him with all people of color: "Let all of his complexion choose me so" (II.7.80). The Jew Shylock is banned after his daughter Jessica has been kidnapped and married to a Christian, after he has been deprived of his wealth, humiliated, and forced to convert; Antonio is welcome inasmuch as he is willing to give up his whole being: his goods, his body and, finally, also his soul. Belmont is as seductive, troubling, and deceiving as a social utopia can be. "Watching *The Merchant of Venice*," writes Auden, "we are compelled to acknowledge that the attraction which we naturally feel towards Belmont is highly questionable."[7] Behind the mask of an idyllic island of marital happiness and wealth, which is typical of traditional comedies, where negative impulses are sublimated and contrasts are made pointless, Belmont reveals a desire to escape from reality into a deathly arcadia. For instance, within the literary *topos* of the night of love that opens the last act of the play, a night when the moon shines bright and a sweet wind gently kisses the trees (V.1.2), seeps the opalescent, sick light of an overcast day; and within the evocation of ancient myths of legendary lovers—Troilus and Cressida, Pyramus and Thisbe, Dido and Aeneas, Medea and Jason—one may hear the echo of their tragic ends. Interestingly, in his famous essay on the scene of the three caskets, Freud interprets the suitors' choice among the gold, silver, and leaden caskets as a choice among three women, the third of whom is death. According to Freud, when Bassanio chooses the leaden casket, which contains Portia's portrait, he is symbolically choosing death.[8]

In this light, it may not be a coincidence that, in Shakespeare's play, the scene of the casket is one of the major variations from one of the play's models—the first novella of the fourth day of Ser Giovanni Fiorentino's collection of tales, *Pecorone*. The scene of the casket was introduced in Shakespeare's play to replace an erotic tale in which a knight was asked to fulfill his sexual obligations although under the effect of a sleeping potion. In the play, the licentious and erotic scene of the tale is replaced by the courtly and chaste scene of the three caskets that, while representing the choice of love, perhaps hints at its opposite.

However, it is in the contrast between Shylock and Antonio, in the sacrifice of the Jewish usurer and in the emotional self-sacrifice of the Venetian merchant, that Shakespeare's play reveals more clearly its malaise: its apparent celebration of wealth, love, and happiness hides a sense of collective uneasiness toward human desires.

In this play, Antonio and Shylock are absolute antagonists, diametrically opposed poles with respect to the thematic center of the comedy, that is, "thrift."[9] One man, Antonio, is completely disinterested since he doesn't lend money for interest but gives away everything he owns for love, without taking anything in return; the other, Shylock, is completely interested since he gives only for profit. On one side there is the champion of gratuitousness and generosity, on the other the personification of untamed self-interest.

The opposition between the merchant and the usurer, however, is not only an economic matter but an emotional one. In the play, the treatment of the theme of thrift pertains to both commercial affairs and love matters, and, interestingly, hints at the economy of love, at the right management of one's own emotional life. Again on the one hand is Antonio who, by putting on Shylock's scale his "pound of flesh," both his heart and his sexuality, gives away all his being without asking anything in return and embraces what, in Christianity, is the most noble way to administer one's emotional life, that is, eros sublimated and deprived of its carnality. On the other hand is Shylock who, with his knife, threatens Antonio's heart and sexuality since he doesn't speak the language of emotions and mercy but only that of dry legality. An "unfeeling man" is Shylock for Bassanio (IV.1.63); for Gratiano, he is a man whose soul is as hard as leather, whose envy is sharper than the metal of the hangman's axe (IV.1.125). Antonio is "the kindest man, / the best conditioned and unwearied spirit / in doing courtesies; and one in whom / the ancient Roman honour more appears"

(III.2.291). "The paper as the body of my friend, / and every word in it a gaping wound, / Issuing lifeblood." (III.2.263) says Bassanio when he shows Portia a letter that Antonio has just sent him to inform him that his ships have sunk and that he is financially ruined. With a sentimental metaphor, Bassanio points to his friend's body as if reduced to paper and to his bleeding wounds as if reduced to letters, and seems to allude to the triumph of Shylock's legalism over Antonio's body and feelings.

As Leslie Fiedler has observed in his essay on the roots of European anti-Semitism, in *The Merchant of Venice,* Shylock not only incarnates the usurer's lust for money and the legalistic spirit of the Talmud despised by the Church fathers, but he also represents scorn for the values of courtly society and aversion to all pleasure: Antonio's and Bassanio's friendship, Jessica's and Lorenzo's conjugal love, as well as the pleasant and carefree life led by the youths who, at the end of the play, gather in Belmont.[10] Shylock's knife brandished against Antonio's flesh is the symbolic materialization of this aversion, which, according to Fiedler, has roots in popular interpretations of the Bible. In the scriptures, Abraham is twice described in the act of lifting a knife against his son Isaac: once for the sacrifice from which his son comes out unharmed and next for the rite of circumcision. During the Middle Ages, in the deepest part of the psyche of European gentiles, the incomplete sacrifice of Isaac becomes confused with circumcision and translates into the threat of castration. In a form of collective paranoia, the circumcised body of the Jew is perceived as a castrated and feminized body, and the blade that Shylock brandishes against Antonio becomes the symbol of a threat to love and fertility. Thus, for the first time in Shakespeare's play, two anti-Semitic myths intertwine. In Shylock, lust for money is associated with the "pound of flesh"; the myth of the Jewish usurer is combined with that of the Jewish blade that threatens love.[11]

Thus at the thematic center of this play is not only, as critics have often remarked, the superiority of mercy over pure law or the anti-Semitic Christian opposition between Christianity as a religion of the heart, of gratuitous, disinterested mercy, and Judaism as a religion of law, of dry, interested legalism. Inscribed in this play is also the ancient Christian uneasiness toward pleasure and, in particular, its polemic against usury and sodomy as extreme forms of the subject's satisfaction: pleasure in gain without common profit, and sexuality without reproduction.[12] Beginning in the eighth century, the councils of the Catholic Church forbade Christians from practicing usury, leaving to the Jews—a people, from the point of view of Christian theology, already excluded from eternal salvation—the opportunity of practicing it. More precisely, beginning in the fourteenth century, the punishments against usury devised by ecclesiastical legislation show striking resemblances to those against sodomy: the Church considered both to be unnatural behaviors. Unsurprisingly, in Dante, sodomites and usurers are found in the same circle of Hell, where the violent against nature are punished.[13] The pairing of usury and sodomy, which finds an echo in the opposition of Shylock and Antonio, implies that, both in the management of goods and of emotion and one's body, ethical behavior must correspond to a presumed naturalness, must adhere to a presumed state of nature; and this naturalness must coincide with the act of giving freely, lending money and loving without interest. It must therefore coincide with a form of interpersonal relation that sublimates not only the impulse toward monetary or carnal gain but also any form of reciprocity. At the base of this gratuitousness, of course, there is the evangelical precept expressed in Luke 6:35: "But love ye your enemies, and do good, and lend, hoping for nothing again; and your reward shall be great, and ye shall be the children of the Highest: for he is kind unto the unthankful and (to) the evil."

But what happens to subjective impulses, to individual desires, when the moral imperative on which society is founded is the completely disinterested love of others, even of one's enemies? "When once the Apostle Paul had posited universal love between men as the foundation of his Christian community," writes Freud in *Civilization and Its Discontents*, "extreme intolerance on the part of Christendom towards those who remained outside became the inevitable consequence."[14] In Freud's interpretation, if we are asked to unconditionally love our neighbors, to contain and repress impulses and inclinations that lead to the satisfaction of our desires, we transform our sense of guilt for our inclinations into aggression, push those same inclinations toward the outside, and impute them to others.[15]

From this interpretative perspective, in *The Merchant of Venice*, the denial of the existence of an impulse toward economic, emotional, or

sexual gain translates into Antonio's melancholic self-laceration and Shylock's legalistic aridity, into a negation of that impulse, and into its attribu-
tion to the phantasms of the *feeling* Venetian merchant and of the *unfeeling*
Jewish usurer. Antonio is Shylock's upside-down image. Shylock the usurer
is the target of a mercantile society that practices commerce but is ill at
ease with its impulse toward money, interest, and possessions and therefore
needs to create a scapegoat, the myth of an unfeeling, interested Jewish
usurer, to free itself of its sense of guilt for that very impulse. At the same
time, Shylock the dry man of law is the target of a Christian society that
knows and practices the pleasures of the courtly lifestyle but is ill at ease
with its impulse toward gain in love and sex. Therefore, in order to think
of itself as disinterested, altruistic, and giving and to free its conscience of
its sense of guilt for its own interested desires, it needs to create the myth
of an unfeeling, dry man of law. While Shylock becomes the target of this
sense of shame turned into aggression, Antonio voluntarily makes himself
the target of that same aggression and agrees to transform his affection for
Bassanio into a form of total altruism that is a prelude to the annihilation
of his needs and his persona. His sadness, therefore, is also an effect of the
role that he agrees to play in his society. Antonio himself underlines the
social and theatrical nature of this condition when he describes his sadness
as inevitable, as a part he has to take on, a social role he has to play: "I hold
the world but as the world, . . . / a stage where every man must play a part,
/ and mine a sad one" (I.1.77).

Thus, it is not a coincidence that, Antonio and Shylock are antagonists. Society needs both to repress and hide its uneasiness toward its own
impulses. Antonio and his sublimated, disinterested sensuality are necessary to represent and mask the uneasiness toward those instincts. The more
Antonio is willing to give up his needs and his well-being, the more he is
welcomed by Portia's dubious embrace within the small circle of friends
that gathers at Belmont. In the end, once he has crossed Belmont's threshold, he will even be willing to give up his soul: "I once did lend my body
for (Bassanio's) wealth; / . . . I dare be bound again, / My soul upon the
forfeit, that your lord / Will nevermore break faith advisedly" (V.1.249).
At the same time, to assert the superiority of uninterested, altruistic, platonic love, to remove reciprocity and pleasure from the ethical horizon, to

cut the pound of flesh, society cannot operate by itself but hypocritically needs Shylock: it needs to put the knife in the hand of the Jewish usurer, to deprive him little by little of his humanity and to force him to play the part of the executioner. By depriving the Jew of his faculty to feel and of his humanity in order to accuse him later of being heartless, and by pretending to set the merchant free while not actually giving him the possibility of being requited, society gets rid of both and puts to rest its own uneasiness toward human desires and pleasures in the dim light of Belmont.

Nearly four hundred years later, these two literary myths born of the Western imagination return in a novel by Giorgio Bassani, *The Gold-Rimmed Spectacles*. Bassani's book recounts the parallel lives of two outsiders: Dr. Athos Fadigati, a well-respected homosexual doctor, and a young Jew, both of whom live in the small, comfortable, although stifling, town of Ferrara in the years preceding World War II. Here the homophobia and anti-Semitism of a small provincial society mirror the uneasiness of Elizabethan society toward diversity that characterizes Shakespeare's play. Nevertheless, in *The Gold-Rimmed Spectacles*, the opposition between Antonio and Shylock that characterizes *The Merchant of Venice* does not result in an irreconcilable opposition. Unlike Antonio and Shylock, Dr. Fadigati and the young narrator of *The Gold-Rimmed Spectacles* are not antagonists but deuteragonists. As Bassani says in a commentary to the cinematic version of the novel, "The two find themselves together, and they understand each other because they are different, and yet similar. . . . Two outcasts, who derive their strength to stay together precisely from their marginalization, and who in fact sense that they are the same precisely because they are persecuted differently."[16] While "Shylock and Antonio are at one in refusing to acknowledge a common brotherhood,"[17] Dr. Fadigati and the young narrator are often described in attitudes that emphasize the parallelism of their conditions: they stroll side by side along the beach at Riccione, go for walks through the streets of Ferrara, and gradually build a form of solidarity among outsiders that is completely absent from Shakespeare's play.

A brotherhood between the two is possible also because, in Bassani's work, the literary myths of the Jew and the homosexual become historical figures. They cease being figures outside of time, immutable masks condemned to play the same role over and over again, and rather become literary figures within time, characters with a social background, a psychological depth, a voice and a chance to tell their personal story. While Antonio and Shylock, as Sartre has said, are "irrevocable" characters in that they cannot cease to be what they are and are therefore deprived of free will, Dr. Fadigati and the narrator of *The Gold-Rimmed Spectacles* are figures who begin to free themselves from the rough stone of myth, who step out of legend in order to enter history and narrate it from their point of view. Consequently, *The Gold-Rimmed Spectacles,* as well as its sequel *The Garden of the Finzi-Continis,* are bildungsromans that help to construct the Jewish literary character as a historical subject. While Shylock is a myth, a character stripped of all attributes that could establish a communion with his environment, the young narrator of *The Gold-Rimmed Spectacles* is a character that is deeply rooted in a solid historical terrain.

Of course the picture that Bassani paints in *The Gold-Rimmed Spectacles* is not idyllic: the understanding between the two men is gradual, the symmetry of their solidarity imperfect. Like Shakespeare's Antonio, Dr. Fadigati too represents a devaluing of one's own self that almost comes to coincide with a death instinct. At the end of the story, in fact, while the boy crosses a symbolic threshold and finds his own identity in proud opposition to the discrimination of Fascist society, the doctor disappears into the fog of the Ferrara night and throws himself into the waters of the river Po.

In Bassani, the representation of Jewish identity is also established through this imperfect symmetry: in the solidarity between the homosexual doctor and the young Jew, the stereotyped, anti-Semitic opposition between emotion and legality is freed. At the same time, the narrator's Jewish identity takes shape as a choice of life and memory in opposition to the death instinct that permeates Fascist society, and which the doctor ends up incarnating.

The Gold-Rimmed Spectacles is a novel rich in intertextual references. At times they consist of explicit references to other literary texts made directly either by the author or the narrative voice, at others they consist of implicit markers, coded citations, or simple allusions interspersed in the characters' dialogues.

The first edition of the novel, for instance, has as its epigraph a quotation from Sophocles' *Philoctetes*—the play named after the Greek hero who, before the start of the Trojan War, was exiled by his countrymen to the island of Lemnos because of a purulent, incurable snakebite to his foot. The quotation is taken from the central part of the play when the old Philoctetes asks Neoptolemus—the young son of Achilles who has been charged to bring the hero back to Troy—to kill him and thus free him from the pain that torments him:

> I am done for, my son, and I shall not be able to hide my distress from
> > you. Oh! it is going through me, going through me,
> Poor miserable wretch. I am done for, my son. I am being devoured, my son.
> (Cries of pain)
> By the gods, if you are carrying a sword ready to your hand, my son,
> strike at my heel,
> cut it off at once—
> be merciless—strike hard. Go on, boy.[18]

By quoting a passage from *Philoctetes* as the epigraph of his novel, Bassani draws our attention to the similarities between the events represented in Sophocles' play and those narrated in *The Gold-Rimmed Spectacles*. In both texts, for example, there is a mysterious wound caused by an equally mysterious transgression, there is a character exiled from society, there is a dialogue between an old and a young man that creates a bond between two outcasts. However, in spite of these similarities, the two texts speak two different literary languages: the play speaks the symbolic language of myths, the novel the realistic language of history. In Bassani's novel, myths become stories, and the images in Sophocles' play lose the dense, mysterious character of symbols to take on the social, historical, or psychological depth of realism. Philoctetes stands in the same relation to the homosexual doctor Athos Fadigati as the epigraph to the literary text, as an archetype does to a specific idea, behavior, or personality.

What takes place in *The Gold-Rimmed Spectacles* is almost an unveiling of the symbolic mechanism that characterizes the functioning of both myths and dreams. In this novel, in place of raw symbols in need of interpretation, the reader is invited to read another literary text, which in turn recalls another literary text, in an intertextual progression that enriches the meaning of the novel and, at the same time, provides the reader with an interpretation of the texts to which it refers and of the symbols that they contain. Here intertextual references take the place of symbols; the intellectual fascination for intertextual references is privileged over the fascination that symbols exert in myths and dreams; a more transparent literary memory is privileged over an opaque symbolic one. Thanks to the complex network of intertextual references, the wound of the main character, whose meaning in *Philoctetes* remains vague and has been read as an allusion to various transgressions, gains historical, social, and psychological meanings in Bassani's novel.

In Sophocles's play, there are two symbolic images that are particularly important for my reading of *The Gold-Rimmed Spectacles*: the image of the hero's dwelling and that of poison.

Both Sophocles' play and Bassani's novel are centered on the theme of dual personalities. Both Philoctetes and Fadigati lead a mysterious life. One side of their lives is visible, the other side is hidden from view. Philoctetes is an honest man who has been banned from society, he has a wound that smells terribly, but his bow and arrows are necessary for the Greeks to win the Trojan War. Fadigati is an esteemed doctor by day and a closeted homosexual by night. The double lives of Philoctetes and Fadigati are reflected in the symbolic structure of their homes. Philoctetes' cave has two entrances. "There is a rock-cave with two entrances,"[19] says Ulysses in the prologue to the tragedy, evoking right away the anomalous and mysterious nature of Philoctetes' dwelling, its being both a confusing and a vulnerable space.

The house of another doctor, named Jekyll, also has two entrances. There is the mysterious door by which Mr. Hyde comes and goes in order to perform his crimes, and there is the respectable entrance to the house in which the esteemed professional Dr. Jekyll lives. His house is a place with two natures: a house and a laboratory, a den and a hunting field. Significantly, the beginning of *The Gold-Rimmed Spectacles* alludes to the main character of Stevenson's famous story: "Like Fredric March in *Dr. Jekyll and Mr. Hyde,* Dr. Fadigati had two lives."[20]

Equally mysterious is the house of Dr. Fadigati, who, like Jekyll, "lived and had his surgery" in the same building in via Gorgadello.[21] In the description of Fadigati's house, we find the same element of mystery, inviolability, and vulnerability present in his illustrious predecessor's home. There is a little, inviting, half-open door, two flights of stairs that lead to the "magical luminous square" of a French window;[22] there are the windows with half-open blinds through which only a scrap of light filters, and echoes of music that rise to the gothic eaves of the dome where the owls perch. And then there is via Gorgadello, the little street where on winter nights the wind whips whistling, and in which the doctor disappears after his evening walks; a street whose name, moreover, seems to allude to the *gorgo*, the vortex into which Fadigati gradually disappears, and to the waters of the river Po into which he finally lets himself fall at the end of the novel. These spaces metaphorically represent the mystery of lives that seem inviolable but that are, in reality, more vulnerable than ever, that seem hidden from society's gaze, yet open to the destructive criticism of its will to negation.

Society's will to negation, in the literary references contained in Bassani's story, takes the form of a second archetypal symbol, the magic potion. While describing his train journeys between Ferrara and Bologna in the company of his friends and of Fadigati, the narrator opens a peephole into the doctor's artistic and literary tastes: "He began talking of a story by some nineteenth-century English or American writer which was set in Padua about the sixteenth century, he remembered well. 'The main character in this story,' he said, 'is a solitary student like myself thirty years ago. Like me he lived in a rented room which looked out on to a big garden full of poisonous trees.'"[23] The story in question is *Rappaccini's Daughter,* the novella by Nathaniel Hawthorne that tells the story of Giovanni Guasconti, a young student who moves to Padua for his university studies where he rents a room facing the mysterious botanical garden of esteemed Dr. Rappaccini. In this garden, the doctor grows fragrant, poisonous plants from which he distills potions with extraordinary powers. One day, from the garden window, Giovanni notices a young woman of extraordinary beauty named Beatrice, the doctor's daughter, and falls in love with her. Like in Sophocles' play and in Stevenson's novella, in Hawthorne's book there is a double entrance: Rappaccini's garden, which Giovanni can see only from the window of his room, can in fact be reached through a secret door. Once in the garden, Giovanni meets the beautiful Beatrice, and he discovers the poisonous nature of her beauty and begins to suffer from the toxic fumes that emanate from Dr. Rappaccini's plants. Like in Sophocles' play and in Stevenson's novella, in Hawthorne's story there are feelings that conceal a complex emotion of attraction and repulsion:

> It was not love, although her rich beauty was a madness to him; nor horror, even while he fancied her spirit to be imbued with the same baneful essence that seemed to pervade her physical frame; but a wild offspring of both love and horror that had each parent in it, and burned like one and shivered like the other . . . Blessed are all simple emotions, be they dark or bright! It is the lurid intermixture of the two that produces the illuminating blaze of the infernal regions.[24]

Thus Giovanni begins to suspect that his feelings for Beatrice are an illusion, a fantasy born of an instinct that has nothing to do with love: "And yet, strange to say, there came across him a sudden doubt, whether this intense interest on his part were not delusory—whether it were really of so deep and positive a nature as to justify him in now thrusting himself into an incalculable position—whether it were not merely the fantasy of a young man's brain, only slightly, or not at all, connected with his heart!"[25]

In the end, in order to save both himself and the girl from the garden's poison, the young man takes the advice of Dr. Baglioni, one of Rappaccini's rivals, and persuades Beatrice to drink a potion that is meant to free her from the poison's evil. Nevertheless, immediately after drinking the potion, the girl dies. A human being cannot survive a potion that tries to clearly separate the good and bad instincts, and to transform the human into a being that is either completely good or completely bad.

In this novella, the poison is a symbolic archetype that hints at the human desire to clearly divide good from evil. As such, it ties together all of the literary works so far mentioned. In each of them, there is a poison, a philter, a potion or a drug that has the power to change human nature, revealing to the world man's impulse toward evil. There is the potion that Dr. Jekyll drinks in order to separate his good from his evil natures, there is the helpful philter that Giovanni gives to Rappaccini's daughter in order to heal her from the garden's toxic fumes, there is the love and death potion of Wagner's *Tristan*, which Fadigati greatly admires, and there is the poison of the snake that bites Philoctetes, causing the untreatable wound in his foot. In the device of the potion that is meant to separate good from evil, society conceals its own uneasiness in accepting the idea that human beings have a natural inclination toward evil, and it reveals the desire to preserve intact the illusion of a natural goodness in mankind. "But this is an illusion," Auden writes in his commentary on the *Merchant of Venice,* "no hatred is totally without justification, no love totally innocent."[26]

There is no symbolic poison in Bassani's novel; there is, instead, the doctor's literally poisonous feelings for the young Eraldo Deliliers that gradually isolate him from society and finally lead him to death; there is Fadigati's interiorization of the hatred of a society that tries to delude itself into believing that good is all on one side and evil is all on the other, and so needs a scapegoat. In the movement from Sophocles' tragedy to the novellas of Stevenson and Hawthorne, and from these to Bassani's novel—that is to say, in the movement from myth to literature, and from this to autobiographical recollection—the mechanism of symbolic substitution gradually dissipates, symbols become ever more transparent, and, in the end, are present in the text only through a mechanism of intertextual references. Thus in Bassani's novel what remains of the mystery of the snake's poison, of the spell of Tristan's love philter, of the allure of Dr. Baglioni's potion and of Jekyll's drug, is the intellectual fascination of intertextual echoes that openly allude to the poison that afflicts Fadigati, namely his self-destructive passion for the young Deliliers.

Fadigati's attraction for Deliliers resembles a malaise more than an erotic desire. It recalls the erotic shading of the impulse toward self-destruction that I discussed at the beginning of this chapter with respect to Shakespeare's Antonio. Obviously I do not mean to imply that Fadigati's desire represents a form of self-destruction inasmuch as it is homoerotic, rather that the desire that Bassani represents in *The Gold-Rimmed Spectacles* is a dark, sadomasochistic aspect of homoeroticism or, more generally, a form of eroticism that reflects a collective impulse toward death.

A few examples from the text should make this clear. While giving an impassioned account of a production of Wagner's *Tristan,* Fadigati delightedly weaves love and death together. Thinking of the opera's second act, in which Tristan and Isolde "plunged, entwined, into a night of sensuousness that was as eternal as death," Fadigati "smiled enraptured."[27] And the funeral bed of the two lovers seems to act as a prelude to the doctor's gradual decline into his unrequited passion for the young Deliliers and subsequently into death. Fadigati's tragic end is also foreshadowed in the reference to the destiny of a girl who, a few years earlier, had committed suicide for Deliliers—she too a victim not of a form of love but of a form of "idolatry" for the young man. As the narrator comments, "The fact was that even among us, in our student circle, Eraldo Deliliers was not just loved, but downright idolized."[28] Thus when Deliliers harshly insults Fadigati, the doctor's round eyes don't seem devastated, but shine brightly behind the lenses of his gold-rimmed glasses, "full of bitter satisfaction, of childish, inexplicable blind gaiety."[29] This unpleasant taste, like an archaic, incomprehensible, and unreflective instinct for destruction, leaves its traces in the doctor's glittering eyes; it is a flash of lightning in which an instinctive and internal joy of emptiness moves forward disguised as desire.

Similarly, when the doctor tells the narrator that he has been robbed and abandoned by his young lover, his tale does not end in a complaint for his misfortune, but with "a strange, almost exultant shout: as if, in a final count, the list of objects that Deliliers has stolen had the effect of turning his distress into something stronger, something filled with pleasure and pride."[30] For Fadigati, as for Shakespeare's Antonio, the fact of being deprived of goods and gradually stripped of his own person turns into a sense of pride and pleasure. The doctor's awkward, cumbersome body is ready for martyrdom, his hotel room is open to be sacked: "they all lie unlocked" to the occasions of his friend, as if the tirade of the lover and the compliance of the beloved were signs of love. As if what is at play here were not so much a story of homoeroticism, or of transgressive eroticism, but the phenomenology of a confusion between domination and love.

Toward the end of the novel, during a late-night walk through the foggy wintry streets of Ferrara, the narrator meets Fadigati in the company of a stray dog. Even the animal seems to incarnate a sadomasochistic instinct of submission and death: "'Beat me, kill me if you like,' [the dog] seemed to be saying. 'It's quite right for you to do so, and anyway, I like it!'"[31] "Look at her," Fadigati remarks, pointing to the dog, "perhaps we ought to be like that, to be able to accept our own nature. Besides, what is one to do? Can one possibly pay such a price? There's a great deal of the beast in man: can a man give way to it? Can he admit he is an animal, only an animal?"[32] The doctor is naturally thinking of homosexuality, but homosexuality understood strictly as an instinct and not as consciousness and freedom. A much wider eroticism is reflected in the sadomasochistic phenomenology of his feeling and in the hatred of the Ferrarese society that condemns it: an eroticism that conceals the temptation toward the abyss, the impulse to bring life back to materiality, to what is indistinct, to its "primaeval, inorganic state."[33] The doctor adds immediately afterward, "For me . . . there is absolutely nothing more to be done."[34] Fadigati's person can exist only as Deliliers' victim, and as a target for the propriety of Ferrarese society.

Beneath the mask of the man with the hat, the cloak, and the gold-rimmed glasses, beneath the doctor's public persona, now there is only an impulse toward self-destruction. "If only I could dress in some other way! But can you see me without this hat . . . this cloak . . . these respectable-looking spectacles?"[35] Fadigati asks the narrator. But the latter remains silent. "I thought of Deliliers and of Fadigati," the narrator remarks, "one, the butcher, the other, the victim."[36] Then he goes back into his house, he says good-bye to his friend and symbolically crosses a threshold. At this point he is aware of the existence of a self-destructive, sadomasochistic mechanism that brings together the doctor and his young lover, but also of a more general desire for the abyss that runs through the little community of Ferrara, conscientiously preparing the storm of the coming years. As we shall see, he also possesses a will to escape from this mechanism and to make a distinction between himself and the world that surrounds him. It is precisely through this distinction that the narrator finds his sense of belonging to Judaism, both as a reaction to a collective death instinct, as an affirmation of life, and as a salvaging of a collective Jewish memory.

"I would have been much more successful as a sea gull or a fish" the young Edmund says in Eugene O'Neill's *Long Day's Journey into Night*. "As it is, I will always be a stranger who never feels at home, who does not really want and is not really wanted, who can never belong, who must always be a little in love with death!"[37] The alternative to belonging is the impulse to dilute one's own self within matter, the temptation to identify with everything, to become a sea gull or a fish. Thus without a house or a family, without a group to belong to, during a journey on a square rigger bound for Buenos Aires, Edmund imagines himself to be sun, sand, green seaweed; he imagines himself dissolving his consciousness into the ocean: "And for a moment I lost myself . . . [I] became moonlight and the ship and the high dim-starred sky . . . I became the sun, the hot sand, green seaweed anchored to a rock, swaying in the tide."[38] And in this deceptive sense of freedom and fullness, he thinks he has found a sense of belonging: "I belonged, without past or future, within peace and unity, and a wild joy."[39]

In Judaism, as well as in other ancient religions, the sea is often a symbol for the indistinct. It represents a negative and shapeless force that is opposed to creation.[40] In several books of the Bible, the roaring waters of the abyss aim at submerging the works of God. The waters of the Red Sea part so that the people may find salvation in the Promised Land. In order to escape the divine call, the prophet Jonah does not go into the desert but into the sea, for the sea is not a propitious place for revelations; it is a place in which God's glory has not been proclaimed. In *The Gold-Rimmed Spectacles* too, the Adriatic Sea is a dark, silent, and menacing presence, whose waters exercise a mysterious allure. The "dark blue, almost black" sea that Fadigati contemplates in the summer afternoons of 1938, "our divine Amarissimo"[41] as he calls it, the "empty sea" with "no sails at all on it . . . " that at times looks "dark: a thick, leaden color" and at times "unquiet and green, a vegetable green," is what has not yet been separated. And dark waters are also at the end of Fadigati's life: the waters of the river Po, at Pontelagoscuro, in which he will drown himself.

Inscribed in Jewish monotheism, and in its prohibition against idolatrous identification with creation, is the theme of separation, of forced exile from what is indistinct and from the temptation to return to it. From this perspective, notes Levi Della Torre, Judaism has chosen the fundamental direction of life, which is to react and combat the entropic fall into indistinctness. In different historical periods, Judaism has represented the theme of separation that is at the base of civilization—its original drama of separation from the natural elements and its repeated relapses in it—and has exalted, instead, the possibility of choice, of free will, of individual responsibility.[42]

A similar historical drama is taking place in Bassani's literary works, in particular in *The Gold-Rimmed Spectacles* and *The Garden of the*

Finzi-Continis. These works also recount the formation of a Jewish consciousness in a young man from Ferrara during Fascism—a period of Italian history that can be interpreted as a form of political idolatry inasmuch as it represents a collective fear of individual freedom and responsibility as well as a collective impulse to negate the role of the individual in an anonymous, indistinct mass. As I will show in the second part of this chapter, the construction of this consciousness unfolds in two stages: the first, in *The Gold-Rimmed Spectacles,* as resistance to the impulse to negate oneself and to fall into the indistinct, represented in the opposition of the narrator to both his father and Fadigati; next, in *The Garden of the Finzi-Continis,* as the salvaging of a sense of belonging to a collective Jewish history, represented by the Finzi-Contini family.

The meeting point of these two stages is to be found in the last pages of *The Gold-Rimmed Spectacles,* which describe the tranquility of an afternoon in a well-to-do household upset by a small family drama and by the echo of the larger political tragedy that struck the whole of Italian society during the 1930s and '40s.

It is the winter of 1938, only a few days away from the promulgation of the Fascist racial laws that discriminated against Italian Jews, forcing them into a state of vulnerability that was the prelude to deportation. Full of good humor and optimism, the narrator's father has just launched into a naïve speech about the improbability that Italian Fascists will promote racial legislation. The father appears naïve in his son's eyes for his inability to understand the meaning of Fascist discrimination and its consequences, to grasp what it means to be Jewish in a totalitarian state, and also for his tendency to make compromises and his inability to oppose discrimination. "But I," the narrator says, "would never have returned from my exile. Never again."[43] Unlike his father, who sinks into an unfounded historical optimism, the son has become aware of the existence of evil in history, understood that perhaps human consciousness coincides with exile. Against his will, he has been thrown into Jewish history as exile and Diaspora; but by proudly accepting this condition, he rejects his father's vain hopes, his attempts at compromising with injustices, and opposes Fascist discriminations and the collective impulse to death that drives the society around him.

A few pages earlier, the narrator had described his last attempt at reconciling his Italian identity with Judaism, his city with Jewish memory, and his hopes for a different future. Just back from holidays at the seaside, he goes for a bike ride through the streets of Ferrara, and, once he reaches the top of the city walls, he contemplates his city's Jewish cemetery. From that high up he is able to see the small cemetery as part of the whole urban topography: "the Jewish cemetery at my feet, the apse and campanile of the church of St. Christopher a little farther away, and in the distance, high above the dark extent of houses, the distant bulk of the castle and the cathedral."[44] The sun's embrace at dusk joins the Jewish memory of Ferrara with that of the Christians, and the narrator feels himself penetrated "with great sweetness, with peace and tender gratitude."[45] For the last time, he is able to find "the motherly face of [his] city,"[46] to see Jewish memory as an integral part of the history of Ferrara. But now, in the winter of 1938, everything has changed irrevocably.

The lunch is over. As the father lingers at the dining table to chat with his wife, the son imagines him sleeping, taking his afternoon nap in the parlor, "separate, shut in, protected, as if in a glowing pink cocoon,"[47] with his naïve face turned up toward the rays of the afternoon sun that pierce the shutters. Then the son takes up the newspaper, where he reads the news of Dr. Fadigati's death by drowning. "I looked down. Gradually my heartbeats grew more regular. I waited for [the maid] to shut the kitchen door and then, quietly, but at once: 'Doctor Fadigati is dead,' I said."[48] While announcing the death of the doctor, while announcing the drowning of his heavy, bulky, heart patient's body, the narrator announces, for himself and for all, his consciousness of the existence of an individual and collective impulse to annihilation—the individual, emotional evil that led Fadigati to death and the larger collective, historical evil that is lying in wait. Between the body of his father, closed in his cocoon, willingly unaware of the existence of a historical evil, and the corpse of Fadigati, floating in the waters of the river, a victim of that same evil, the narrator finds a conscious position: not only in the awareness of the existence of an impulse to death, in individuals and in groups, in feelings and in history, but also in the form of a proud marginality. While opposing an impulse to death, he asserts his exile and difference, and in doing so, he rejects inequality.

On the basis of this awareness, the narrator of *The Garden of the Finzi-Continis* tells of a renewed sense of belonging to Jewish history as memory. To Fascist discrimination that would like him to be either fully assimilated or exclusively Jewish, as well as to his "crude and 'assimilated'" father, he opposes the rich, varied, and cultured world of the Finzi-Continis; to the sense of death that surrounds Fadigati, he contrasts Micòl's vitality and sense of the past.

In the fourth chapter of *The Garden of the Finzi-Continis*, the narrator describes the link between himself and the young Finzi-Continis, and between himself and Judaism, as a type of intimacy:

> As far as I personally am concerned, there had always been something more intimate, in any case, about my relation with Alberto and Micòl . . . Something more intimate. But what, exactly?
>
> It's obvious: in the first place we were Jews, and this, in itself, would have been more than enough . . . Between us there might have been nothing in common, not even the scant communion derived from having occasionally exchanged a few words. The fact, however, that we were what we were, that twice a year at least, at Passover and Kippur, we appeared with our respective parents and close relations at the same doorway on via Mazzini . . . this would have been enough that we young people met elsewhere, and especially in the presence of outsiders, there would immediately appear in our eyes the shadow or the smile of a certain special complicity and connivance.[49]

This is far from the stereotypical opposition between Judaism as a religion of law and Christianity as a religion of the heart. In the narrator's words, in fact, Judaism immediately presents itself as an intimate, indefinite emotion of complicity and connivance, as a feeling of silences, smiles, confidential nods, but also of ritual and family. It is the emotion of a single person who finds his individuality in discovering that he is part of a family or group with its own language, rites and history. In comparison with this emotion, the bureaucratic, legal, or administrative aspect—that is, whether or not one is registered as a member of the Jewish community of Ferrara—counts for almost nothing: "That we were Jews . . . and inscribed in the ledgers of the same Jewish community, still counted fairly little in

our case."[50] The words "Jew," "Jewish community," and "Hebrew university" lose their meaning if separated from the intimate, secret emotion of
sharing with others the same collective memory, the same rituals, the same
school: "What meaning could there be, for us, in terms like 'community'
or 'Hebrew university,' for they were totally distinct from the existence of
that further intimacy—secret, its value calculable only by those who shared
it—derived from the fact that our two families, not through choice, but
thanks to a tradition older than any possible memory, belonged to the same
religious rite, or rather to the same 'school'?"[51]

In these pages, Judaism is not described as an identity but as a sense
of belonging. It does not have the rigid and immutable character of a concept defined by an external, often hostile gaze. It is rather the feeling of
a single person who sees himself as a part of a history that is larger than
himself, of a collective history whose origins are older than any memory.
Moreover, what the narrator is talking about in this passage is not only
the affirmation of a generic belonging to Judaism but also the more precise affirmation of belonging to its various schools—in particular, to the
Italian school of Judaism that, at the levels of religiousness, rituals, and
social extraction, is so different from the German or Levantine schools.
Thus in the microcosm of Ferrarese Judaism, through the narrator's gaze,
the reader perceives the macrocosm of the Jewish Diaspora with its differences between Sephardic and Ashkenazi Jews, the differences between Italian, German, and Levantine schools, between assimilated and orthodox,
between the Hebrew of the rabbis, the half-Venetian, half-Spanish dialect
spoken by the Herreras—"tall, thin, bald, with long pale faces shadowed
by a growth of beard, dressed always in blue or black"—and the Italian of
the Finzi-Continis—with their "sweaters and tobacco-colored long stock-
ings . . . English woolens and tan cottons" of the type worn by country
gentlemen.[52] "And yet, different as they were," the narrator remarks, "I felt
a deep solidarity among them."[53] In the small Ferrarese synagogue of the
Italian school, the remains of a millenarian history pass before his eyes,
one that in its extraordinary variety and solidarity is a lesson in unity and
multiplicity for the individual.

Thus, through a gradual process of differentiation, the individual
begins to take shape, inasmuch as he is a member of a community, a

memory within which an infinity of others are distinguishable, none of which counts by itself for its specific differences, but all of which count for the generative process of distinction that allow them to exist. Differentiation is a central aspect of Judaism: it descends directly from the idea of divine transcendence, from the notion that the divine and the human are always separate. The universe, animals, human beings and all that is created are born through differentiation. In Genesis, God's first act is a sign of differentiation, a separation of unformed matter and the void that open up before him, a separation of light from darkness, of the waters above from those below, the seas from the emerging lands. Through this process of differentiation between groups and individuals, and of complicity between groups and individuals, the individual discovers his own subjectivity not as an idolatrous identification or as a conflictual opposition, but as part of a collective history.

The second part of this chapter will therefore be dedicated to the analysis of this process of formation of individuality. As we shall see, in *The Garden of the Finzi-Continis,* this formation takes place through two modes of gazing. There is a nostalgic gaze and a compassionate one: one that threatens the subject's wholeness, the other that protects it through the construction of a relationship between the other and the group. These are two ways of looking at the past that will bring us to the Jewish idea of history as memory that informs the pages of the novel.

At the moment of solemn benediction, when all children are gathered beneath the paternal tallith as beneath so many tents, the narrator turns to look at the Finzi-Continis who are on the bench directly behind his. Through the holes and tears wrought by the years in the fragile cloth of his coat, the narrator sees Professor Ermanno pronounce the words of the *beruha* and returns the smiles and the curiously inviting winks that Alberto and Micòl send him through the holes in their tents. Under paternal guidance, beneath the limits of the tent, the contours of subjectivity and the sense of belonging to a collective history take shape.

In the scriptures and in myth, a backwards glance is often the sign of the violation of a pact. One such violator who comes to mind is Lot's wife who in Genesis 19:26 looks back at Sodom and Gomorrah in flames beneath the rain of sulfur and fire, or Orpheus who breaks the pact established with

Hades that he will not turn around to look at Eurydice until she has left the underworld: he turns to see if his beloved is following him and loses her forever. And for their transgressions Lot's wife is turned into a pillar of salt and Orpheus is dismembered and scattered by the Furies. These are subjects who have been scattered by the force of nostalgia for the past, or by a desire of identification with that which has been left behind, or by a form of curiosity that reifies and scatters. As if that backward glance were a threat to the subject's integrity.

The narrator of the Finzi-Continis is also continually looking back. "As usual, I had turned to look."[54] But the tallith, the paternal embrace, limits and protects him. It signals the limits of one's subjectivity, preventing the subject from being scattered and from disappearing in a desire to identify with the world, in the doing and undoing of oneself. As the shining surface of Perseus's shield allows the hero to confront the Medusa's gaze—by reflecting it—without being turned to stone, the threading of the paternal cloak filters the narrator's curious glances around the room, revealing his urge to satisfy an innate desire to be other than himself: his impulse is to identify himself with the richness and refined culture of the Finzi-Continis, with the delicate, singsongy, intoned voice of Professor Ermanno, with his clear pronunciation of Hebrew, or with the religious zeal of the Herrera brothers—all of whom are so different from his "crude and *goyishe*" father and from the anonymous mass that fills the little synagogue in Ferrara.[55] But here, in Bassani, we are no longer on the terrain of myth: we are in historical time. What is being described is not an individual heroic feat but an ordinary, collective practice, a ritualistic gesture repeated throughout the centuries by which life is defended from the temptation of a complete identification with the other and from a spontaneous relapse into indistinctness through the affection and guidance of a father for his son.

The subject in Judaism, as Stefano Levi Della Torre reminds us in *Mosaico,* is both collective and individual. On the one hand, the minyan is prescribed—the quorum of ten adult males from whom the community is built. On the other, the tallith is prescribed—the liturgical cloak that circumscribes and isolates, within the community act, the space of the single person, his gathering and his personal relationship with the Torah.[56] In Bassani too, the subject takes shape in the tension between the individual dimension and the collective one, between the definition of subjective impulses and the construction of a relationship with the collectivity, understood first of all as the memory of a common history. It is this second way of gazing that I drew attention to, a second glance backward, but one whose purpose is to preserve memory.

The garden of the Finzi-Continis is truly a space of memory. The intricate geography of trees, paths, and canals that cross it, just as the labyrinthine structure of the *magna domus,* where every corner recalls a moment of the past, are almost a spatial translation of the complexity of memory and of the biblical imperative to remember the past: "And thou shalt repeat [these words] when thou sittest in thine house, and when thou walkest by the way, and when thou liest down, and when thou risest up. And thou shalt bind them for a sign upon thine hand, and they shall be as frontlets between thine eyes. *And thou shalt write them upon the posts of thine house, and on thy gates"* (*Deut.* 6:7–9; emphasis is mine).

Even space carries the signs of memory. And everything in the Finzi-Contini house religiously recalls the past. The garden and the villa are filled with "venerated testimonials", that is to say, they abound with memories that one cannot and must not forget. For example there are the old, luxurious objects that are preserved with the greatest care by the gardener Perotti: the dark blue brougham, "with large rubber wheels, red shafts, all glistening in fresh paint, crystal, nickel,"[57] in which Alberto and Micòl Finzi-Contini go to school, or the house's antiquated elevator, "all wine-colored gleaming wood, glistening crystal panels adorned with an M, an F, and a C elaborately intertwined."[58] These precious old objects not only represent the wealth that surrounds the Finzi-Continis, but they allude indirectly to the recent history of Italian Judaism. In their capacity as signs of the standing that the family has achieved in the last hundred years, these objects tell the story of the rapid integration of the Jews into Italian society after the emancipation of 1848. Their preservation is a way of guarding the memory of an era of great hopes and great social changes. In addition, perhaps, these same objects, in their closed and inviting character, preserve an indefinable memory of the ghetto experience: "To be seized by the pungent, somewhat stifling odor, of mold, perhaps, and turpentine, which impregnated the air enclosed in that small space, was to feel suddenly an unmotivated sense of calm, of fatalistic tranquility, of actually ironic detachment."[59]

One even breathes the same stagnant, comfortable air—slightly oppressive and protective—in the villa's old garage, where a strange and pleasant odor floats, a mixture of gasoline, oil, old dust, citrus ("the smell was really good—Micòl said at once, noticing how I sniffed . . . —she also liked it very much").[60] Or again in the dining room that looks onto the park: it is intimate, separate, and buried "like the porthole of the *Nautilus*";[61] or again in Professor Ermanno's office, a narrow little room crammed with an incredible quantity of books and the most varied objects.

Preserved in Professor Ermanno's office, however, are not only the traces of a recent history, the vague and indefinable memories of a life in the ghetto and the unequivocal signs of the conquest of freedom; he tries to preserve a specifically Jewish memory as well. Among the professor's books stand out a collection of volumes on Jewish antiquities and two small works on the history of the Venetian Jews: the one contains all the inscriptions of the Jewish cemetery of the Lido, gathered together and translated; the other is on the Jewish poetess Sara Enriquez Avigdor who lived in Venice in the first half of the seventeenth century. The garden and the *magna domus* of the Finzi-Continis thus present themselves as spaces in which an ambivalent memory is reflected: on the one hand, they reflect the desire to integrate into Italian society, to leave the past behind; on the other, they reflect the desire to resist a complete assimilation, to preserve a memory of the past and of Jewish history. They express the Jewish freedom described by Vladimir Jankélévitch in "Ressembler, dissembler": the desire to resemble others and adapt to the culture of a majority and, at the same time, the desire to preserve a sense of religious or cultural difference; the human freedom to be at once equal and different, oneself and something other than oneself.[62]

Professor Ermanno's decision to have the little Spanish synagogue in via Mazzini restored at his own expense must be read in this light. In 1933, Mussolini made political changes to increase the number of people registered in the Fascist party. Even in the small Jewish community of Ferrara, notes Bassani, the number of people registered increased to 90 percent. Professor Ermanno and the Finzi-Continis, however, did not register. Instead he has an old synagogue restored, one that for at least three centuries was used as a storeroom rather than for worship. The small Spanish synagogue in via Mazzini, the professor's collection of books on Jewish antiquities, and his whole house, pregnant with memories, represent small acts of resistance to Fascism and a call to the Jewish community of Ferrara not to allow the integration into Italian society, which had begun with the Risorgimento, to translate, under Fascism, into a complete assimilation and a total cancellation of Jewish memory.

But the figure that more than any other represents memory in *The Garden of the Finzi-Continis* is Micòl. As a foreshadowing of her approaching end, Micòl doesn't love the future, "preferring to it by far *'le vierge, le vivace et le bel aujourd'hui,'* and, even more, the past, 'the dear, sweet, sainted* past.'"[63] This religious sense of time, the idea of a *sainted* past that conceals the possibility and impossibility of the present, is the distinctive key to her character. For Micòl, "pious pilgrimages" are long walks to the places of her childhood, to the corners of the garden where one can still make out the remains of a past life. These places, objects, and situations transmit less a sense of nostalgia for the past or the idea that revisiting it may lead us to a different future as they do the idea of a liberation of a past that has remained hidden, unexpressed, forgotten, or simply dormant: a small launching point hidden amid the thick vegetation where Alberto and Micòl left for long canoe trips when they were children; the Perotti's colonial house where they stayed to eat extraordinary non-kosher bean soups; the garden wall against which a spiral staircase generally leaned, which they used for their brief flights from the paternal house. These were three small transgressions whose remains—the launching point, the colonial house, the garden wall—bear witness to all of the possibilities that have remained unexpressed in the past. Like Benjamin's angel of history, pushed toward the future by a storm that it is unable to oppose, and with its face turned toward a past in ruins, Micòl lifts her gaze from a future that she cannot know and turns it pitifully onto the ruins of the past, on the catastrophe of objects, places, and situations that still preserve, in their abandonment and in their being, remains of something that is no longer, a ray of light of all the possibilities of life that were interrupted in the past, of all that which could have been and did not become.[64] It is not simply a question of a nostalgic re-evocation of the past. For Micòl, as well as for Bassani, memory is an active recollection in which the remains of the past are restored, making possible a different development of the present and another possibility for the future.

Precisely because of her sensibility with regard to the past, Micòl escapes the nostalgia for old things; she escapes from memories of a time gone by, from the antiquated memories that seem to surround the Finzi-Continis. She does not like the dark blue carriage that is used for special occasions, the brougham that the coachman Perotti continues to polish like new, and that Micòl thinks should be left to sink into oblivion. "Objects also die, my friend," Micòl says to the narrator, "and if they also must die, then that's it, better to let them go."[65]

Where her friend Malnate, who believes in the future and progress, would see a necessity, Micòl sees only a pile of ruins. But they are ruins that in their state of abandonment can reveal the traces of a forgotten or dormant life. The dark, oblong outline of the canoe, for example, in its loss of function, in its capacity as a leftover of history—now nothing more than a "ghost canoe"—reveals the life that passed through it through the gaze that snatches it from the past. "Look instead at the canoe, I beg you, and observe its honesty, dignity, and moral courage; it has drawn all the necessary conclusions from its own total loss of function."[66]

For this reason too, perhaps, Micòl is a passionate collector of *làttimi*, that is, cups, goblets, flasks, bits of glass of every type that could have become precious objects but that were instead thrown out and forgotten. And now, lined up on the shelves of her room, they emanate the weak, milky light of a past that has not been expressed but that never completely died.

At other times, Micòl's gaze lingers on the trees in the garden, on "the great, calm, strong, pensive" trees that she can recognize and name one by one.[67] Even in the trees, Micòl sees the remains of an archaic, dormant past, a suspended and immobile life that is waiting to be reawakened. The seven *Washingtoniae graciles,* the beloved desert palms with their "dark, dry, curved, scaly" trunks,[68] remind her of the seven hermits of the Thebaid, dried by the sun and by fasting, or seven St. John the Baptists, feeding only on locusts. Micòl seems to call upon the trees to speak as if she were trying to take nature out of its silence, out of the muteness and deep sadness in which, as Benjamin writes, nature finds itself after the Fall.[69] And perhaps it is for this reason that Micòl's speech is woven with fragments of literary and artistic quotations—from Mallarmé to Baudelaire to Debussy—as if language were a way to salvage other suspended discourses that were never finished, of which only a broken, spread-out memory remains, an anthology of quotations.

On the other hand, Micòl's temporal dimension is the present, as her vitality and uneasiness demonstrate. Micòl is an active, uneasy character, animated by a strong will to preserve and affirm life at times when life seems seriously threatened. The "beloved earthquake," as her father calls her, finds the time to look after everything. She takes care of her studies and the general management of the household, her own learning and her family. And despite the discrimination introduced by the racial laws that exclude Jews from the professions, she nevertheless goes to Venice to write her thesis on Emily Dickinson and then graduate. Her Italian translation of a poem by Dickinson tells of a dialogue between two lives that tenaciously resist silence and death as far as they are able. "And so, as kinsmen met a night, / We talked between the rooms, / Until the moss had reached our lips / And covered up our names."[70]

But of course Micòl's vitality is incomplete. Her gaze also transmits an awareness of the precariousness of the future. Despite the loving care of the gardeners who bind them in straw every year, Micòl does not know whether her beloved *Washingtoniae graciles* will survive the cold winter of 1938. And in the foggy days that the winter promises, when the circle of discrimination slowly tightens around the Finzi-Continis, Micòl looks past the panes of the window, she fixes the horizon, she pushes her gaze beyond the treetops, onto the roofs of the houses, the towers of the castle, onto the marble of the Duomo of Ferrara. But the thick fog of history blocks her view.

All the same, despite the tragedy of history, Micòl's vitality is in some sense opposed to Fadigati's melancholy; it is opposed to the waters of the Pontelagoscuro in which the doctor drowns and into which, at times, the narrator himself would like to let himself fall. Her vitality is a paradoxical form of hope in contrast to the impulse to self-annihilation that the doctor represents. "For me . . . there was no hope, no hope for *anything*," says the narrator as he looks at himself in the opaque water of the kitchen mirror and he imagines that a hurricane is about to scatter his little family that has gathered to celebrate the first evening of Pesach, to scatter it "like fragile leaves, like scraps of paper, like hairs from a head whitened by years, or by terror. . . . But who could tell? What can we know . . . of what lies ahead of us?" he adds.[71] And in fact the phone rings, Alberto invites him to visit the Finzi-Continis and, after a happy bike ride through the deserted streets of Ferrara, he distinguishes Micòl's familiar outline on the threshold of the *magna domus*: her "small dark form, engraved on a background of very white light" that rekindles hope despite the historical period.

Of course the narrator's hope will prove vain. The future will present itself to him precisely as a storm that scatters lives. "What we call progress," Benjamin writes, "is *this* storm."[72] History for Micòl, and for Bassani, is not progress; it is neither the naïve, optimistic history of the narrator's father, nor Malnate's utopia, whose future Micòl abhors, but the paradoxical history that, by turning its back on the future, sets its gaze on the ruins of the past, on the remains of all that could have been and was not and, by looking at them, gives them a possibility. In her gaze, there is more than a passing resemblance to the Jewish idea of history as memory, remains, and possibility, history as a construction of hope. It is an idea of history that informs Bassani's own writing.

When the narrator, as a Jew, is expelled from Ferrara's municipal library, Professor Ermanno puts at the young man's disposal his personal library so that he might finish his thesis. It is the last days of the winter of 1939 and the garden of the Finzi-Continis, all white, "buried beneath a blanket of snow,"[73] appears to the narrator as an anchor to hang on to in order to stop the inexorable flow of time: "My heart inhabited by a dark, mysterious lake of fear, clung to the little desk which Professor Ermanno . . . had had placed for me in the billiard room, beneath the central window, as if, in doing so, I were able to resist the irresistible advance of time."[74]

It is in this context that the narrator receives a gift from the professor of the two short works on the history of the Venetian Jews that the professor had worked on in his youth. The two texts are mentioned several times throughout the novel. The first time is when the narrator and the professor are taking a walk around the tennis courts and talking about Italian culture and ancient Jewish remembrances—the walk and the conversation almost seem to be an apotropaic wall against the *new* that is advancing, represented by the tennis courts. "He was still saving for me the copies of his little essays on Venetian history, I was not to forget,"[75] the professor reminds the narrator several times as he guides him along the row of bedrooms and corridors that lead to Alberto's room. And it is finally here, in the large, warm, silent parlor of the Finzi-Contini house, where the professor, both loving and respectful, showers him with sympathy and admiration for his tenacity in his work: "He looked at me with glowing, shining eyes: as if from me, from my future as a man of letters, as a scholar, he expected who knows what; as if he were counting on me for some secret ambition of his, that transcended not only himself, but me as well."[76]

There is a light irony in the tone of this passage. Professor Ermanno's "glowing, shining eyes," which rest on the narrator and on his "future as a man of letters," and on the scholarly research that should fulfill a "secret," transcendent ambition, hint at a sense of embarrassment on the part of the narrator—as if he, perceiving a lack of proportion between the professor's expectations and the task of completing a scholarly research on local Jewish history, were taking a step back; and as if he sensed that what is expected of him, of his future as writer, is memory—what is passed on to him is the task of transmitting Jewish memories to new generations and the commandment to always remember the past, any past.

At the end of the short story "Argon," Primo Levi too masks with light irony the embarrassment that he felt as a child every time his grandmother Màlia offered him an old, stale chocolate. Perhaps, like the gifts from Professor Ermanno, this chocolate too represents the passing of time and the importance of memory; the act of passing it on to the child represents the transmission of memories to new generations, and its sweet, sour flavor represents the pleasant and difficult task of remembering. The grandmother's chocolate is stale and worm-eaten, but the child quickly hides it away in his pocket. No matter how hard it is to swallow, nor how difficult they are to transmit, the child holds on tight to his chocolate, and the adult to his memories.

Perhaps, like Levi in "Argon," in this passage of *The Garden of the Finzi-Contini*, Bassani too hints at the ambiguity of gifts and, in particular, at the double nature of the gift of memory that is at once a lightness and a burden, a freedom and a responsibility, a vital possibility and a difficult, unavoidable duty. He seems to invite us to interpret all of his works as the completion of the ellipsis placed at the end of the paragraph, as the realization of Professor Ermanno's hope that someone make another attempt, give himself another possibility and continue his work on memory. In this light *The Garden of the Finzi-Continis,* as well as the other five volumes that compose the *Romanzo di Ferrara,* can be read as a series of works that preserve Jewish memories, not simply because they recount Jewish stories but because they share a way of remembering the past that is central to Jewish history and thought: memory as an attempt at salvaging the past and changing the present.

As Levi Della Torre remarked in *Mosaico,* this attempt, this constantly renewed possibility, is central to Judaism and to the biblical notion of the remnant. In his interpretation, the remnant does not so much refer to those who have been saved through their goodness as to those who have had the privilege of surviving and who therefore have the responsibility to bear witness to the past and put history back into motion.[77] Perhaps both Ermanno's historical research and the tale of Bassani's narrator reflect, in different ways, a similar chance, a similar duty, to salvage the past. Perhaps the secret design that transcends both Professor Ermanno and the narrator, and that is sealed by the gift of the two works on Venetian antiquity, coincides with this possibility, effort, and hope. The professor has not managed to finish the research he began in his youth, namely to write a history of the Jews of Venice, he knows that his son Alberto is not interested by historical and literary studies, and he will not live long enough to see the project through. Possibility and effort reappear however in the narrator, who is passionate about study and literature.

The Garden of the Finzi-Continis, however, is a work of fiction. As such, it deals with the past in ways that are different from pure historical research, traditional literary criticism, or from the kind of learned, scholarly writing favored by Professor Ermanno. Unlike narratives that aim at an entirely objective discourse, literary texts combine history and autobiography with fiction and imagination; they mix collective and individual history, objective and subjective narratives. Thus, in Bassani, the recovery of the Jewish past does not so much unfold under Professor Ermanno's

objective, historical gaze as under the subjective gaze of memory—as if
the narrator of *The Garden of the Finzi-Continis* had picked up the thread
of Jewish history that, years before, Professor Ermanno had had passed
on to him and used it to weave a narrative work peopled with imaginary
characters, fictitious settings, made-up events that give readers a kind of
knowledge of that same past that is not merely factual.

On the one hand, *The Garden of the Finzi-Continis* is characterized
by precise references to historical facts, real places, names, and dates, and
by a degree of concreteness and precision in describing reality that has led
readers to wonder how much of the novel's plot is fictional, how much is
real, whether or not its characters are inspired by real people, where to
draw the line between history and literature, reality and imagination. The
presence of historical events in the novel, as well as the author's attention
to their exactness, is certainly linked to the fact that among these events
is the Shoah: there is a history that can no longer by ignored by a writer
and that requires care and attention in order not to betray its historical
truth. On the other hand, the novel seems to evince a need for concreteness and precision even in detailing events that are likely to be the product
of imagination. At the beginning of the novel, for instance, the narrator
names the members of the Finzi-Contini family one by one, and he mentions the address where they lived and the day that he found the impulse to
write down his memories, a Sunday in April 1957. Here, concreteness and
precision acquire a meaning that goes beyond attention to the veracity of
historical facts and has to do, instead, with the way that the figurative use
of language can preserve a memory of the past and provide a different, not
strictly historical knowledge of the past. Without betraying the veracity of
historical facts, the use of literary tools and imagination—that intimate
and slightly melancholic list of names, the concreteness and specificity of
that address and that date—gives to the narrative a historical concreteness
that brings the story of the Finzi-Continis closer to the novel's readers and
may have consequences on their emotions and their ethical sense. Thus, the
inclusion of history within a fictional narrative counts not only as a way to
bear witness to the past but also as a way to transform that same history
into a paradigm for the present. What counts in this novel is not only the
historical datum but its actualization, not only the fact but the possibility

of transforming it into memory of the past in the present, not only the historical past that Professor Ermanno studies but the past that Micòl evokes and makes alive in the present by her language, her mood, her pilgrimages to the dear places of her childhood, her memory.

At issue here is a kind of writing that bears witness to the past without renouncing the resources offered by imagination. It is a literature that includes historical facts without suppressing the subjective gaze on those facts, without denying that other not purely factual, not purely objective elements of writing—such as the author's gaze, the narrator's and the character's voices, as well as the readers' reactions—may also contribute to knowledge of reality. Although history is necessary for knowing the past, historical facts are not enough. For sorrows and joys, justice and injustice, emotions and ethics to be carried from the past to the present, for suffering to come out of the past and be put back within the circle of life, as Appelfeld writes, for history to be memory, it is necessary to have a type of writing that, without posing a threat to the integrity of the historical discourse, does not suppress the subjective gaze on the past or sharply oppose historical and literary discourse but sees them as two equally important sides of the knowledge of the past. In Judaism, history is necessary because meaning is not ahistorical: meaning is not an eternal, immutable entity, as it is in myths, but it happens in history and in its becoming. At the same time, writing and interpretation of history are necessary so that that history can be saved and transmitted and so that it can acquire different meanings in different times for different generations.

As Young has remarked, history and literature, reality and writing have never been diametrically opposed; they are interdependent, they permeate one another like the past and our response to it. Writing remembers the past so that the past can find its voice in the present; literature incorporates historical facts and characters so that they can become the inspiration and paradigm of resistance in the present. In this light, the narrative voice is not just the descriptive, analytical voice of a detached observer; it is rather a performative voice of memory and healing.

During a visit to an Etruscan cemetery, the vision of the ancient tombs of a lost civilization remind the narrator of the Finzi-Continis and of the other families in the small Jewish community of Ferrara, and of their lives before the Shoah. The monuments to a lost civilization remind him of another civilization, persecuted and dispersed too, but still living and present. So begins *The Garden of the Finzi-Continis*. It begins with a witness who tries to gather and connect the fragments of the past, with a voice that tries to tell their story today, a Sunday in April 1957, so that their story can find expression in the present, and perhaps both past and present can be healed. From the very beginning of *The Garden of the Finzi-Continis*, the act of writing is an act of remembering, a response to the storm of the past, to the catastrophes of history, to inscrutable matter. Memory, here, reconnects reality and writing, history and literature, facts and their interpretations, past and present. It turns the opposition between history and imagination into a vital tension: no longer the rights of history *versus* the rights of imagination, but the right of history *and* the rights of imagination. Here, within memory, the tigers and kittens of Ginzburg's poetics, the burden of writing the truth and the lightness of writing fiction, seem to find a possible reconciliation.

For the narrator, the Etruscan tombs count not so much for their historical, archeological, or documentary meaning as for their ability to remind him of the Finzi-Continis and compel him to tell their story. Likewise for Bassani, the recovery of the Jewish past, of any past, is not just history, archeology, or antiquarianism; rather, it has the richness of the subjective gaze with its emotions, its joys and sorrows, and its ethics, its desire to call out injustices and its longing for justice, that are characteristic of literature, art, or psychology. It has the historical and eschatological depth that the human voice gains once it is within time—a voice that tries to bring back to the present fragments from the past and postpone at the horizon of time what may be the ultimate meaning of those fragments and those lives. Thus recovering the past is inspiration and paradigm, memory and hope. It is an inspiration to gather the fragments of the past, to listen to its voices and bring them back to life in the present. And it is a paradigm for action in the present inasmuch as these fragments and these voices, in their historical concreteness and specificity, become models for resistance in the present, hope for the future. In this historical specificity, in this temporal concreteness, they find a second chance of life. While remembering the story of the Finzi-Continis, "Micòl and Alberto . . . Professor Ermanno and Signora Olga—and all the others who inhabited or, like me, frequented the house in corso Ercole I d'Este, in Ferrara, just before the outbreak of the last war," while giving voice to the concrete story of a Jewish family from Ferrara during World War II—Bassani also tells a universal story.[78] Thanks to its historical specificity and concreteness, his imaginary tale takes on a universal meaning, becomes part of a collective memory and an abstract paradigm for humankind.

4

The Modesty of Starbuck

ON HYBRIDS, JUDAISM, AND ETHICS IN PRIMO LEVI

IN THE SPRING OF 1980, Giulio Bollati, chief editor of the Italian publishing house Einaudi, asked several Italian writers to compile an anthology of books that had played an important role in their intellectual development. Originally conceived as textbooks for high school students, these anthologies were meant neither as traditional manuals of exemplary compositions nor as collections of illustrious quotations drawn from the classics of world literature. Rather, they were intended as anthologies of excerpts that would constitute literary self-portraits of their compilers. Primo Levi accepted Bollati's proposal with enthusiasm and readily began to work on his project. In the spring of the following year, he had completed a manuscript that was published in May 1981 under the title *The Search for Roots.*[1]

At first glance, what stands out in Levi's anthology is its hybrid nature, its combination of writers of very different traditions and characters such as Rabelais and Darwin, Homer and Eliot, Lucretius and Celan. Such a bold juxtaposition of literary and scientific texts, contemporary authors and classics of ancient literatures speaks of Levi's vivid intellectual curiosity and independent mind, but it also reflects the hybrid condition that is at the core of Levi's creativity: his being writer and witness, scientist and humanist, Italian and Jew; or, as Levi himself said, his being like a centaur, a hybrid creature in tension between two different conditions. Like the mythological centaur who was divided into two halves, Levi aspired to be both author of memoirs and fiction writer, historian and storyteller; he freely mixed disciplines that are traditionally seen as opposed, such as science and literature, and combined Italian and Jewish traditions into a whole and coherent intellectual experience.[2]

Both Levi's notion of writing and his relationship with Judaism develop within this vital tension between different aspirations, disciplines, and traditions. For Levi, the possibility of looking at the world from different points of view, of resorting to various skills and traditions in order to interpret reality, translates into a form of intellectual freedom and responsibility. As a witness and a fiction writer, Levi was always attentive to the thin border between history and imagination, and felt responsible for the veracity of the facts he presented in his books; as a scientist and a humanist, he placed exactness and clarity of expression at the center of his poetics; as an Italian and a Jew, he enjoyed the freedom of combining the modern, liberal ideals of Risorgimento and anti-Fascism with the depth and wisdom of ancient Jewish traditions; or, as Vladimir Jankélévitch says, the freedom of being the same and different, himself and other than himself.

At the same time, for Levi, both writing and Judaism are experiences linked with the Shoah. On more than one occasion, when he was asked about the source of his writing, he traced it back to the experience of the concentration camps and said that, without Auschwitz, he would never have become a writer. Similarly, when he was asked about his relationship with Judaism, Levi said that, before being deported to Auschwitz, he was just an Italian who had grown up in a secular and integrated Jewish family from Turin. For him, Jewish identity came mostly as the result of the promulgation of the 1938 racial laws and then from his deportation to the concentration camp; his identity was born out of the response of an integrated and nonreligious Jew to anti-Semitism.

Nonetheless, his interest in Judaism grew steadily over the years and, through a gradual rediscovery of his family's Jewish roots, turned into a vivid interest in various aspects of Jewish culture.[3] In general, Levi rejected a notion of Jewish identity based on race, embracing instead a sense of a cultural belonging to Jewish tradition. To him, Judaism was a tradition that he did not want to renounce and whose heritage he proudly began to claim as his own after the war. In 1986, in an interview with the journal *Qol*, he said, "For me, Judaism is a tradition and a culture. Both aspects interest me and I think that they would interest me even if I were not Jewish."[4] He also described himself as "un esempio tipico di ebreo di ritorno," a typical example of a Jew who had returned to his roots and renewed his interest in Judaism only at a later stage in his life.[5] In particular, Levi spoke of Judaism as an *impurity,* as "the grain of salt or mustard" that "makes the zinc react," referring to the fertile role played by an imperfect minority in the development of contemporary Western cultures,[6] and of the possibility, from that point of view, of reclaiming a Jewish heritage characterized by a strong emphasis on ethics.

Our discussion of the relationship between Levi and Judaism develops precisely within this tension: on the one hand, the hybrid character of Levi's writing and his notion of Jewish identity, and, on the other, the emphasis he placed on ethics and their consonances with Jewish ethical traditions. From a methodological point of view, this approach has two main advantages. First, the notion of a hybridized history allows us to go beyond the dichotomy that often characterizes the bibliography on Jewish literature, namely the extreme choice between an essentialist specificity of Judaism and no specificity whatsoever; it allows us to go beyond either a fixed and determined history or no history at all. Secondly, focusing on ethics may help to situate Levi in a larger cultural context and gain a better critical perspective on his works. Levi seems to share the tension of other nineteenth- and twentieth-century Jewish intellectuals who, while being modern, attempt to adhere to Jewish traditions, a tension they resolve by emphasizing the ethical core of such traditions. Ethics can also be described as a development of a world outlook that has its sources in religion but eventually goes beyond it. From this perspective, I see Levi's work as a secular reappropriation of Judaism that, by means of a reactualization of Jewish themes within contemporary Italian culture, represents an active and alternative response to Auschwitz and a reminder of the importance of ethics within literary discourse.[7]

In *The Search for Roots,* Levi reserves a small but significant place for his Jewish roots. Although he included in his ideal library only three Jewish writers and one character from the Bible—Isaac Babel, Sholem Aleichem, Paul Celan, and Job, a distant and proximate Jewish kinship, as Levi calls it—the presence of Jewish cultural memory resonates throughout the text. There is, for instance, an excerpt from *Joseph and his Brothers,* Mann's novel that recounts the biblical story of Joseph as told in the book of Genesis and that was published between 1933 and 1943, when Hitler was in power. In his comments on contemporary literature, Levi makes various references to the Bible, for example, when he compares some characters in Porta's dialect poems to small Jobs: "Giovannin, Ninetta, Marchionn, are Jobs in miniature, good human material that, for others' pleasure, is worn down, torn, and finally ripped to shreds."[8] These and other scattered references to the Bible, to Jewish history and culture, are characterized by a strong focus on ethics. It is precisely in his focus on the ethical dimension of writing, and on its consonances with Jewish ethics, that Levi's relationship to Judaism becomes particularly evident. A look at the drawing placed by Levi at the beginning of his anthology will help to clarify this point.

As a visual and conceptual preface to *The Search for Roots,* Levi drew the figure of an ellipse whose northern pole he made coincide with the biblical book of Job and the southern pole with the astronomical concept of the black holes. In between the two poles, Levi traced four curved lines along which he placed the names of some exemplary authors included in his anthology who had dedicated their works to the themes of knowledge, laughter, unjust human suffering, and moral stature. In Levi's drawing, the northern pole of the ellipse represents Job, the just man oppressed by injustice; the southern pole represents Auschwitz and other forms of annihilation of human consciousness; and the four lines connecting the two poles represent four different narrative itineraries, four different ways in which reading and writing can become an inspiration to resist against evil: ways of strengthening Job's sense of justice and of rescuing humans from drifting into the blind matter of the black holes.

Inscribed within this drawing, there may be an idea of ethics that has more than a consonance with Jewish morality, with its focus on the themes of emancipation and human action. The spatial opposition between Job and the black holes, between the theme of justice and the theme of emptiness, between the work of the just man and the concrete existence of evil, recalls the theme of emancipation that is at the center of Jewish history. The Exodus of the Jewish people from Egypt, celebrated every year at Pesach as the record of human emancipation from slavery, is also a metaphor of every exit from a present state of things, of every birth and deliverance of life from matter, of the people from the indistinct mass of peoples, of the person from the slave. In Levi's drawing, in his four possible routes to salvation (laughter, knowledge, and awareness of unjust human suffering and of the moral stature of humans), human life also takes on the form of a deliverance from matter as represented by the black holes. On the one hand, what is represented in Levi's drawing is clearly an Exodus *in negativo*: the four arrows that connect Job to the black holes, the four routes to salvation, point downward and are turned toward the black holes. The Exodus here is a form of resistance to our natural and spontaneous drift into blind matter. On the other hand, awareness of the existence of evil doesn't mean absence of hope: the opposition between Job and the black holes is not simply a fatalistic opposition between ethics and Auschwitz but rather a tension between human consciousness of the existence of evil and the possibility of vanquishing it. "If the human mind has conceived black holes," wrote Levi at the very end of his anthology, "why should it not know how to conquer fear, poverty and grief?"[9]

At the center of the resistance that we can put up to this drift, there is human action. As Levi Della Torre has observed, in Judaism, in contrast to Greek culture, truth is not something that is known but something that is done.[10] In Exodus 24:7, when Moses comes down from Mount Sinai with the Torah and reads it to the people, they answer, "All that the Lord hath said *will we do and will we listen*:" *na'ase venishma*. According to a common interpretation, the fact that in this passage the "doing" precedes the "listening" is a way of underlining the strict connection between listening and acting, and the primacy of action over pure theology. Only when we put into practice the teachings we have received will we be able to understand, that is, *listen to,* their deeper message, because their meaning can be fully understood only when it is tested against reality. While the Greeks speak of *physis,* of the autonomous generative power of nature, the Jews speak of creation, of forces that are making the world. Unlike in the Greek universe, where our task is to observe and understand the given world, in the Jewish world the task is to continue the work of creation in collaboration with its Creator. Similarly, in the Kabbalah, creation is not cosmos—that is to say, perfection—but an imperfect outcome, a catastrophe that we must remedy in collaboration with the Creator.

In Levi, the work of man is at the center of his ethical vision of human life. In a brief essay on the Schulchan Aruch, a sixteenth-century Hebrew code of Jewish law composed by Rabbi Josef Karo, Levi compares the work of the scientist to that of the rabbi who compiled the manual: both seem to him valuable activities inasmuch as they share the common art of making distinctions to make order in a chaotic universe in need of human intervention. For Levi, work is in general the very point of human existence. Tino Faussone, the skilled rigger who is the hero of Levi's 1978 novel, *The Monkey's Wrench*, says:

> We agreed then on the good things we have in common. On the advantage of being able to test yourself, not depending on others in the test, reflecting yourself in your work. On the pleasure of seeing your creature grow, beam after beam, bolt after bolt, solid, necessary, symmetrical, suited to its purpose; and when it's finished you look at it and perhaps you think it will live longer than you, and perhaps it will be of use to someone you don't know, who doesn't know you.[11]

This eulogy to work is perhaps Levi's strongest ethical response to Auschwitz. In a famous interview published in November 1986 in *La Stampa*, Philip Roth asked Primo Levi:

> Work would seem to be your chief subject, not just in *The Monkey's Wrench* but even in your first book about your incarceration at Auschwitz. *Arbeit Macht Frei*—"Work Makes Freedom"—are the words inscribed by the Nazis over the Auschwitz gate. But work in Auschwitz is a horrifying parody of work, useless and senseless—labor as punishment leading to agonizing death. It's possible to view your entire literary labor as dedicated to restoring to work its humane meaning, reclaiming the word *Arbeit* from the derisive cynicism with which your Auschwitz employers had disfigured it. Faussone says to you, "Every job I undertake is like a first love." He enjoys talking about his work almost as much as he enjoys working. Faussone is Man the Worker made truly free through his labors.[12]

Levi responded to the observation in the following way:

I am persuaded that normal human beings are biologically built for an activity that is aimed towards a goal and that idleness, or aimless work (like Auschwitz's *Arbeit*) gives rise to suffering and to atrophy . . . At Auschwitz I quite often observed a curious phenomenon. The need for *lavoro ben fatto*—"work properly done"—is so strong even to induce people to perform even slavish chores "properly." The Italian bricklayer who saved my life by bringing me food on the sly for six months hated Germans, their food, their language, their war; but when they set him to erect walls, he built them straight and solid, not out of obedience but out of professional dignity.[13]

Here work is not only an activity directed toward construction, it is a form of freedom inasmuch as it helps the individual to maintain his integrity as a subject resisting slavery, annihilation, relapse into the nothingness of matter and the black holes of history. From this perspective, the work of the chemist and that of the writer, like the work of the master bridge builder Faussone, is a continual birth and deliverance, the Exodus that man celebrates every year and remembers and repeats every day of his life. The Jewish notion that man's task is to continue the work of creation in collaboration with its Creator is celebrated in Levi in its secular and ethical meanings of the responsibility to complete one's work well and the freedom that may result from it. In this sense, this notion takes on a universal value.

It is not by chance, then, that Levi places a literary character who stands up for his ethical virtues at the center of *The Search for Roots*— Starbuck, the first mate of the *Pequod* in Melville's *Moby-Dick*. A native of Nantucket and a Quaker by descent, Starbuck is the virtuous and sober man who represents a degree of containment against Ahab's maniacally obsessive hunt for the white whale. He is the man who reasons rather than emotes, who questions Ahab's judgment and balances his thirst for vengeance. Many of his qualities recall the ethical virtues that Levi praised in his writings: sobriety and a sense of limit, craftsmanship and reasonability, fortitude and cautiousness. From this perspective, Starbuck may even be read as an American ancestor of Tino Faussone. Starbuck's appearance right at the center of Levi's anthology, then, cannot be accidental.

In Levi's anthology, texts are not organized by subject or chronological sequence but are listed in the order in which Levi read them. The chapter that precedes the excerpt about Starbuck is dedicated to Roger Vercel's *Tug-Boat,* a French novel that Levi read in Auschwitz on the day the Nazis fled the camp. The Allies had not yet arrived, and he expected to die. The chapter after Starbuck's is dedicated to an excerpt from Saint-Exupéry's *Wind, Sand, and Stars* that, significantly, is entitled "Survivors in the Sahara."[14] In other words, the portrait of Starbuck stands between the experience of the prisoner in Auschwitz and that of the survivor: "I prefer to pass over the pages, at the same time Biblical and barbaric, in which the sacred terror of the hunt is portrayed, to note instead the portrait of a man in 'full fig,' replete with modesty and presentiment."[15]

Between the experience of the concentration camp and that of survival, Levi seems to suspend his narration, passing over the immeasurable pages that tell of the white whale and the folly of Captain Ahab, choosing instead to privilege Starbuck and give us a full portrait of a just man. In a certain way, the choice to anthologize a passage from Melville, and in particular the portrait of Starbuck, is a form of expressive reticence. Instead of quoting the terrible pages about the whale hunt, instead of referring directly to the unspeakable experience of the concentration camp, Levi emphasizes its opposite: a life-sized portrait of a man. Starbuck's chapter is significantly entitled "The Dark Well of the Human Spirit." Against Ahab's journey into the dark side of the human spirit, Levi opposes Starbuck's ordinary virtues, his modesty and presentiment. Their place at the very center of Levi's anthology signifies the preeminence of the ethical discourse in Levi's search for roots and, more generally, in his conception of writing. As has been noted by Robert Gordon in his *Primo Levi's Ordinary Virtues*: Levi's "writing marks out and maps a terrain whose coordinates can be best described as a catalogue of virtues . . . [whose] persistent and fundamental feature . . . is their rather stubborn ordinariness."[16]

In the following discussion, the ethical character of Levi's Judaism provides my theoretical framework. First, I will focus on his treatment of the notion of the shame of the survivor in order to show how he contributes to the reconstruction of Jewish cultural memory through his secular, rational recovery of Jewish religious themes. Then, through a comparison with the work of the philosopher Günther Anders, I will put Levi's work in a larger cultural context and show that he was not alone in his return to Judaism. Finally, through a comparison with Kafka, I will analyze how an ethical and hybrid notion of Judaism may challenge consolidated notions of literature and writing.

IT HAS BEEN CONFIRMED by numerous testimonies that prisoners in concentration camps experienced a feeling of shame during their time of imprisonment. According to Primo Levi, who dedicated the third chapter of his last book, *The Drowned and the Saved,* to this subject, prisoners became aware of this feeling when the brutish routine of the camps was briefly suspended and they could regain consciousness of the state to which they had been reduced. "During the very few Sundays of rest, the fleeting minutes before falling asleep, or the fury of the air raids," prisoners were granted a reprieve from the inhuman conditions to which they had been confined, and they measured their diminishment in its entirety and felt ashamed.[17]

Nor—however strange it may seem—did this feeling vanish after liberation. Rather, it grew ever stronger and more intense. According to many who survived, liberation was not joyful but was accompanied by a feeling of vague discomfort. When one came out of Auschwitz and returned to so-called civilian life, the reacquired consciousness of having been diminished caused sufferance. This absurd and paradoxical pain was not exactly shame, specifies Levi, but it was perceived as such. It was an intricately composite feeling that contained diverse elements and came in diverse proportions depending on the individual.

First, there was the shame of not having done anything, or not enough, against the system of the concentration camp. When hearing the news that another prisoner had had the chance and the strength to revolt, many experienced a feeling of shame over their own inability to act. Levi gives such an example in the sixteenth chapter of *Survival in Auschwitz,* which recounts how a prisoner was publicly hanged for taking part in a revolt that led to the explosion of one of the Birkenau crematoria: the other prisoners remained silent as they were forced to witness his execution and went back to their huts oppressed by a sense of shame.

Of course, such a feeling can hardly be rationally justified, for in the Lager, resistance was almost impossible and limited to the political prisoners. And yet, even though the vast majority of prisoners did not have the opportunity to act, after their liberation many among them felt guilty as a consequence of their inaction. Conversely, prisoners who had the opportunity and the strength to act against the concentration camp machinery were sheltered from this feeling. Political prisoners like Sivadjan, the quiet man briefly mentioned in *Survival in Auschwitz* who introduced explosives into the camp in order to start an insurrection, or those who worked to eliminate a new particularly fearsome *kapo* who indiscriminately beat all his subjects with the intention of inflicting pain, or those who had the power of switching the registration numbers on the lists of prisoners who were destined for the gas chamber—none of these experienced the feeling of shame described in *The Drowned and the Saved*. They may have experienced another feeling, Levi notes, but they were protected from shame by the fact of their action.

Perhaps more reasonable is the self-accusation of having failed in terms of human solidarity. Sent with his squad to clean out a cellar on a very hot summer day, Primo found a source of water and decided to share it only with his friend, Alberto, excluding the rest of the squad of thirsty prisoners. After the war, that unshared glass of water stood between Primo and his fellow prisoners as a perceptible act of omission. Yet, rationally, in none of these instances can one make a strong case justifying shame.

Nevertheless, some survivors experienced shame even when they had committed no evident transgression. For survivors, shame may just be the awareness of being alive instead of someone who was not so fortunate, and, in particular, instead of someone more generous, more sensitive, more deserving of life, for one can never completely rule out the possibility of having usurped one's neighbor's place, living on *instead* of the other.

You review your memories . . . No, you find no obvious transgressions, you did not usurp anyone's place, you did not beat anyone (but would you have had the strength to do so?), you did not accept positions (but none were offered to you . . .), you did not steal anyone's bread; nevertheless you cannot exclude it. It is no more than a suspicion, indeed the shadow of a suspicion: that each man is his brother's Cain, that each one of us (and this time I say "us" in a much vaster, indeed, universal sense) has usurped his neighbor's place and lives in his stead.[18]

With a twist that is typical of a reasoning that draws a universal lesson from the experience of the concentration camp, Levi moves from the notion of shame felt due to an actual transgression to shame felt in the absence of evident transgression, from shame as a form of guilt to shame as consciousness of the existence of evil. In this form, Levi adds, shame may also contain the survivor's impulse to testify to his experience in the concentration camp. It may be the other side of testimony.

In order to explain this third type of shame, Primo Levi resorts to a gradual methodological shift across disciplines. First, he tackles and refutes two possible ways of interpreting and healing the anguish of the survivor: religion and psychoanalysis. He could not accept the relief that may come from a providential vision of history according to which his own survival was not the work of chance but rather of providence, that he had been saved in order to write and bear witness. Neither could he share the rationale of those psychoanalysts who sought to describe the anguish of prisoners and survivors as a response to traumas of the camps, a form of curable neurosis. The first concept seemed monstrous to Levi. He could find no proportion between the privilege of surviving and its outcome, namely his testifying. The second attempt at explanation, the psychoanalytical, struck him as approximate and simplistic insofar as it had its origin outside of the concentration camp universe and had been conceived for patients whose mental mechanisms, physiology, and pathologies were quite different from those of the prisoners.

Unsatisfied with both religious and psychoanalytical approaches, Levi turns to a written text and connects the prisoners' anguish to the second verse of Genesis, one that is key to understanding Levi's treatment of shame as well as his relationship with Judaism: "Now the earth was unformed and void, and darkness was upon the face of the deep; and the spirit of God hovered over the face of the waters" (Genesis 1:2). In the shame of the survivor, Levi writes, one may hear an echo of the atavistic anguish inscribed in everyone of the *tohu-bohu,* of the empty and deserted universe "crushed under the spirit of God but from which the spirit of man is absent: not yet born or already extinguished."[19] Thus testimony is neither a portion of a larger providential design nor a means of healing a neurosis, but a response to a more ancient, larger, and deeper anguish. What is the meaning, then, of this reference to a verse of the Bible right at the climax of his discourse on shame? What is the meaning of a gradual shift from historical facts to religion, from psychoanalysis to ancestral collective memory and finally to the text where a trace of that memory may be recorded?[20]

Let's take a closer look at Levi's words and at his paraphrase of the second verse of Genesis. The Hebrew verb *rahaf*—which in Genesis 2 refers to the spirit of God and in English is usually rendered as "to hover," "to move," or "to flutter," and in Italian as "librarsi," "muoversi," "aleggiare"— is translated by Levi with a verb of opposite meaning: "to crush," turning the lightness of the spirit of God that hovers over the waters into a crushing cumbersome presence.[21] Levi had already dwelt upon this same verb in "Argon," the first chapter of *The Periodic Table* dedicated to an ironic and affectionate literary portrait of his Jewish ancestors. In this text too, Levi's translation of the verb *rahaf* differs from the common one, being rendered as *alitare*: "to breathe," "to stir." "From *rúakh* . . . which means 'breath,'" writes Levi, "the illustrious term that can be read in the dark and admirable second verse of Genesis ('The wind of the Lord breathed upon the face of the waters'), was taken *tiré 'n rúakh,* "make a wind," in its diverse physiological significances."[22] Years of history seem to separate these two references to the second verse of Genesis. Levi's ancestors' familiarity with God, their domestic and homely theology, are in sharp contrast to the presence of God evoked by the verb "to crush." But Levi's original translations register something more than the rational approach of a nonbeliever to a religious text. They may also speak of the fracture that occurred between the divine and the human after Auschwitz and of an attempt at filling that void. By means of a secular and rational resumption of Jewish religious themes, through their reactualization, Levi contributes to the reconstruction of Jewish cultural memory. From this perspective, Levi's reference to

Genesis, his use of a religious text, is similar to what he does with his poem "Shemà," in which the Jewish prayer of faith in the unity of God is turned into a secular call not to forget Auschwitz:

Shemà

You who live safely
In your comfortable houses,
You who find in the evening
Warm food and friendly faces:
   Consider if this is a man
   Who works in the mud
   Who knows no peace
   Who fights for a small piece of bread
   Who dies for a yes or a no.
   Consider if this is a woman,
   With no hair and with no name
   With no more strength to remember
   Her eyes empty and her womb cold
   Like a frog in winter.
Consider that this has happened:
I command you these words
Carve them in your hearts
When you sit in your house, when you walk by the way,
When you lie down, when you rise up.
Repeat them to your children.
Or may your house be undone,
Disease may impair you
Your offspring turn their faces away from you.

                    10 January 1946[23]

Even in the form of a negative theology, Levi's references to Genesis call into question three aspects that are at the foundations of Judaism: a text, a collective, and a relationship with God; three fundamental aspects whose survival is in an echo, in an impression ("perhaps," "one may hear" . . .), in a feeble memory. Fractured is the relationship with God after Auschwitz;

scattered is the collective; elusive and deceptive is memory. And yet, the text is there as an anchor against our forgetfulness.[24] The Hebrew Bible does not hesitate to command memory. As Yosif Yerushalmi writes in his book on Freud's Moses, the verb *zakhar* is used throughout the text whenever Israel is admonished to remember, and appears in its various declensions no fewer than 169 times. It often describes the double injunction to remember the past and to be open to the future.[25] Primo Levi wrote eloquently about the traps of memory, but all his memoirs, as well as his other literary works, develop within this same double tension. On the one hand, he foregrounds the duty to remember the past, a moral obligation that, for him, mostly consists of witnessing the Shoah and restoring a Jewish cultural memory that had previously been forsaken. On the other hand, he is acutely aware of his duty to the future, seen as the obligation to anticipate, hence to construct hope in the future. Turning to the third section of *The Drowned and the Saved,* to the organization of its different sections, we can see how the treatment of shame may also be fruitfully inscribed within this double obligation.

Once again, the rational writer focuses his writing on a nonrational aspect of history: contrary to what might be expected, concentration camp survivors did not experience joy at liberation but a feeling of shame. As in a novel by Joseph Conrad, an author whom he greatly admired, Levi adopts a strategy of writing that ventures into the heart of darkness of human experience. This time, what is at stake is the opaque and paradoxical character of a feeling of anguish. On other occasions, it will be similarly complex and obscure notions, such as the existence of a grey zone between victims and persecutors, the coexistence of compassion and brutality in the *sonderkommandos* (those prisoners in Auschwitz who were entrusted with the running of the crematoria), or the figure of the drowned as the real witness to Auschwitz. Nonetheless, what is at stake for Levi is not a romantic lure toward the dark side of human experience but the full awareness of its existence as an irredeemable scandal. And in order for someone to become aware of it, to fathom it in full, he or she has to resort to multiple disciplines at one and the same time. No discipline alone will suffice. One may start from a romantic impulse toward irrationality and, by way of science, history, psychoanalysis, and religion, one may end up with a wisdom that is already recorded in the Bible. It is the subject itself, its nonrational character, that requires this gradual methodological shift from history to religion, from psychology to biblical interpretation, from the fact per se to the text, to an archival memory where a trace of the fact may be recorded. As Derrida has significantly noted in his reading of Yerushalmi's book on Freud's Judaism, it is necessary for the historian to make way for the anthropologist, the psychoanalyst, and the biblical scholar, not only because different approaches can give a better understanding of the subject matter but because shame as such is not readable as ordinary history. It is a symptom of a collective archival memory, whose echo may be recorded in Genesis, and that may contain the anticipation of a hope in the future.[26]

It is not by chance, then, that Primo Levi has chosen this specific verse from Genesis. By means of this textual reference, Levi retraces the roots of the feeling of anguish all the way back to the origin of creation, to the moment that precedes creation, to the very beginning of biblical Jewish history: as if the anguish felt by the prisoners in the concentration camps were already inscribed in that original anguish before the emptiness of the universe, and as if both contained, or as a matter of fact were themselves, the first signs of a reaction against blind matter and the dehumanized universe—as if they were the very anticipation of a specific hope for the future.

Significantly, in the following and concluding paragraph of the essay, Levi effects a reversal of the negative meaning of shame, or rather, he creatively turns it into the repository for the anticipation of a hope in the future. There is also another vaster shame, the shame for the existence of evil in the world. "The just among us . . . felt remorse . . . for the misdeeds that others and not they had committed, and in which they felt involved, because they felt that what had happened around them and in their presence, and in them, was irrevocable. Never again could it be cleansed."[27]

Here the discourse on shame is overturned and what is usually perceived as a limitation becomes a strength: the feeling of shame, the painful emotion arising from the consciousness of something that limits our self, is turned into a sign of consciousness of the evil committed by others and of the righteousness of the victim. As such, concludes Levi, shame may also work as an immunization against the possibility that tragic events, like the Shoah, may occur again in a near or distant future:

> In my opinion, a mass slaughter is particularly unlikely in the Western world, Japan, and also the Soviet Union: the Lagers of World War II are still part of the memory of many, on both the popular and governmental levels, and a sort of immunizational defense is at work which amply coincides with the shame of which I have spoken. As to what might happen in other parts of the world, or later on, it is prudent to suspend judgment. And the nuclear apocalypse, certainly bilateral, probably instantaneous and definitive, is a greater and different horror, strange, new, which stands outside the theme I have chosen.[28]

Victims can be bearers of hope: not on account of their innocence, as would be the common Christian understanding, but rather on account of their consciousness of the existence of evil and their memory and sense of justice. "Is it possible," asks Yerushalmi at the end of *Zakhor*, "that the antonym of 'forgetting' is not 'remembering,' but *justice*?"[29] If justice is synonymous with memory, then hope does not consist in an aspiration toward an innocent world in which humans live in a state of forgetfulness, innocent and unaware of evil, but in an ethical universe where individuals, aware of the existence of evil, are dedicated to its containment through justice.

Primo Levi's creative interpretation of the shame of the survivor may also be read as an attempt to sketch a new ethical map of the world after Auschwitz. His reference to the second verse of Genesis, his juxtaposition of the anguish felt by humans before an empty universe with the shame of the survivor, and his conclusive finding of consciousness enclosed within this same feeling also work as a compass to orient oneself in a territory whose ethical reliefs have not been charted yet and whose ethical horizon is blurred. Levi reminds us that there is a text, an archive where the collective memory of a feeling of anguish has been recorded. Within this memory, perhaps, there is the first sign of a reaction in the face of an empty universe, awareness that something in the world is not quite right, that the universe is not a cosmos, an orderly and harmonious creation as suggested by the original Greek word but rather an imperfect creation that needs to be improved by the active participation of humans. The shame of the survivor, the nameless pain felt before the silence and the void of Auschwitz, may also be an echo, a reverberation, of a more ancient anguish felt before an empty and silent universe; in both there may lie a consciousness of the existence of an incurable evil and, therefore, a hope for a better future. By means of a meditation on Auschwitz, by a reference to the Bible and to some fundamental concepts of Jewish ethics (Genesis, the double duty to memory and hope, and consciousness), Levi delineates an ethical horizon in which a text, a collective memory, and a relationship with God—or with the silence of God—stand as fragile but visible sign posts in an ethically uncertain future.

Such an attempt at rebuilding the foundations of ethics by means of both a meditation on Auschwitz and the recovery of a Jewish cultural memory is an enterprise that Primo Levi shares with other Jewish intellectuals of his generation such as Günther Anders, the Viennese philosopher best known as a theorist and an activist in the antinuclear movement.[30] Like Levi, Anders was an integrated and nonreligious Jew who began to consider himself Jewish only when faced by anti-Semitism. Like Levi, he developed a strong cultural interest in Judaism at a later stage in his life, praised mostly the cultural contribution of the Jewish Diaspora to European societies, and used the metaphor of the grain of salt to describe Jews' impure and fertile role in the development of contemporary Western cultures. In his 1978 essay entitled "My Judaism," Anders writes, *"But to be salt in the flour, and not simply flour,* this has been the role that the Jews have had in the last hundred or hundred and fifty years in Europe and America. And in this role of salt I recognize myself."[31] In particular, similarly to Levi, Anders discussed his renewed interest in Judaism and his sense of Jewish identity by dealing with the shame of the survivor. In "My Judaism," he writes about the shame of still existing today as a Jew—of not being among those who were annihilated at Auschwitz:

> If . . . you ask me on which day I was most deeply ashamed, no, not of being Jewish (of which I am not in the least ashamed except when I encounter a Jew who is ashamed of being Jewish), but on which day I was most deeply ashamed of still being here as a Jew, then I will respond, It

was that summer day . . . when I found myself at Auschwitz in front of mountains of shoes, eyeglass frames, broken dentures, locks of cut hair and suitcases now devoid of owners. And among these things my eyeglasses might have also been found, my teeth, my shoes, my suitcase. At that moment I—who had not been deported to Auschwitz, who had come out of all this as if by coincidence—I felt like a deserter. And I hadn't the courage to think, "Thank God I'm still here."[32]

Anders' refusal to thank God for his own survival reminds us of Levi's contempt for Kuhn's prayer—the fellow prisoner in *Survival in Auschwitz* who thanked God for being alive after the Nazis fled Auschwitz. "If I was God," Levi wrote, "I would spit at Kuhn's prayer."[33] Anders and Levi share the conviction that surviving Nazi persecution and extermination in concentration camps was a product of chance. Theirs is the refusal to believe in the existence of a providential design behind survival. Their connection with Judaism does not have a religious character but an ethical one.

In Levi and Anders, the treatment of shame is framed within the same double ethical duty toward the past and the future. On the one hand, as in Levi, Anders' shame is a feeling with a history and a prehistory. It is the visible sign of a larger and deeper collective feeling: the astonishment of *still* being alive not only as an individual Jew but also as a member of a larger collective with a long history: "Such a shame has a prehistory. It is in fact the most obvious point of an amazement that has always been at the foundation of my being Jewish, the amazement at having come to the world already as a Jew . . . Naturally, this didn't have to do only with my personal 'still being here' but the fact that we still exist."[34]

By linking his feeling of shame to a larger and deeper feeling of astonishment, Anders reawakens consciousness of Jewish history and actualizes memory of a Jewish past, a step that is reinforced by a reference to the Bible: "And that still today there exists this *remnant of remnants,* this is the thing at which I am continually astounded and from which I would under no circumstances wish to redeem myself."[35] While connecting shame to a historical collective memory, Anders, like Levi, quotes a verse from the Bible. Before the emptiness of Auschwitz, before the tragic Jewish prehistory and history—"an uninterrupted chain of separations" as he euphemistically refers to it—he too makes a textual reference to the Bible where a sense of this tragic history is recorded. This time the reference is to an enigmatic verse from the prophet Isaiah: "[yet] a remnant of them shall return."[36]

Perhaps, as Giorgio Agamben suggests in *The Time That Remains*, here the word "remnant" does not refer only to a numerical portion.[37] The remnant is neither the part nor the whole; it neither coincides with that portion of Jews who survived the biblical catastrophes nor is it simply identical to Israel, as the chosen people who survive the final destruction of all peoples. Rather, it is the impossibility, for both the whole and the part, to fully coincide with themselves and the lack of a complete coincidence of the modern Jew with himself. Perhaps it hints at the fracturing of Jewish identity in modern times, at the problem of the modern Jewish intellectual who, while being modern, still tries to adhere to Jewish traditions, or at the distance and proximity between the secular and the religious Jew. Anders is convinced that there is a mutual interdependence between the two, that the existence of the former depends also on the survival of the latter: "I who do not recognize any God direct my gratitude to my bearded brother in caftan, and not only to him but to the 70 generations who preceded him. Yes, to them I must direct my thanks, because without their persistence, I too, on the way, would have been lost in some way."[38]

On the other hand, if this feeling has a past—if it is also the surprise at being part of a history of survival, the consciousness of a chance for survival—then this same feeling holds in itself the possibility of hope for the future. Anders wrote, "I felt myself attached for the first time to the Jewish past in 1958, on the market square in Kyoto, lecturing to a group of Buddhist priests on the first evening of the anniversary of Hiroshima Day."[39] In Kyoto, for the 1958 commemoration of the Hiroshima bombing, he talked to a group of Buddhist monks about the task of confronting the ethical void created by Hiroshima. But the possibility of talking about this task lies also in the existence of a Jewish past, in a reference to an archival collective memory and to the text where that memory may be recorded: "And while I preached—even though I'm an atheist personally—so, while I preached like that, in the boiling heat of the south Japanese August, I felt I was not alone, but that these admonitory words came to me like the whisperings of the Prophets of misfortune in the Old Testament."[40] How can one not think here of Primo Levi's surprise at the thought that he, a nonreligious Jew, had been chosen by destiny to retell the kabbalistic legends of Lilith and the Shekinah? "It is inexplicable," Levi writes at the end of his short story dedicated to the figure of Lilith, "that fate has chosen an un-believer to repeat this pious and impious tale, woven of poetry, ignorance, daring acumen, and the unassuageable sadness that grows on the ruins of lost civilizations."[41] Once again, from a secular point of view comes an original reactualization of Jewish memory within modernity and also a treatment of the Jewish past as a historical experience that, while remaining the experience of a minority, takes on universal ethical values.[42]

A clear example of this can be found in Anders' writings on Claude Eatherly, the pilot who gave the command to drop the first atomic bomb on the city of Hiroshima. After the war, unlike the other members of the crew who returned to their lives as civilians without any apparent second thoughts, Eatherly could not forget the bombing of Hiroshima. He suffered from depression and tried several times to commit suicide. Tormented by insomnia and nightmares, he developed behavior that bespoke his incapacity to return to normal civilian life: he crammed bank notes into envelopes and sent them to Japan by way of apology for his action; he committed futile acts of rebellion like small robberies. Finally, Eatherly was arrested, brought before a court of psychiatrists nominated by the military authority, declared insane by these medical experts, and condemned to incarceration in the military hospital for mental ailments in Waco, Texas.

In the spring of 1959, after reading a report in *Newsweek* magazine, Günther Anders took interest in his case and started a correspondence with him that lasted from June 1959 until July 1961. In his correspondence with Anders, Eatherly presented himself as a thinking man, but his tormented conscience, his shame for what he had done at Hiroshima, was interpreted by the authorities as pathological. For the authorities, acknowledging Eatherly's shame would have meant a judgment against the bombing of Hiroshima and against its perpetrators. "The truth is," wrote Eatherly in one of his letters to Anders, "that society cannot simply accept the fact of my guilt without at the same time recognizing its own far deeper guilt."[43]

In his letters to Eatherly, Anders seeks also to outline in wider terms a general theory of morality in the nuclear age. He writes of a general condition of *guiltless guilt* that would characterize human life in our highly technological times. In a world ruled more and more by technology, humans can be used in actions whose effects and consequences are beyond their understanding and imagination and against their moral principles. It is a form of mechanization of our beings that did not exist in less technically advanced times and that can change the moral foundations of our existence inasmuch as it makes us guilty of actions that we have not directly committed.[44] But shame, in Eatherly's case, is also the sign of the survival of a vigilant conscience. Although one may have simply functioned as a little screw in a huge machine, shame, the survivor's feeling of uneasiness, is the proof that one has been able to keep one's conscience alert. The fact that Eatherly could not master what he had done showed that he was trying to cope with the moral implications of his action. His, as Primo Levi wrote in *The Truce,* is the shame that the Germans never knew, the shame of the just man who feels remorse for the existence of evil.

Anders is aware of the dangerous implications of his notion of *guiltless guilt.* When Anders was corresponding with Eatherly, Adolf Eichmann was on trial in Jerusalem. Anders' idea of a collective condition of guiltless guilt could include and justify the line of defense adopted by Eichmann during his trial: he said that he was not guilty because he had just been a tool in the machine of terror that carried out the orders of the Third Reich. As Levi noted in his essay on the grey zone, these notions can lead to a blurring of the distinction between innocent victims, guilty perpetrators, and executors of orders who were only partially aware of the consequences of their actions. Anders, though, makes a distinction. Eatherly, he writes, is not the twin of Eichmann but precisely his opposite. He is not the individual who resorts to technology as a way of silencing his consciousness but the one who is able to perceive in this blind machinery a great danger to the integrity of conscience. Not knowing, Anders concludes, is not an excuse for a crime, and he adds, "I am a Jew, I lost my friends in Hitler's gas chambers."[45] A larger and deeper consciousness of history is born out of a response to Auschwitz.

THERE IS AT LEAST one literary precedent to the feeling of anguish described by Primo Levi and Günther Anders. It can be found in Kakfa's 1914 novella, *In the Penal Colony*.[46] There too, in a deserted valley on a tropical island, a machine called the *apparatus* performs the blind duty of torturing and executing human beings. It is an old and worn-out machine that looks both modern and primitive and executes prisoners by carving onto their bodies the law that they have transgressed. Whatever commandment the prisoner has disobeyed is written upon his body by a glass harrow that hangs at the center of the apparatus.[47] All around the machinery, as on a minimal Beckettian stage, lies a wasteland scattered with few humble objects—a ladder, a bucket of water, a heap of cane chairs—and peopled by four nameless characters: the explorer, the officer, the soldier, and the condemned man. The plot of the novella is equally minimal. The unseen commandant of a tropical island has invited a visitor from a foreign country, called the explorer, to judge the method of executing prisoners practiced in the penal colony. While the explorer prepares himself to witness the execution of a man condemned to death for disobeying a superior, an officer explains the functioning of the machine in detail to the explorer and tries to persuade him to recommend to the commandant not to discontinue such a method of execution. But when a part of the old machinery breaks down, the execution of the condemned man is suspended. The officer, who has thrust himself into the machine, dies, and the explorer leaves the penal colony.

The penal colony has been interpreted as a judicial universe without justice: a world where judgment has regressed to a stage in which a verdict is passed without a real trial and in the absence of a proper jury. There is no interrogation, discussion of evidence, or testimony. The court has been reduced to the person of the officer. Only his opinion counts. The condemned man does not know the sentence that has been passed on him nor, as a matter of fact, is he aware that he has been sentenced. Persecutors and victims can easily shift their roles. And, in the end, the witness can give no testimony and quits the penal colony, leaving behind the soldier and the condemned man who had followed him with the vain hope of being taken along.

Here, on this tropical island, we are in a universe that precedes or follows justice. Trial, verdict, and law enforcement have all imploded into the mere mechanical actions performed by the machine. Transgression, guilt, and shame have faded away in the background. Justice has become only a meaningless machinery, its consciousness a distant echo from the past. In the penal colony, paraphrasing what Levi wrote in regard to Auschwitz, we are on this side of good and evil. However, unlike in Levi, in the Kafka novella there is no trace of shame, no sign of that feeling of anguish felt by the prisoners in the desolate universe of the concentration camps. None of the four characters in the novella seems to be fully conscious of the horror that surrounds them. Their consciences, like their names, are reduced to the roles they perform in the judicial process. Even the explorer, a visitor who comes from a foreign country and on whom one would expect the horror of this penal system to register, shows a certain detachment and numbness. His reactions are limited to a frown, a certain embarrassment, and a series of inconsequential thoughts on the possibility of intervening with the commandant to stop the judicial process performed by the machinery. All characters behave as if their actions were somehow disconnected from their ethical implications.

On the other hand, unlike its four characters, readers of Kafka's novella perceive that in the penal colony, shame is absolute. Even though shame is never mentioned or expressed, it shrouds the landscape entirely. Stemming from the four characters' enigmatic actions and words, it filters through the naked crags that surround the small sandy valley on all sides. It reverberates under the strong glare of the sun that parches the shadeless hollow where the machinery lies. Its pervasiveness reminds Kafka's readers of the last sentences of *The Trial* when K., the novel's main character, at the moment of his own death, feels overwhelmed by a strong sense of shame for the injustice he has suffered and wonders if such shame is the only thing that will outlive him: "But the hands of one of the men were closing around K.'s throat, while the other drove the knife deep into his heart and turned it there twice. With failing sight K. could still see the two men right in front of him, cheek pressed against cheek, as if they observed the final act. 'Like a dog!' he said, as if the shame would outlive him."[48] At the end of *The Trial*, the feeling of his own humiliation is so profound that K. wonders whether only an abstract conscience of injustice will survive him. Yet shame is still named. In *In the Penal Colony,* Kafka takes us a step forward. On the tropical island, shame is immanent to the point of not needing to be named or even perceived anymore. And when it is mentioned, it is only in its trivialized meaning of "pity." It is reduced almost to a minor transgression or a missed opportunity: "The explorer wanted to withdraw his face from the officer and looked round him at random. The officer thought he was surveying the valley's desolation; so he seized him by the hands, turned him round to meet his eyes, and asked: 'Do you realize the shame of it?' But the explorer said nothing."[49] What in the eyes of the officer is pity for the malfunctioning of the apparatus and a sense of nostalgia for the good old days in which the machine performed its duty flawlessly, in the eyes of the readers registers as a major shame.

It has been noted numerous times that Kafka's literary imagery can be read as an allegorical anticipation, almost a prophecy, of a totalitarian society. And indeed, it is not difficult to see in the nightmarish image of the penal colony an allegory of the dehumanization of Auschwitz. Whether this is a viable interpretation or not, it is clear that, in many of his literary works, Kafka provides his readers with images of a universe on the verge of being entirely deprived of justice and emptied of consciousness. It is a world, as Elias Canetti has noted, in which power, taking on increasingly evasive forms, withdraws from the scene; in which the individual's relationship with power becomes one of waiting and longing for a superior entity that manifests itself only in incomprehensible and capricious ways and ultimately stands out as absence, silence, and void.[50]

Kafka and Levi share this notion of the religious as absence. But, whereas for the former, shame at the existence of evil in the world and God's silence remain enigmatic, for the latter, shame is overcome and turned into an answer. Unlike Kafka, Levi doesn't present his readers with raw enigmatic images that need to be interpreted. As a rationalist, he likes to tackle, deconstruct, and make creative use of anything obscure, pushing his readers to gain consciousness of the existence of an atavistic sense of guilt and of the disgrace that wraps the dark side of living. This is why the dark irrational feeling Levi calls *shame* becomes the signal that the conscience of the witness remains vigilant and leads to the impulse to testify to the horror felt before the void.

It is not by chance, then, that Levi felt the need to make a sharp distinction between Kafka's way of writing and his own. In 1982, the Italian publisher Einaudi asked Levi to translate Kafka's *The Trial* for a new collection of classics of world literature translated by Italian writers.[51] Levi accepted the task, and his new translation came out in Italian bookstores at the end of April 1983. But in an interview with the local newspaper *La Stampa,* he underlined the differences between his prose and the prose of the Czech writer:

> Now, I love and admire Kafka because he writes in a way that is totally unavailable to me. In my writing, for good or evil, knowingly or not, I've always strived to pass from the darkness into light, as . . . a filtering pump might do, which sucks up turbid water and expels it decanted: possibly sterile. Kafka forges his path in the opposite direction: he endlessly unravels the hallucinations that he draws from incredibly profound layers, and he never filters them. The reader feels them swarm with germs and spores: they are gravid with burning significances, but he never receives any help in tearing through the veil or circumventing it to go and see what it conceals.[52]

Literature, for Levi, was and had to remain a dialogue between the writer and the reader. For him, even the enigmatic image in the last sentence of Kafka's *Trial* should be tackled and explained. At the very the end of the novel, Levi notes, what K. is ashamed of is the existence of an occult and corrupt tribunal that pervades everything that surrounds him: not a divine jury but a tribunal of men made by man. With a knife already planted in his heart, concludes Levi, K. feels ashamed of being a man.[53]

Another good example of this difference between Levi and Kafka may be found at the conclusion of *In the Penal Colony,* when the explorer leaves the island and starts walking toward the harbor where he will take the steamer to return to his country. At this point, the soldier and the condemned man run after him in an attempt to force him to take them away. But by the time they reach the dock, the explorer is already onboard and lifts in the air a heavy knotted rope to prevent them from jumping onto the boat. So ends

Kafka's novella. It closes suddenly with the images of the explorer sailing away and of the two clumsy characters gesturing in vain on the island shore. Perhaps the soldier and the condemned man—like Arthur and Jeremiah in *The Castle,* as well as all other characters in Kafka's prose—represent our relation with what is forgotten and lost and with what exceeds our capability to feel piety toward the past. As has been beautifully suggested by Agamben, these literary characters seem to translate for us, as in a language for deaf-mute people, the text of what has been forgotten and lost but still demands to remain within us in a perceptible form.[54] This would explain their strange mimicry, their obstinate gesturing, their clumsy restlessness and ambiguity— as if parody were the only possible representation of what cannot be fulfilled anymore but still demands not to be forgotten. Perhaps, in the figures of the soldier and the condemned man, as well as in Kafka's other assistants, one may see something comparable to Primo Levi's drowned—the prisoners who never returned from Auschwitz. They both may represent what has drowned within our memory and we have totally forgotten, and hence forever lost, but who themselves demand not to be forgotten. A lasting memory of the drowned testifies to the persistence of our consciousness. Unlike Levi, though, who made a point of remembering, Kafka's drowned seem also to be forgotten by the witness. The explorer sails away from the penal colony threatening them, so as to prevent them from jumping onto his boat.

It may be, as Levi has subtly noted, that witnessing is nothing but a way of freeing oneself from the memory of those who were drowned. Nonetheless, whatever the impulse to write may be, written testimony survives and lasts as a possible memento for future generations. Whereas Kafka's novella closes with the image of the boat that departs from the shore of the penal colony leaving the soldier and the condemned man behind, and also leaving the reader in a meaningful and menacing universe of silence, Levi's last writings remind their readers of the duty to take back the memory of the drowned from the hell of Auschwitz, to carry them over the waters of oblivion to our weak memory. In Levi's works, in spite of the existence of a grey zone, one ought to always draw a distinction between persecutors and victims; in spite of the existence of the drowned, he always responds to the impulse to recount their tragic fate; in spite of the anguish felt by prisoners before the meaningless void represented by the concentration camp, there is shame—the feeling of discomfort at the existence of evil in the world and the sign that their consciences are still alive and that humans have not been completely destroyed. The witness can take off from the island of Auschwitz, come back to his life as a civilian, look at the perilous waters he has left behind and be haunted by a feeling of anguish while still being able to turn that feeling into the story of those who didn't come back.

There exists a stereotyped picture consecrated by literature and poetry: at the end of the storm all hearts rejoice. Judging by the stories told by many who came back, the hour of liberation was neither joyful nor lighthearted. So begins Primo Levi's essay on the shame of the survivor. It begins with a warning about the ethics of writing. Writing shall not falsify the truth and, in particular, shall resist the temptation to use stylizations and clichés to ornament a grim and ineffable reality. It is well-known that Levi's stylistic resource to attain this goal consisted mostly in clarity of expression. In addition, his writing shows us that a lesson can be drawn from tackling a dark, irrational feeling like shame. Levi's interpretation of the shame of the survivor is an ethical response to Auschwitz. And as such, it is also a Jewish answer: not only as an ethical answer that is born out of the tragic history of Judaism in twentieth-century Europe but also as a reactualization of Jewish memory.

As Yerushalmi reminds us in his *Zakhor*, one of the first ritual acts to be performed at Passover is the lifting of a piece of unleavened bread. What both the language and the gesture invoke is not so much a leap of memory as a fusion of past and present. Here, memory is not the recollection of a distant past but its reactualization. Levi's reference to Genesis and the references to Jewish themes scattered throughout his works should be read not simply as erudite allusions but as forms of reactualization of Jewish memory, as an active use of memory in the present that incites meaningful encounters between past and present. From this perspective, testimony is neither a portion of a larger providential design nor a means of healing a neurosis, but may be an echo of the anguish recorded in Genesis, an answer to the anguish felt by humans before an empty and deserted universe. Confronting the anguish felt before the void, the writer gives a creative answer, generating both the writing of an ethical universe and an ethical universe of writing.

From a literary point of view, the idea that Levi's writing and his relationship with Judaism are ways of responding to Auschwitz has several implications. If writing is born out of a need to testify, if creativity is a response to ethical urgency, then a tension between witnessing the truth and telling stories, between the work of the witness and that of the fiction writer, between a notion of writing as a purely aesthetic use of language and writing as the site where ethics and aesthetics meet, becomes unavoidable. The inclusion of ethics within literary discourse opens up the literary text to the rhetorical needs of the witness and sets it free from the strict rules that tend to confine writing to a purely aesthetic and self-referential use of language. Consequently, the act of writing will be characterized by the imperfection, by the multiplicity, or—to follow the parallel that I used at the beginning of this chapter—by the same hybridism that characterizes the history of Judaism.

Therefore, when one talks of Judaism and Jewish identity in Primo Levi's work, one talks of a subject that is wider and more complex than just inclusion and treatment of Jewish themes in a literary work. What matters is not only the critical reappropriation of a cultural tradition or the references to Jewish culture that are scattered throughout his works but the hybrid character of Levi's writing, its "imperfection," its tension between testimony and narrative that reveals deep consonances between his writing and his Jewish background. It is through this hybrid character, through this explicit and implicit dialogue with Judaism that Levi's works reawaken the ethical dimension of writing and challenge consolidated notions about literature. If writing is primarily an act of testimony, the very act of writing becomes a way of bringing to light the limits of a practice that goes under the name of Literature. From this focus on hybridism and the ethical dimension of writing comes Levi's indirect criticism of a traditional notion of Literature and his most interesting observations about writing. I will limit myself to three examples.

In reading Levi's works, one has the impression that literature does not consist only in the aesthetic use of language but in a broader search for the resources that language makes available to attain ethical goals. In Levi's works, the *perlocutionary* use of language, namely the attempt to produce an effect upon the listener that would cause the listener to act, prevails over *elocutio,* namely the search for beautiful words. In both his memoirs and prose, as well as in his poetry, words are not pure ornaments but tools to attain clarity of expression and, more importantly, a call to engage the reader in an ethical response. Writing, in other words, becomes a way of expanding consciousness. Moreover, Levi's style questions writing as we know it or, at least, as we have learned to consider it: its strict hierarchy of literary genres, its careful distinction between what can be considered literature and what cannot, its privilege of form over content, of Aesthetics over Ethics. A few concrete examples should suffice.

First, Primo Levi's work invites its readers to consider the rigid classification of texts into literary genres. *Survival in Auschwitz, The Periodic Table,* and *Moments of Reprieve* are literary works that can hardly be ascribed to a traditional literary genre. They are halfway between narrative and philosophy, science and literature, history and fiction and seem to set up a new literary form that almost constitutes a genre in itself. Precisely because of their hybrid character, their unclassifiable nature, these books unhinge the rigid taxonomy of literary texts that has characterized Italian (and European) literature for centuries and invite us to ask what Literature is and, consequently, what the meaning of writing is. In a certain way, his works take us back to the boundary line between writing and Literature, between the free act of writing and its codification in a genre: they take us to the moment in which writing becomes an artistic form, to the place where one starts questioning the balance between ethics and aesthetics.

Second, if inspiration is born out of a need to testify, if creativity is a response to an ethical urgency, then literature cannot be a self-referential act that feeds only on other literary texts. "The kernel of my writing," notes Levi in the preface to *The Search for Roots,* "does not derive from what I have read."[55]

Third, from a historical point of view, Levi's critique means distancing oneself from both the Romantic and the Decadent literary traditions, from those writers who have favored the use of aestheticisms, stylizations, literary topoi such as the conjunction of love and death, and all those shortcuts of thought that can easily turn into falsifications of the truth. The experience of the concentration camps, the urgency to recount events as they happened and to analyze their meaning, or their absence of meaning, transfers itself directly onto the page and takes on concrete form in new modes of writing that unveil the deceits and the traps of literature.

Levi offers us an outline of what some of these traps might be in his *Other People's Trades*, where he comments on some of the classics of literature.[56] In Alessandro Manzoni's *The Betrothed*, a gesture made by Renzo as he attempts to defend himself from the city crowd seems to Levi to be modeled on "an illustration in keeping with the taste of the time." Renzo pushes his way through the crowd and escapes at a gallop, his fist in the air, tight, knuckled, ready for who ever else may get in his way:

> Now, it is completely unnatural to run while holding one's fist in the air. . . . There are other images like this in the novel, unreal, mannered; they make one think of an indirect mental process, as if the author, faced by an attitude of the human body, strove to construct an illustration in keeping with the taste of the time and then, in the written text, tried to illustrate the illustration itself instead of the immediate visual datum.[57]

This, then, was a stylized image that revealed Manzoni's uneasiness about the representation of gestures and the human body.

Similarly, in Giacomo Leopardi's *In Praise of Birds*, Levi sees a romantic falsification of the natural world.[58] The happiness of birds, "the most joyful creatures in the world," is nothing other than the effect of a poetic look on the world, a look that mediates between the world and the subject through distortion and deceit. Such taste for literary conventions, clichés, stylizations, and aestheticisms is the result of a notion of literature that valorizes the primacy of emotions over other human faculties and makes the heart the site where truth resides:

> It is not true that the only authentic writing is that which "comes from the heart," and which actually comes from all the distinct ingredients of consciousness mentioned above [ego and id, spirit and flesh, and furthermore, nucleic acids, traditions, hormones, remote and recent experiences, and traumas]. This time-honored opinion is based on the presupposition that the heart which "dictates inside" is an organ different from that of reason and more noble, and that the language of the heart is the same for everyone, which it is not.[59]

Contrary to what is commonly believed, the language of the heart is far from being the noblest and is certainly not the same for everybody. To put into discussion the authentic and universal character of the heart means remembering that the heart, namely our emotional experience, is not necessarily part of our consciousness; it also means questioning those writers who make of the emotions and of all the irrational "ingredients" of consciousness their favorite theme, their privileged means of expression, as well as the foundation of their works.

The witness knows that, after Auschwitz, every virtue is questionable, particularly the virtues of the heart. Knowing that in the Nazi criminal, the love for his family or the passion for good classical music can live comfortably alongside the horror of the concentration camps means wondering what words like "love" and "beauty," what emotional and aesthetic virtues really mean. Heart and beauty are not exempt from an ethics that is *more Auschwitz demonstrata*.[60] Neither does their presence testify to the supposed humanity of a human being, nor to his or her sense of justice, nor to the humanity and the sense of justice of a writer and his works. Moreover, the politics of the heart may also be regressive. "The heart is not progressive," says a character in a play by Tony Kushner. "The heart is conservative, no matter what the mind may be ... Love is profoundly reactionary, you fall in love and that instant is fixed, love is always fixed on the past."[61]

It is well-known that the primacy and universality of the heart are arguments used by Christian polemicists to assert the spiritual superiority of Christianity over Judaism, to construct the myth of Christianity as the newer and freer religion of love opposed to Judaism as the older and drier religion of law. This distinction is one of the strongest and most ingrained commonplaces in the history of Christianity; it has lasted until the present and helped to feed centuries of Christian anti-Semitism, in spite of its manifest incompatibility with Mark 12:28–31, where the love of God and the love of one's neighbor are not antithetical but are juxtaposed as two of the most important commandments:

> And one of the scribes came, and having heard them reasoning together, and perceiving that he had answered them well, asked him, Which is the first commandment of all?

And Jesus answered him, The first of all the commandments [is], Hear, O Israel; The Lord our God is one Lord:

And thou shalt love the Lord thy God with all thy heart, and with all thy soul, and with all thy mind, and with all thy strength: this [is] the first commandment.

And the second [is] like, [namely] this, Thou shalt love thy neighbor as thyself. There is none other commandment greater than these.[62]

By means of a curious philological oblivion, conscious censorship, or unconscious textual repression, Christianity has neglected the fact that in this passage Jesus is quoting Leviticus 19:18 and has arrogated to itself the primacy of the heart and the right to be the religion of love: "Thou shalt not avenge, nor bear any grudge against the children of thy people, but thou shalt love thy neighbor as thyself: I [am] the LORD." This seemingly accidental omission may be a good example of what Derrida would refer to as *le mal d'archive,* archive fever: a Freudian death drive whose aim is not only to incite forgetfulness but also to demand the complete effacement of the archive, meant as the accumulation of memory on some external substrate such as the printable and reproducible surface of a text. In Derrida's formulation, archival memory does not correspond to a living, spontaneous, and internal memory, to what the Greeks called *mneme* or *anamnesis.* Rather, the archive takes shape where such memory begins to fade. There is a desire of the archive, a desire to record and preserve memory, as well as a drive to destroy it. What is at issue here is not only a question of historical revisionism but a collective psychological malaise toward one's negative impulses. By repressing or suppressing the paternity of the text, by effacing its archive and by depriving Jews of their faculty to feel, Christianity gives voice to its *mal d'archive* and manages to mask its own uneasiness toward emotions. It is not by chance that while he is struggling to define the notion of a death drive, and mentions his own defensive attitude toward this idea, Freud in *Civilization and Its Discontents* refers to the myths of the devil and of the Jews as playing the part of an economic discharge in the world of the Aryan ideal:

I remember my own defensive attitude when the idea of an instinct of destruction first emerged in psychoanalytic literature, and how long it took before I became receptive to it . . . "Little children do not like it" when there is talk of the inborn human inclination to "badness," to aggressiveness and destructiveness, and so to cruelty as well. God has made them in the image of His own perfection; nobody wants to be reminded how hard it is to reconcile the undeniable existence of evil . . . with His all-powerfulness or His all-goodness. The Devil would be the best way out as an excuse for God; in that way he would be playing the same part as an agent of economic discharge as the Jew does in the world of the Aryan ideal.[63]

Thus the law of the primacy and universality of the heart turns into its opposite, hatred.

It is no surprise then if, in response to anti-Semitism and to its extreme and dreadful ramifications in the twentieth century, Jewish intellectuals began to write on the existence of a discontinuity in what was once called the Judeo-Christian tradition and to elaborate on the existence of an ethical Jewish legacy in modern times. In *Judaism and Christianity,* for instance, the Jewish reform thinker Leo Baeck argued that Pauline Christianity is a Romantic religion valuing feelings and ecstatic abandonment, thereby devaluing action and the ethical enterprise. His work, published in 1958, can be read as a consequence of the Shoah inasmuch as it signals a distancing from the once-prevalent notion of the existence of a common Judeo-Christian tradition in which there was harmony between Jewish and Christian ethics. In Primo Levi's works, unlike in Baeck's, there is no direct textual evidence for what I'm suggesting here, namely that there may be consonances between his criticism of the primacy of the heart, as well as of a Romantic notion of art, and his Judaism. Of course, Levi's scientific background plays an important role in shaping this particular aspect of his poetics. Nonetheless, at the root of Levi's discontent with the opaqueness of the heart is also the need to testify to the truth of what happened in the concentration camps. As in Baeck, Levi's criticism of the primacy of the heart and the Romantic artistic sensibility is also a response to the Shoah, as well as an attempt to delineate a cultural horizon in which the heart is no longer the primal and universal site of authentic experience nor the touchstone of moral actions; it is just an aspect of the human experience that, although important, has to be treated as an integral part of the ethical discourse.

Thinking about the Shoah and questioning the existence of evil puts into question the primacy and universality of the heart and reveals their lack of any historical and psychological ground; it unties the hierarchical opposition of heart and law, as expressed in Paul's Epistle to the Galatians, by making both heart and law, action and feeling, integral and questionable parts of any enterprise that wants to call itself human and ethical;[64] and finally, it points toward a new consciousness of language characterized by a deeper awareness of memory and reality and by an enhanced attention to clichés and other stylistic traps that may result from forgetfulness and imagination. Clichés, stock phrases, and commonplaces—as Hannah Arendt has poignantly noted in her essay on the Eichmann trial—are also the main words in the vocabulary of evil. Eichmann's deposition at his trial in Jerusalem was neither demonic nor monstrous: it did not have the negative grandeur, the Luciferian quality that traditionally is associated with extreme evil; instead, it was riddled with banality, ordinary expressions, and stereotypes. For Arendt, evil talks in clichés and commonplaces. Their use may reveal the radical danger of our inability to think critically and of our need to protect ourselves from reality. Levi's criticism of the language of the heart is also a warning against ways of writing and thinking that mirror our need to remove ourselves from reality and drift into a state of thoughtlessness. "Aesthetics by itself is not . . . reliable or sufficient," Levinas noted in *Beyond the Verse*, "There is in it—Talmudists have always thought so—a possibility of rhetoric and pure courtesy, a 'courtly language' which veils cruelties and malevolence, the extreme fragility of all this refinement capable of ending up in Auschwitz."[65]

Once again, it is Starbuck, in Levi's *Search for Roots*, who warns us of the alleged universality and nobility of emotions. To him, Ahab's obsessive pursuit of the white whale is not right: it contrasts with his own reasonableness, consideration, and tender feelings about home. He joined the *Pequod* to hunt whales, not to satisfy his commander's thirst for vengeance. And when he is confronted by Ahab's boundless drive and by his own conflicted feelings, Starbuck blushes.

Toward the end of *Moby-Dick*, when the *Pequod* is sailing to Japan, Starbuck discovers that the precious oil casks stored in the ship's hold are leaking. He informs Ahab and suggests that he stop their hunt to fix them.

But Ahab rejects Starbuck's suggestion and threatens his first mate with a gun. His hubris leads him to believe that he is above humans: as God is the Lord of the earth, he is the lord of the *Pequod*. With a cautious and respectful boldness, betrayed only by a blush, Starbuck warns Ahab, "I ask thee not to beware of Starbuck; but let Ahab beware of Ahab."[66] Although the captain's conscience is clouded by his dark obsession with the hunt for the whale, when Starbuck leaves his cabin, Ahab orders the casks to be repaired. For the moment, the ship's load is safe and the *Pequod* can continue on its crazy rush. Starbuck's words have the temporary effect of distancing the moment in which the *Pequod*, hit by the fury of the white whale, will sink. His blush, his feeling of shame, work as a force of containment and a warning. Unlike Ahab, Starbuck's vigilant conscience or, to use Levi's words, his modesty and premonition, put him in a place where emotions and consciousness are not opposites but are combined, where a feeling like shame, even in its apparent insignificance, can be a step toward the construction of consciousness. It is through this hybrid figure of a Quaker having landed in an adventure bigger than himself, as the figure of a hybrid Jew in the Europe of the past century, that Primo Levi reminds us of the ethical dimension of writing and responds to our elusive and fragmented reality by resorting to an ethical tradition whose hybrid roots are also Jewish.

Epilogue

OUR JOURNEY through the relationship between Judaism and writing in the works of four twentieth-century Italian authors bring us to some provisional conclusions. Although it would not be accurate to talk of a coherent and cohesive Italian Jewish literary tradition spanning from the Middle Ages and the Renaissance to the time of emancipation, the historical changes that occur in the eighteenth and the nineteenth centuries being too deep, one can certainly talk of a rich and fruitful exchange between Judaism and writing in contemporary Italian literature. Our itinerary confirms our premise that it is possible to reconstruct a Jewish cultural legacy in Italian literature by tracing the Jewish idea of history as memory in the works of four contemporary Italian writers. Through examining Saba's ambivalence towards his Jewish past and Ginzburg's hesitation between two cultural traditions, through Bassani's construction of a Jewish narrative self and his rediscovered sense of belonging to a collective history and Levi's hybrid and ethical Judaism, it can be seen that between emancipation and the Shoah, some Italian writers reconsidered their relationship to Judaism and regained a sense of belonging to Jewish history and cultural traditions and that, furthermore, this process is reflected in an idea of writing as emancipation. By writing about Jewish history and themes, by making historical memories the subject of their narratives, these four writers set their narratives free from traditional literary genres and create new hybrid forms of literary expression.

Our theoretical approach helps to draw attention to the fact that the relationship between Judaism and writing in twentieth-century Italy involves theoretical and literary questions that pertain to a wider subject. First, it underlines the limits of commonly accepted definitions of the particular and the universal and hints at the ethical and political implications of these limits in contemporary culture. As mentioned in the introduction, the two main historical events that frame the modern history of European Jews, emancipation and the Shoah, represent the fulfillment and the failure of the egalitarian principles of the Enlightenment. The eighteenth-century ideals of freedom, equality, and fraternity that led to the demolition of the ghetto walls and to the extension of fundamental rights to minorities did not ultimately protect European Jews from the resurgence of anti-Semitism in the nineteenth and twentieth centuries. In 1894, the French Jewish officer Alfred Dreyfus was unjustly accused of espionage and sentenced to life in prison. From a high-ranking position in the military—which represented one of the highest possible degrees of assimilation in Western society of that time—Dreyfus was singled out, marginalized, and turned into an outcast.

Only a hundred years after the declaration of the rights of man, the principles of the Enlightenment were overturned and became their opposites, revealing that an aversion towards difference lay at the root of those principles. The efforts necessary to adapt to the new world of progress and equality fueled a sense of resentment and revenge towards that very process. That resentment took form in a particular sense of revulsion towards those people who, although fully integrated into society, could still represent the old world of religious rituals and customs surpassed by emancipation. Paradoxically, within the Enlightenment ideal of tolerance towards all men as abstract human beings festered a hidden intolerance of individuals in their concrete historical differences; an intolerance that perhaps was a reflection of discomfort with one's own irreducible differences. It is from this perspective that the search for the universal human being beyond all particular individuals shows its stronger limitations, inasmuch as it fails to represent every *imperfect* being, or, as Levi put it, the "tender and delicate" particle of zinc, the grain of salt or seed that doesn't mix with the whole but is needed for the wheel to turn, for life to be lived.

Thus, what can be drawn from the relationship of these four writers with Judaism is not a clear and self-evident understanding of the universal and the particular, of what it means to be a Christian or a Jewish secular writer in contemporary society. What we are left with is rather this *imperfection,* this impossibility for an individual to utterly mix with a collective, for a minority to completely assimilate to a majority, for the part to entirely coincide with the whole. But also for the whole and the part to fully coincide with itself. In other words, what is at stake here is a discussion not only of the limits of the commonly accepted concept of the universal but also of the limits of the notion of the particular as seen from the majority's point of view: an entity that remains immutable and fixed throughout history.

The variety of points of view explored in this book suggests that Judaism is not one but many different historical and theoretical traditions. As our intellectual syncretism of the works of these four writers and the evidence in the brief history of Italian literature we have outlined in the introduction both demonstrate, Judaism is not the "other," but one very important component of the cultural heritage of the West. "There exists an ancient triangular culture—composed of Jewish, Greek, and Latin intellectual products—a *collegium trilingue* [that] dominates up to today . . . our cultural heritage,"[1] wrote Arnaldo Momigliano in *Alien Wisdom,* disproving the myth of Judaism as a set of fixed religious and cultural traditions that developed in complete isolation from other traditions and remained impermeable to any external influence. To paraphrase the words of Clara Sereni quoted in the preface, Judaism can also be interpreted as a constant gathering and reassembling in an unfinished mosaic of the fragments of an ancient history that is never linear and fully coherent but often uneven and contradictory. From this perspective, Judaism is not a form of objective and fixed identity but the result of a constant negotiation between the subject and the surrounding world: a subjective and mutable sense of belonging in whose fragmentary and imperfect character lies its richness.

To illustrate this modality and to explore how it articulates itself in the works of our four writers, we have turned to the biblical notion of the *remnant*—as both the part that survived a catastrophe and the part that didn't, as the people who had the privilege to survive, and who therefore have the responsibility to testify, and those who didn't survive and who in their muteness, in the impossibility of their ever telling their own story, ask not to be forgotten. At the same time, for the very reason that this remnant has survived, that it questions us with its mute presence, it is also a carrier of hope. It represents the possibility of putting the past, through an active act of memory, back into the flow of life. Traces of this synergy between remembrance and hope—between past to be remembered and future to be anticipated—that is central to both Judaism and its history can be found in the works of our four writers. All the half-forgotten, half-remembered words that echo in Natalia Ginzburg's stories, the old and worn objects that inhabit Giorgio Bassani's pages, and the lives of the submerged in Primo Levi's memoirs are also these remnants of the past: all the voices, customs, habits, and lives that have been swept away by history but still question us with their silence and ask not to be forgotten.

It should not be difficult to find traces of this synergy between memory and hope in the works of Italian Jewish writers of the new generation. Lia Levi, Clara Sereni, Moni Ovadia, and Elena Loewenthal, to name just some of the most important contemporary Italian Jewish writers, share a deep interest in ancient Jewish traditions and in reviving them within the cultural context of Italian society today. Unlike their predecessors, though, these writers don't have a direct experience of the time of emancipation, nor of World War II, nor of anti-Semitism and the Shoah. Thus in their works, the synergy between cultural heritage and historical conditions does not undergo the strong tension that characterized the lives and works of the writers of the previous generation. Their sense of belonging to Judaism is not characterized as much by the contrast between the religious and the secular, or by a need to recuperate a lost sense of belonging, as by a meditation on how to preserve that memory and how to inflect it along the major themes and events that have characterized Italian society in the last fifty years: the ideological struggle between Catholicism and Communism and the role of political engagement, the condition of women, the education of children, the deep transformation of the Italian family.

Israel, of course, plays a larger role in their works than it did in the lives and works of Saba, Ginzburg, Bassani, and Levi—none of whom was a Zionist—as well as in their definition of what it means to be a twenty-first-century Jewish writer of the Italian Diaspora. But the synergy between Judaism and Jewishness that has characterized the lives of Jews for centuries still provides them with a theoretical and historical model to add new chapters to the long and rich history of Italian Jews, as well as to the history of other social and cultural forms of imperfection.

Notes
Bibliography
Index

Notes

INTRODUCTION

1. See Arnaldo Momigliano, *Alien Wisdom: The Limits of Hellenization* (Cambridge: Cambridge Univ. Press, 1975); and *Essays on Ancient and Modern Judaism*, ed. Silvia Berti (Chicago: Univ. of Chicago Press, 1994).

2. Yosif Hayim Yerushalmi, *Zakhor: Jewish History and Jewish Memory*, intr. Harold Bloom (Seattle: Univ. of Washington Press, 1982), 16.

3. Stefano Levi Della Torre, *Mosaico: Attualità e inattualità degli ebrei* (Turin: Rosenberg and Sellier, 1994), 42.

4. For this information see Attilio Milano, *Storia degli ebrei in Italia* (Turin: Einaudi, 1963), xiv–xv. For a general introduction to the history of the Jews of Italy, see Cecil Roth, *The History of the Jews of Italy* (Philadelphia: Jewish Publication Society of America, 5706 [1946]); and Milano, *Storia degli ebrei in Italia*. For a detailed exploration of Jewish life in Renaissance Italy, see Robert Bonfil, *Jewish Life in Renaissance Italy*, trans. Anthony Oldcorn (Berkeley: Univ. of California Press, 1994). Bonfil's book questions conventional interpretations of the Italian Renaissance as a period of peaceful cohabitation between Christians and Jews. On Italian Jewish culture during the Renaissance, see also David Ruderman, ed., *Essential Papers on Jewish Culture in Renaissance and Baroque Italy* (New York: New York Univ. Press, 1992). For the emancipation period, see Giorgina Arian Levi and Giulio Disegni, *Fuori dal ghetto: Il 1848 degli ebrei*, pref. Guido Neppi Modona (Rome: Editori Riuniti, 1998). For a historical account of the Shoah in Italy, see Susan Zuccotti, *The Italians and the Holocaust: Persecution, Rescue, and Survival*, intr. Furio Colombo (Lincoln: Univ. of Nebraska Press, 1996). On the subject of Italian Jewish history in the twentieth century, Susan Zuccotti is also the author of *Under His Very Windows: The Vatican and the Holocaust* (New Haven: Yale Univ. Press, 2000). Recent contributions on Italian Jewish history and culture include Thomas P. DiNapoli, ed., *The Italian Jewish Experience* (Stony Brook, N.Y.: Forum Italicum, 2000); Stanislao G. Pugliese, ed., *The Most Ancient of Minorities: The Jews of Italy* (Westport, Conn.: Greenwood, 2002); Alexander Stille, *Benevolence and Betrayal: Five Italian Jewish Families under Fascism* (New York: Summit Books, 1991); David Kertzer, *The Kidnapping of Edgardo Mortara* (New York: Vintage Books, 1998); and

Kertzer, *The Popes against the Jews: The Vatican Role in the Rise of Modern Anti-Semitism* (New York: Alfred A. Knopf, 2001).

5. Primo Levi, *The Periodic Table*, trans. Raymond Rosenthal (New York: Schocken Books, 1984), 3–20. A linguistic universe comparable to the one described by Levi in the first chapter of *The Periodic Table* can be found in the literary works of Crescenzo del Monte (1868–1935), the author of satirical sonnets on Jewish subjects written in the ancient dialect of the Roman ghetto. See del Monte, *Sonetti giudaico-romaneschi, sonetti romaneschi, prose e versioni*, ed. Micaela Procaccia and Marcello Teodonio (Florence: Giuntina, 2008). Another interesting example of the usage of Italian Jewish words is reported in a review by Edouard Roditi, who could remember his grandfather swearing in the Livornese-Jewish dialect: "Te lo giuro su tutti i sefarimmi," "I swear it to you on all the books" (Roditi, "The Great Tradition of Italian-Jewish Literature," *Midstream: A Monthly Jewish Review* [November 1984]: 53–55).

6. The text of the "Jewish-Italian Elegy" can be read in its entirety in Gianfranco Contini, ed., *Poeti del Duecento*, vol. 1 (Milan: Ricciardi, 1960), 35–42.

7. Immanuel Romano's journey through hell and paradise can be read in a recent annotated Italian edition: Immanuel Romano, *L'Inferno e il Paradiso*, ed. Giorgio Battistoni, trans. Emanuele Weiss Levi, pref. Amos Luzzato (Florence: Giuntina, 2000). See also Romano, *Mahbereth Prima (Il destino)*, ed. Stefano Fumagalli and M. Tiziana Mayer (Milan: Aquilegia, 2002). Romano's poem can be read in English translation in Immanuel Ben Solomon Romi, *Tophet and Eden (Hell and Paradise): In Imitation of Dante's "Inferno and Paradiso,"* ed. and trans. Hermann Gollancz (London: London Univ. Press, 1921). A selection of poems by Romano in English translation was published by T. Carmi in *The Penguin Book of Hebrew Verse* (New York: Penguin, 1981), 119–20, 421–27.

8. Umberto Cassuto, *Dante e Manoello* (Florence: Israel, 5682 [1921]), 73. Unless otherwise noted, all translations are mine.

9. See Amos Luzzato, "Prefazione," in Romano, *L'Inferno e il Paradiso*, x.

10. Yosef Hayim Yerushalmi, *Freud's Moses: Judaism Terminable and Interminable* (New Haven: Yale Univ. Press, 1991), 89–90.

11. For the following paragraphs I am highly indebted to Vladimir Jankélévitch, "Ressembler, dissembler (la conscience juive)," in *Sources: Recueil* (Paris: Seuil, 1984), 37–121; Stefano Levi Della Torre, *Mosaico*; and to Giorgio Agamben, *The Time That Remains: A Commentary on the Letter to the Romans*, trans. Patricia Dailey (Stanford: Stanford Univ. Press, 2005).

12. Jankélévitch, "Ressembler, dissembler," 44.

13. Ibid., 96.

14. Ibid., 97.

15. Giorgio Bassani, *The Gold-Rimmed Spectacles*, trans. Isabel Quigly (New York: Atheneum, 1960), 103.

16. Jankélévitch, "Ressembler, dissembler," 40.

17. Ibid., 100.

18. See Max Horkheimer and Theodor W. Adorno, *Dialectic of Enlightenment: Philosophical Fragments,* ed. Gunzelin Schmid Noerr, trans. Edmund Jephcott (Stanford: Stanford Univ. Press, 2002).

19. Jankélévitch, "Ressembler, dissembler," 44–45.

20. Joan Ross Acocella, *Twenty-Eight Artists and Two Saints: Essays* (New York: Pantheon Books, 2007), xviii.

21. Giorgio Bassani, *Opere,* ed. R. Cotroneo (Milan: Mondadori, 1998), 313.

22. Sergio Quinzio, *Radici ebraiche del moderno,* (Milan: Adelphi, 1990), 20–27.

23. Jankélévitch, "Ressembler, dissembler," 50.

24. As quoted in Michel David, *Letteratura e psicoanalisi* (Milan: Mursia, 1967), 44. See also Michel David, *La psicoanalisi nella cultura italiana* (Turin: Boringhieri, 1966), 44 (hereafter David, *La psicoanalisi* 1). Significantly, the entry "psychology" written by the psychoanalyst Edoardo Weiss was censored in the *Enciclopedia Treccani* edited by Gentile (see David, *Letteratura e psicoanalisi,* 65). A detailed analysis of the relationship between fascism and psychoanalysis can be read in a newer, expanded version of David's essay: *La psicoanalisi nella cultura italiana* (Turin: Bollati Boringhieri, 1990), 23–89 (hereafter David, *La psicoanalisi* 2).

25. David, *Letteratura e psicoanalisi,* 45.

26. Jankélévitch, "Ressembler, dissembler," 41.

27. Ibid., 41.

28. Agamben, *The Time That Remains,* 55 (emphasis in the original).

29. Primo Levi, *The Drowned and the Saved,* trans. Raymond Rosenthal (New York: Summit Books, 1988), 83–84.

30. Jankélévitch, "Ressembler, dissembler," 60.

31. Ibid., 60.

32. See Walter Benjamin, *Selected Writings,* vol. 4, *1938–1940,* ed. Howard Eiland and Michael W. Jennings (Cambridge, Mass.: Harvard Univ. Press, 2003), 392–93 (emphasis in the original).

33. Umberto Saba, *The Stories and Recollections of Umberto Saba,* trans. Estelle Gilson (Riverdale-on-Hudson, N.Y.: Sheep Meadow Press, 1993), 9.

34. Levi, *Periodic Table,* 17.

35. Ibid., 19.

36. Ibid., 34.

37. Natalia Ginzburg, "Portrait of a Writer," in *Never Must You Ask Me,* trans. Isabel Quigly (London: Joseph, 1973), 168.

38. Jean Améry, *At the Mind's Limits: Contemplations by a Survivor on Auschwitz and Its Realities,* trans. Sidney Rosenfeld and Stella P. Rosenfeld (Bloomington: Indiana Univ. Press, 1980), 94–95.

39. See James E. Young, *Writing and Rewriting the Holocaust: Narrative and the Consequences of Interpretation* (Bloomington: Indiana Univ. Press, 1988), 189 (emphasis in the original).

40. Roland Barthes, "Historical Discourse," in *Introduction to Structuralism*, ed. Michael Lane (New York: Basic Books, 1970), 149.

41. Young, *Writing and Rewriting*, 43.

42. Ibid., 4.

43. Ibid., 50.

44. Ibid., 192.

45. Aharon Appelfeld, *Beyond Despair* (New York: Fromm International, 1994), xiv.

46. Young, *Writing and Rewriting*, 16. On the links between representational techniques and ethical concerns in the representation and transmission of extreme experiences, see also Geoffrey Hartman, *The Longest Shadow: In the Aftermath of the Holocaust* (Bloomington: Indiana Univ. Press, 1996).

47. See Gianfranco Contini, "Preliminari sulla lingua del Petrarca," preface to Francesco Petrarca, *Canzoniere* (Turin: Einaudi, 1964), x: "Let us not forget that the notion of literary genre has been derived from classical poetics with the notorious theoretical poverty connected, as it was, with a canon of imitation, which justifies itself in the undifferentiated unity of transcendental language and, as such, stands in opposition to plurality."

48. David Ward, interview with Clara Sereni, Wellesley College, spring 1999.

49. Franz Kafka, *Letters to Milena*, ed. and trans. Philip Boehm (New York: Schocken Books, 1990), 55.

50. Jankélévitch, "Ressembler, dissembler," 60.

51. Vittorio Foa, *Il Cavallo e la Torre: Riflessioni su una vita* (Turin: Einaudi, 1991), 326–27.

1. THE MATERNAL BORDERS OF THE SOUL: IDENTITY, JUDAISM, AND WRITING IN THE WORKS OF UMBERTO SABA

1. Giacomo Debenedetti, "Ritrattino del '45," in *Intermezzo* (Milan: Mondadori, 1963), 29–34. Originally published as Giacomo Debenedetti, "Umberto Saba legge *Ultime cose*," *Epoca*, Mar. 15, 1945.

2. Umberto Saba, *Atroce paese che amo: Lettere famigliari (1945–1953)*, ed. Gianfranca Lavezzi and Rossana Saccani (Milan: Bompiani, 1987), 6. Saba's poem can be read in Umberto Saba, *Songbook: Selected Poems from the "Canzoniere" of Umberto Saba*, trans. Stephen Sartarelli (Riverdale-on-Hudson, N.Y.: Sheep Meadow Press, 1998), 241. There are several anthologies of Saba's poems in English translation. Unless otherwise noted, I quote from Umberto Saba, *Songbook*.

3. Born in Vienna in 1880, Otto Weininger was the author of *Geschlecht und Character* [Sex and Character] (Vienna: Braumüller, 1903)—a theoretical essay on gender differences that would gain wide popularity in European intellectual circles after Weininger's theatrical suicide in 1903 at the age of twenty-three. In his book, Weininger aims at constructing a theory of the sexes by arguing that all individuals are a biological combination of male and female

components—where the first would correspond to positive traits, such as reason, culture, and logic, and the second to negative ones, such as irrationality, nature, and amorality. By means of an abstract analogy between the Jew and the feminine principle, Weininger concludes that modernity, with its privileging of economics and technology over art, philosophy, and genius, is the product of a feminine and Jewish spirit. Although what was presented as a scientific and philosophical analysis of genders reminds us more of a polemical and, at times, even deranged pamphlet, Weininger's conclusions are also an anticipation of the misogynistic, homophobic, and anti-Semitic imagination that would dominate Europe in the following decades.

According to some Italian literary critics, the presence of misogynistic and anti-Semitic themes in Saba's poems also derived from his reading of *Geschlecht und Character,* published in Italian translation in 1912. On December 4, 1912, Aldo Fortuna, one of Saba's closest friends, wrote in his journal that Saba had just finished reading *Geschlecht und Character* and that it had "made a big impression, an almost decisive impression, and he has almost declared that, if he had read it ten years earlier, he would have committed suicide as well." According to Fortuna, in April 1913, Saba still thought that Weininger's theories were "indisputable." This testimony can be found in Saba, *Lettere sulla psicoanalisi: Carteggio con Joachim Fliescher 1946–1949,* ed. Arrigo Stara (Milan: SE, 1991), 119–20. "Saba spent entire nights on Weininger," wrote Giacomo Debenedetti in 1946, "champion of a revolt against himself, resulting in checkmate." For Debenedetti, Weininger, together with Nietzsche and Freud, was one of Saba's "bad masters" (Debenedetti, *Intermezzo,* 42). On September 3 of that year, Saba would reply to the literary critic: "Why do you tell me that I have chosen bad masters for myself? Weininger never was a bad master for me: I used him to torment myself and Lina [Saba's wife] when I was writing *Serene Desperation* in Bologna. And Nietzsche and Freud are not bad masters." A little more than a year after the end of the war and the defeat of Nazism, Saba understandably distanced himself from the anti-Semite Weininger and reconstructed his own intellectual genealogy, basing it on Nietzsche and Freud.

On Otto Weininger's influence on Italian culture, see Nancy Harrowitz and Barbara Hyams, eds., *Jews and Gender: Responses to Otto Weininger* (Philadelphia: Temple Univ. Press, 1995); Alberto Cavaglion, *La filosofia del pressappoco: Weininger, sesso, carattere, e la cultura del Novecento* (Naples: L'ancora del Mediterraneo, 2001); and Michel David, *La psicoanalisi 2.* David's hypothesis is that, in their resistance to psychoanalysis, Italian intellectuals used Weininger as a surrogate for Freud. Weininger's work can now be read in a new English translation by Ladislau Löb: Otto Weininger, *Sex and Character: An Investigation on Fundamental Principles,* ed. Daniel Steuer and Laura Marcus (Bloomington: Indiana Univ. Press, 2005).

4. Cynthia Ozick, "Who Owns Anne Frank," in *Quarrel and Quandary* (New York: Knopf, 2000), 74–102. The first edition of Anne Frank's diary was published in 1947.

5. Saba, *Songbook,* 241. Saba's complete poems in Italian can be read in Umberto Saba, *Tutte le poesie,* ed. Arrigo Stara (Milan: Mondadori, 1988).

6. Umberto Saba, preface to Federico Almansi, *Poesie (1938–1946),* (Florence: Fussi, 1948), xi.

7. Ibid., x.

8. On this notion, see Susan Sontag, *Illness as Metaphor* (New York: Farrar, Straus, and Giroux, 1978).

9. See Joseph Cary, *Three Modern Italian Poets: Saba, Ungaretti, Montale* (New York: New York Univ. Press, 1969), 106.

10. On Saba as an example of Jewish anti-Semitism, see Dario Calimani, "Saba e la capra semita," in *Appartenenza e differenza: Ebrei d'Italia e letteratura*, ed. Juliette Hassine, Jacques Misan-Montefiore, and Sandra Debenedetti Stow (Florence: Giuntina, 1998), 69–89. The starting point of Calimani's article is a letter that Saba wrote to the Jewish psychoanalyst Joachim Fleischer in 1949 in which the poet expressed openly his ambivalence towards Judaism. Here I quote only the most significant passages of the letter: "And now I turn to my 'anti-Semitism.' . . . I shall begin with a memory of childhood . . . I see myself— in that memory of childhood—as a beautiful blond child in the embrace of a young and buxom woman (my deeply beloved nursemaid). On the threshold of a furniture shop stands my mother . . . threatening me and the woman with her hand up because my nursemaid had once again brought me to the church of the 'goyim' . . . At this threat, I burst into tears. I think I was frightened. This is the memory, to which I may add that, when I behaved badly, the nursemaid threatened me to 'make me a Jew' . . . which meant to circumcise me (I wasn't circumcised). It is very probable that I interpreted circumcision as a form of castration (if I was mistaken, I was not much mistaken)." The text of the letter can be read in its entirety in Umberto Saba, *Lettere sulla psicoanalisi*, 34–41. With regard to "The Goat," the famous poem by Saba in which the cry of a goat with a Semitic profile becomes the symbol of fraternal universal pain, I agree with Calimani that it shouldn't be considered among Saba's anti-Semitic writings. On the persistence of the Jewish soul in Saba's literary writings, see Guido Lopez, "Umberto Saba e l'anima ebraica," in *L'ebraismo nella letteratura italiana del Novecento*, ed. Marisa Carlà, Lucia De Angelis, and Daniela Ansallem (Palermo: Palumbo, 1995), 87–99. On Saba's relationship with Judaism in general, see Mario Lavagetto, "Fra gli stessi ebrei," in *La gallina di Saba* (Turin: Einaudi, 1989), 239–51; Mario Lavagetto, "L'altro Saba," in his introduction to Saba's *Tutte le prose*, ed. Arrigo Stara (Milan: Mondadori, 2001), xi–xlvi; Henry Stuart Hughes, *Prisoners of Hope: The Silver Age of the Italian Jews, 1924–1974* (Cambridge, Mass.: Harvard Univ. Press, 1983), 32–33.

11. On the friendship between Umberto Saba and Federico Almansi, and on the latter's only published collection of poems, see Aldo Marcovecchio, "Saba e il 'celeste scolaro,'" *Il Giornale*, Nov. 10, 1985; and Saba's biography by Stelio Mattioni, *Storia di Umberto Saba* (Milan: Camunia, 1989).

12. Umberto Saba, *La spada d'amore: Lettere scelte 1902–1957*, ed. Aldo Marcovecchio (Milan: Mondadori, 1983), 268.

13. Saba, *Songbook*, 99.

14. Saba, *Tutte le prose*, 889.

15. Saba, *Songbook*, 291.

16. Ibid., 281.

17. Saba, *Tutte le prose*, 1022.

18. Saba, preface to Almansi, *Poesie*, ix.

19. Almansi, *Poesie*, 13. See also in the same collection the poem entitled "Ripenso": "I think back . . . to when I saw you, sick, / and like a good god you saved me" (14).

20. Giorgio Agamben, *Genius*, in *Profanations*, trans. Jeff Fort (New York: Zone Books, 2007), 15.

21. Saba, *Tutte le poesie*, 471.

22. Ibid.

23. Agamben, *Genius*, 15–16.

24. Almansi, *Poesie*, 28.

25. Saba, *Songbook*, 99. This poem by Saba can also be read in another English translation by Joseph Cary, 36.

26. Almansi, *Poesie*, 12. On the theme of fatherhood, one may also read in the same collection the following poems: "Addio al padre," "Disegno antico," and "Ho visto."

27. Ibid., 15.

28. Saba, *Songbook*, 281.

29. Ibid., 271.

30. Ibid., 233 (emphasis in original).

31. Saba, *Tutte le poesie*, 538.

32. "But for each person there comes a time when he must be separated from his Genius. It can be at night, unexpectedly, when at the sound of a group of people passing by he feels, without knowing why, that his god has abandoned him. Or perhaps we send Genius away in a moment of great lucidity, an extreme moment in which we know there is salvation but no longer want to be saved, as when in *The Tempest*, Prospero says to Ariel: 'Be free'" (Agamben, *Genius*, 18).

33. See the poem entitled "Caro luogo" [Dear Place] in Saba, *Tutte le poesie*, 467: "A noisy, adult, hostile life / threatened our youth."

34. Saba, *Tutte le poesie*, 509.

35. Ibid., 470.

36. Saba, *Songbook*, 283.

37. Ibid., 241.

38. Ibid., 21. In his correspondence with family and friends, Saba described the creation of the novel *Ernesto* in terms of pregnancy and birth: "The whole story is imbued with maternity: I even had the distinct impression I was pregnant myself as I was writing it," he wrote in a letter to his wife on May 30, 1953. See Umberto Saba, *Ernesto*, trans. Mark Thompson (New York: Carcanet, 1987), 123. In a letter to the novelist Piero Quarantotti Gambini, written in August of the same year, he said, "If you come to Trieste I'll read you an episode: so far, in three months roughly, I've done a hundred pages: I should have finished it in Rome, in the clinic where I began it in a fit of maternity" (Saba, *Ernesto*, 125). It should

also be mentioned that in his 1946 essay entitled *Il grembo della poesia*, Giacomo Debenedetti interpreted Saba's poetry as a maternal womb. According to Debenedetti, Saba treated poetry as a principle of maternal and protective goodness: "For him, poetry plays the role of the one who rubbed a hand over the skinned knee and put the uncertain little walker back on his feet. It is still the same, still that which re-enacts every time the miracle of birth, restoring the unhurt son to that 'bad' world which has inflicted on him insults and scorn . . . Poetry is called upon still to lend its maternal offices—of repair, of reconciliation, of encouragement" (Debenedetti, "Il grembo della poesia," in *Intermezzo*, 40).

39. Saba, *Tutte le prose*, 888.

40. Umberto Saba and Pierantonio Quarantotti Gambini, *Il vecchio e il giovane: Carteggio 1930–1957*, ed. Linuccia Saba (Milan: Mondadori, 1965), 139.

41. Ibid., 101–2.

42. See ibid., 29: "Dear Friend, While I was eating watermelon (perhaps the last of this year) in piazza del Ponterosso, I found—without looking for it—the title of your book: *The Wave of the Cruiser* ['L'onda dell'incrociatore']."

43. Ibid., 143. See also p. 140: "How could you find such cruelty in yourself . . . to have left a boy like Ario under the impression that he had committed a murder for the rest of his days—Ario, one of the most respectable boys in all of literature, whom you yourself loved so much that you gave him—it's clear—something of yourself, of your childhood and adolescence?"

44. Saba, *Ernesto*, 114.

45. Saba, *Tutte le poesie*, 257.

46. Lavagetto, "L'altro Saba," in Saba, *Tutte le prose*, xli.

47. As quoted in ibid.

48. I take this opportunity to thank Blossom S. Kirschenbaum of Brown University for calling my attention to the meaning of the words inscribed on the plaque.

49. Giacomo Debenedetti, *October 16, 1943: Eight Jews*, trans. Estelle Gilson (Notre Dame, Ind.: Indiana Univ. Press, 2001).

50. Umberto Saba, *History and Chronicle of the Songbook*, trans. Stephen Sartarelli (Riverdale-on-Hudson, N.Y.: Sheep Meadow Press, 1998), 58.

51. Ibid., 59. It is not immediately clear what passage from Nietzsche's works Saba had in mind here. Perhaps Saba's golden drops are a reference to Zarathustra's teachings that fall from the sky like ripe figs for the most select: "'The figs fall from the trees, they are ripe and sweet; and as they fall their red skin splits open. A north wind am I to ripe figs. Thus like figs, my friends, these teachings fall to you: now drink in their juice and sweet flesh! Fall is all around and clear skies and afternoon.' Here is no fanatic that speaks, here nothing is preached, here no *belief* is demanded: from an endless abundance of light and depth of happiness falls drop after drop, word after word: the tempo of these speeches is a tender adagio. Such things reach only the most select; it is a privilege without equal to be a listener here; no one is simply free to have ears for Zarathustra" (Friedrich Nietzsche, *Ecce Homo and The Antichrist*, trans. Thomas Wayne [New York: Algora, 2004], 9–10).

52. The opposition between the will to power and melancholy is represented also in a *Shortcut* in which the poet imagines seeing again, in a blackbird flying in the Villa Borghese gardens, the beloved blackbird, Pimpo, of his childhood: "Early this morning (my 62nd birthday) I saw, at Villa Borghese, the first blackbird. It was Pimpo, the winged friend of my childhood. But he didn't seem nostalgic. He seemed animated by that which Nietzsche calls the will to power. He flew with a snap towards the highest branch of the highest tree, from which—you can be certain—he was about to chase away all the other blackbirds" (Saba, *Tutte le prose*, 56).

53. Nietzsche, *Ecce Homo*, 49.

54. Ibid.

55. The first essay in English on the German cultural obsession with ancient Greece was written by an English scholar, Eliza M. Butler. Published for the first time in England in 1935, *The Tyranny of Greece over Germany* is the reconstruction of the formation and development of the literary obsession with ancient Greece in German culture, a myth that, according to the author, was born with Winckelmann in the mid–eighteenth century and exhausted itself with Stefan George during the Weimar Republic. Eliza Butler began writing her essay in 1933, the year of Hitler's ascent to power, at the moment when the literary passion for an imaginary Greece was taking a political shape. It is not by chance that the author described her book as "a warning." Although in England, only a few grasped the political implications of Butler's essay at the time of its publication, in Germany the book was immediately banned by the Nazi regime. See Mark Lilla, "Slouching towards Athens," *New York Review of Books,* June 23, 2005: 46–48. Lilla's article is a review of the English translation of a recent essay by the German historian Christian Meier, *From Athens to Auschwitz: The Uses of History* (Cambridge, Mass.: Harvard Univ. Press, 2005).

56. Saba, *Tutte le prose*, 71.

57. Saba, *Stories and Recollections*, 110.

58. Ibid., 179.

59. Saba, *History and Chronicle of the Songbook*, 83.

60. Saba, *Tutte le prose*, 79.

61. Saba, *History and Chronicle of the Songbook*, 143.

62. Saba, *Tutte le prose*, 972.

63. Saba, *Stories and Recollections*, 168.

64. Nora Baldi, *Il paradiso di Saba* (Milan: Mondadori, 1958), 22.

65. Saba and Gambini, *Il vecchio e il giovane*, 135.

66. Saba, *Tutte le prose*, 27 and 39. *La Nuova Europa* was the Italian journal in which *Shortcuts* were regularly published.

67. Saba, *Lettere sulla psicoanalisi*, 77 (letter from March 19, 1949, to Edoardo Weiss).

68. Saba, *History and Chronicle of the Songbook*, 143.

69. This information is taken from Saba, *Tutte le prose*, 1293.

70. Saba, *Ernesto*, 124.

2. I KNEW THAT THERE WAS A HOUSE: BELONGING AND NONBELONGING
IN THE WORKS OF NATALIA GINZBURG

1. Ginzburg's two novellas were published in English translation as *The Family and Borghesia,* trans. Beryl Stockman (Manchester: Carcanet, 1988).

2. Natalia Ginzburg, "Autobiografia in terza persona," in *Non possiamo saperlo: Saggi 1973–1990,* ed. Domenico Scarpa (Turin: Einaudi, 2001), 177.

3. Natalia Ginzburg, "Childhood," in *Never Must You Ask Me,* 58.

4. Ibid., 59.

5. Natalia Ginzburg, "White Whiskers," in *Never Must You Ask Me,* 136.

6. See Maja Pflug, *Natalia Ginzburg: Arditamente timida. Una biografia,* trans. Barbara Griffini (Milan: La tartaruga, 1997), 89.

7. Natalia Ginzburg, *It's Hard to Talk about Yourself,* ed. Cesare Garboli and Lisa Ginzburg, trans. Louise Quirke (Chicago: Univ. of Chicago Press, 2003), 52. See also p. 156: "Sinibaldi: You had a Jewish father and a Catholic mother, and have often alluded to your basic extraneousness, when you were a girl, to these religions, together with all that belonging to a religion meant, at that time in particular . . . that is, a social identity. . . .

"Ginzburg: Yes. I feel Jewish and Catholic, both. I don't know why, I couldn't explain it. I don't like priests as a rule, but I do feel a great fondness for a few of them. There are priests who seem extraordinary to me, the ones we read about these days in the papers."

8. Ginzburg, *It's Hard to Talk about Yourself,* 156.

9. Umberto Saba, *An Anthology of His Poetry and Criticism,* trans. Robert Harrison (Troy, Mich.: International Book Publishers, 1986), 26.

10. Peg Boyers, "An Interview with Natalia Ginzburg," in *Natalia Ginzburg: A Voice of the Twentieth Century* ed. Angela M. Jeannet and Giuliana Sanguinetti Katz (Toronto: Univ. of Toronto Press, 2000), 18–19. The interview was previously published in *Salmagundi* 96 (1992): 130–56.

11. See, for instance, Paolo Milano, "Una famiglia come romanzo," *L'espresso,* Apr. 14, 1963; Riccardo Curiel, "Un'autobiografia senza protagonista," *Rassegna mensile di Israel,* July–Aug. 1963, 346–48. On Ginzburg and Judaism, see Hughes, *Prisoners of Hope,* 96–113; Domenico Scarpa, *Cronistoria di "Lessico famigliare,"* appendix to *Lessico famigliare,* by Natalia Ginzburg (Turin: Einaudi, 1999), 247–50; Claudia Nocentini, "Racial Laws and Internment in Natalia Ginzburg's *La strada che va in città* and *Tutti i nostri ieri,*" in DiNapoli, *The Italian Jewish Experience.*

12. Natalia Ginzburg, *Valentino and Sagittarius: Two Novellas,* trans. Avril Bardoni (Manchester: Carcanet, 1987), 43.

13. Ibid., 47.

14. Natalia Ginzburg, "The Child Who Saw Bears," in *Never Must You Ask Me,* 116.

15. Natalia Ginzburg, *Opere: Raccolte e ordinate dall'autore,* vol. 2, ed. Cesare Garboli (Milan: Mondadori, 1987), 643.

16. Ibid., 643.

17. Ibid., 646.

18. Ginzburg, *It's Hard to Talk about Yourself,* 155.

19. Boyers, "Interview with Natalia Ginzburg," 19.

20. Natalia Ginzburg, "Se vien meno la memoria," *Rinascita,* no. 16 (May 27, 1990).

21. Ginzburg, *It's Hard to Talk about Yourself,* 152.

22. On Ginzburg's rejection of Primo Levi's manuscript: "Ginzburg's rejection was like an intimation of the literary scrapheap, yet her reluctance to publish Levi was part of a larger reluctance among Italians to face their brutal and regrettable past" (Ian Thomson, *Primo Levi: A Life* [New York: Metropolitan Books, 2003], 243–44). In an article entitled "The Duty of Identity," the Italian journalist Fiamma Nirenstein writes, "Natalia Ginzburg, who as reader of the publishing house Einaudi first examined the manuscript of 'If This Is a Man,' judged that the message of the book was too Jewish" (Nirenstein, "Il dovere dell'identità," Fondazione Magna Carta, Roma, Dec. 17, 2005, http://www.magna-carta.it/relazioni%20 internazionali%20e%20democrazia/0089_Fiamma_Nirenstein.asp).

23. Ginzburg, *Opere,* 2:1323.

24. Ginzburg, *Never Must You Ask Me,* 58–59.

25. Ibid., 61.

26. Natalia Ginzburg, *Dear Michael: A Novel,* trans. Sheila Cudahy (London: Peter Owen, 1975), 36.

27. Ibid., 45–46.

28. Natalia Ginzburg, *The City and the House,* trans. Dick Davis (New York: Arcade, 1989), 8.

29. Boyers, "Interview with Natalia Ginzburg," 19.

30. Natalia Ginzburg, "My Husband," in *Opere,* 1:202.

31. Natalia Ginzburg, "Portrait of a Friend," in *The Little Virtues,* trans. Dick Davis (Manchester: Carcanet, 1985), 13–20.

32. Natalia Ginzburg, "È davvero una servitù? Essere donna," *La Stampa,* Apr. 15, 1973.

33. Boyers, "Interview with Natalia Ginzburg," 29.

34. Natalia Ginzburg, "The Home," in *Never Must You Ask Me,* 30.

35. Natalia Ginzburg, "Portrait of a Writer," in *Never Must You Ask Me,* 168.

36. "But, when nothing subsists from a distant past, after the death of others, after the destruction of objects, only the senses of smell and taste, weaker but more enduring, more intangible, more persistent, more faithful, continue for a long time, like souls, to remember, to wait, to hope, on the ruins of all the rest, to bring without flinching, on their nearly impalpable droplet, the immense edifice of memory" (Marcel Proust, *Remembrance of Things Past,* vol. 1, *Swann's Way,* trans. C. K. Scott Moncrieff [New York: Modern Library, 1956], 47).

37. Ginzburg, *It's Hard to Talk about Yourself,* 91.

38. Ginzburg, "Portrait of a Writer," in *Never Must You Ask Me,* 168.

39. Ginzburg, *It's Hard to Talk about Yourself*, 98.

40. Giulio Nascimbeni, "Ginzburg: 'Il mio Manzoni giù dal piedistallo?'" *Corriere della sera*, as quoted in Jeannet and Katz, *Natalia Ginzburg*, 190.

41. Ginzburg, *It's Hard to Talk about Yourself*, 96–97.

42. In her preface to *Cinque romanzi brevi* (Turin: Einaudi, 1964), Ginzburg writes, "It pained me to have been born in Italy and to live in Turin, for what I wanted to describe in my books was the Nevsky Prospect, and instead I found myself forced to describe the banks of the Po river. And that seemed a terrible mortification. The name of the city of Turin did not bring forth any melodious echo from my heart, but rather confined me to the narrow lanes of my daily existence, evoking its banality and squalor" (6–7).

43. Eric Auerbach, *Mimesis: The Representation of Reality in Western Literature*, trans. Willard R. Trask (Princeton, N.J.: Princeton Univ. Press, 2003).

44. Eugenio Montale, *New Poems: A Selection from "Satura" and "Diario del '71 e del '72,"* trans. G. Singh (New York: New Directions, 1976), 56.

45. Ibid.

46. It is in this regard, for example, that the story of the Jewish people's exodus from slavery in Egypt has served as a paradigm for the emancipation of African Americans and for their demands for civil rights.

47. Ginzburg, *It's Hard to Talk about Yourself*, 86.

48. Boyers, "Interview with Natalia Ginzburg," 15.

49. Ginzburg, "Portrait of a Writer," in *Never Must You Ask Me*, 168.

50. Ginzburg, *Never Must You Ask Me*, 46.

51. Ginzburg, preface to *Cinque romanzi brevi*, 17.

52. Ginzburg, *It's Hard to Talk about Yourself*, 97.

53. Francesca Sanvitale seems to reach a similar conclusion when she notes that in her writing, Ginzburg "aims at an essence, a kernel that is linked to the universal idea of man and to his destiny and yet inseparable from the single human being in his absolute specificity" ("I temi della narrativa di Natalia Ginzburg: Uno specchio della società italiana," in Walter Mauro et al., *Natalia Ginzburg: La narratrice e i suoi testi*, [Rome: La Nuova Italia Scientifica, 1986], 24). Similarly, David Ward writes that in Ginzburg, "The experiences about which we can be certain are not, then, to be found in the *long durée* of history, but in the specificity and unicity of a particular event" ("Natalia Ginzburg's Early Writings in *L'Italia libera*," in Jeannet and Katz, *Natalia Ginzburg*, 58). In commenting on her activism in defense of the rights of Serena Cruz, a Filipino child taken away from her adoptive Italian parents for their violation of international laws on adoption, Ginzburg returns to the fact that the paradigmatic and universal value of memory resides paradoxically in the specificity and particularity of the historical fact: "It is necessary that we preserve in our memory *that* indignation, *that* offense, as though it were indestructible and unique" (Boyers, "Interview with Natalia Ginzburg," 58).

54. Natalia Ginzburg, *It's Hard to Talk about Yourself*, 99.

55. Belpoliti, Marco, ed., *Primo Levi*, (Milan: Marcos y Marcos, 1998). Ginzburg's review was originally published as "Fra guerra e razzismo," *Corriere della Sera*, May 25, 1975.

56. Natalia Ginzburg, *The Things We Used to Say*, trans. Judith Woolf (Manchester: Carcanet, 1997), 21–22.

57. Sigmund Freud, *Totem and Taboo: Some Points of Agreement between the Mental Lives of Savages and Neurotics*, in Freud, *The Standard Edition of the Complete Psychological Works of Sigmund Freud*, trans. and ed. James Strachey (London: Hogarth Press, 1953–74), 13:xv.

58. Judith Laurence Pastore, "The Personal Is Political: Gender, Generation, and Memory in Natalia Ginzburg's *Caro Michele*," in Jeannet and Katz, *Natalia Ginzburg*, 93–94.

59. Natalia Ginzburg, *The Little Virtues*, 66.

60. Walter Mauro, "Walter Mauro parla con Natalia Ginzburg," in Mauro et al., *Natalia Ginzburg*, 60–61.

61. Natalia Ginzburg, "My Craft," in *A Place to Live and Other Selected Essays of Natalia Ginzburg*, trans. Lynne Sharon Schwartz (New York: Seven Stories Press, 2002), 55.

62. Ginzburg, *Cinque romanzi brevi*, 7.

63. Mauro, "Walter Mauro parla con Natalia Ginzburg," 61.

64. Ginzburg, *Never Must You Ask Me*, 141–42.

65. Cesare Garboli, preface to Ginzburg, *Opere*, 1:65.

66. Italo Calvino, "Natalia Ginzburg o la possibilità del romanzo borghese," *L'Europa letteraria*, June–Aug. 1961, 134.

67. Ginzburg, *Never Must You Ask Me*, 164.

68. See, for instance, Luigi Fontanella, "Natalia Ginzburg between Fiction and Memory: A Reading of *Le voci della sera* and *Lessico famigliare*," 40, and Angela M. Jeannet, "Natalia Ginzburg: Making a Story Out of History," 64, both in Jeannet and Katz, *Natalia Ginzburg*.

69. Ginzburg, *Dear Michael*, 160–61.

70. Quoted in Pflug, *Natalia Ginzburg: Arditamente timida*, 170.

71. Ginzburg, "Fantasy Life," in *A Place to Live*, 191.

72. Ginzburg, *The Little Virtues*, 73.

73. Ibid., 69.

74. Ginzburg, *The Things We Used to Say*, 1.

75. The following considerations on the theme of silence are integrations of Quinzio, *Radici ebraiche*, 155ff.

76. André Neher, *The Exile of the Word: From the Silence of the Bible to the Silence of Auschwitz*, trans. David Maisel (Philadelphia: Jewish Publication Society of America, 5741 [1981]), 136.

77. Sigmund Freud, "The Theme of the Three Caskets," in Freud, *Standard Edition*, 12:295: "Psycho-analysis will tell us that in dreams dumbness is a common representation of death."

78. Sigmund Freud, *Civilization and Its Discontents*, in Freud, *Standard Edition*, 21:119.

79. Walter Benjamin, "On Language as Such and On the Language of Man," in Benjamin, *Selected Writings 1913–1926*, ed. Marcus Bullock and Michael W. Jennings (Cambridge, Mass.: Belknap Press of HUP, 1996), 1:73.

80. Benjamin, "On Language," 1:72–73.

81. Levi, *The Drowned and the Saved*, 93–94.

82. Neher, *Exile of the Word*, 207.

83. Ibid., 143.

84. Benjamin, "On Language," 1:72.

3. FROM MYTH TO HISTORY: THE CONSTRUCTION
OF THE NARRATIVE JEWISH SUBJECT IN GIORGIO BASSANI

1. Pier Paolo Pasolini, "La storia di Bassani scrittore cominciò con un dubbio: F. o Ferrara?" *Il Tempo*, Feb. 8, 1974; also published in Pier Paolo Pasolini, *Saggi sulla letteratura e sull'arte*, ed. Walter Siti and Silvia De Laude (Milan: Mondadori, 1999), 2:1990–94.

2. On Bassani and Judaism, see Ada Nieger, *Bassani e il mondo ebraico*, (Naples: Loffredo, 1983); Hughes, *Prisoners of Hope*, 114–49; Marisa Carlà, Lucia De Angelis, and Daniela Ansallem, eds., *L'ebraismo nella letteratura italiana del Novecento*; Luca De Angelis, *Qualcosa di più intimo: Aspetti della cultura ebraica del Novecento italiano: Da Svevo a Bassani*, (Florence: Giuntina, 2006), 139–71; Lucienne Kroha, "Judaism and Manhood in the Novels of Giorgio Bassani" in DiNapoli, *The Italian Jewish Experience*.

3. I quote from William Shakespeare, *The Merchant of Venice*, ed. M. M. Mahood (Cambridge: Cambridge Univ. Press, 2003).

4. Wystan H. Auden, "Brothers and Others," in Auden, *The Dyer's Hand and Other Essays* (London: Faber and Faber, 1963), 221.

5. Sigmund Freud, "Mourning and Melancholia," in Freud, *Standard Edition*, 14:237–58.

6. See Auden, "Brothers and Others," 221.

7. Ibid.

8. On the theme of the three caskets, see Freud's famous essay, "The Theme of the Three Caskets" (1913) in Freud, *Standard Edition*, 12: 289–301.

9. *Thrift* is one of the keywords of the play; it appears at I.1.174, I.3.42, and I.3.82. See also *unthrifty* at I.3.169. Shylock's daughter Jessica's love is also described as "unthrift" at V.1.16.

10. Leslie Fiedler, *Fiedler on the Roof: Essays on Literature and Jewish Identity* (Boston: David R. Godine, 1991), 20ff.

11. On the perception of the body of the Jew as a feminized body, see also Sander Gilman, *The Jew's Body* (New York: Routledge, 1991); Daniel Boyarin, *Unheroic Conduct: The Rise of Heterosexuality and the Creation of the Jewish Man* (Berkeley: Univ. of California Press, 1997) and *"Goyim Naches*, or, Modernity and the Manliness of the *Mentsh*," in *Modernity, Culture, and "the Jew,"* ed. Bryan Cheyette and Laura Marcus (Cambridge, UK:

Polity Press, 1998), 63–87. In particular, Boyarin argues that the representation of the male Jew as female was not only an external fantasy that originated in the imagination of anti-Semites but also the internal representation of a genuine Jewish cultural difference: the image of the pale, studious, and sedentary yeshiva student as an ideal of manhood.

12. In his *Politics*, Aristotle had already spoken of usury as an unnatural form of commerce: "Hence usury is very justifiably detested, since it gets wealth from money itself, rather then from the very things money was devised to facilitate. For money was introduced to facilitate exchange, but interest makes money itself grow bigger (that is how it gets its name; for offspring resemble their parents, and interest is money that comes from money). Hence of all the kinds of wealth acquisitions this one is the most unnatural" (Aristotle, *Politics*, trans. and ed. C. D. C. Reeve [Indianapolis: Hackett, 1998], 1258b). In ancient Greek, the word *tokos* means both "offspring" and "interest."

13. See John Boswell, *Christianity, Social Tolerance, and Homosexuality: Gay People in Western Europe from the Beginning of the Christian Era to the Fourteenth Century* (Chicago: Univ. of Chicago Press, 1980), 331.

14. Sigmund Freud, *Civilization and Its Discontents*, in Freud, *Standard Edition*, 21:114.

15. According to Theodor W. Adorno and Max Horkheimer as well, whose reflections are also based on Freudian concepts, anti-Semitism is a form of fallacious projection in which the subject attributes to an external object his own impulses, which he is unable to recognize as such (Horkheimer and Adorno, *Dialectic of Enlightenment*, 154, 158–59). Adorno and Horkheimer's reasoning is based on the psychoanalytical theory of morbid projection, by which impulses that are viewed as social taboos are transferred from the subject to the object. The anti-Semite who wants property and possessions and who feels shame for this desire transforms his own sense of guilt into aggression, imputing his own inclinations to the Jews. In particular, the taboo usually has to do with repressed homosexuality, whose repression in the subject translates itself into an aggressive projection towards the outside. According to Freud, too, paranoid projection is a form of defense against homosexual desire. See Freud, *Standard Edition*, 12:59.

16. Bassani, *Opere*, xc. On the representation of outcasts in Bassani's *The Gold-Rimmed Spectacles*, see Mirna Cicioni, "Insiders and Outsiders: Discourses of Oppression in Giorgio Bassani's *Gli occhiali d'oro*," *Italian Studies* 41 (1986): 101–15.

17. Auden, "Brothers and Others," 227.

18. Giorgio Bassani, *Gli occhiali d'oro* (Milan: Mondadori, 1958), 5. For the English translation of the passage, I quote from Sophocles, *Philoctetes*, ed. R. G. Ussher (Warminster, UK: Aris and Phillips, 1990), 742–50.

19. Sophocles, *Philoctetes*, 16. This detail is noted again by Neoptolemus ("His house is this that you see—it has two entrances—a bedroom in the rock," 159–60) and by Philoctetes himself ("My two-doored cave in the rock," 952).

20. Giorgio Bassani, *The Gold-Rimmed Spectacles*, 21. Obviously, Fredric March is the actor who played Dr. Jekyll and Mr. Hyde in the film of the same name, directed by Rouben

Mamoulian in 1931. The reference to the film, rather than to Stevenson's book, is an indication that the comment regarding Fadigati's life is to be ascribed to his neighbors who, if they did not know Stevenson's novel, had certainly heard of the film that was produced and distributed in the years during which Bassani's novel takes place.

21. Ibid., 7.

22. Ibid., 11.

23. Ibid., 44.

24. Nathaniel Hawthorne, *Rappaccini's Daughter*, in Hawthorne, *Selected Tales and Sketches*, ed. Michael J. Colacurcio (New York: Penguin, 1987), 399.

25. Ibid., 402–3.

26. Auden, "Brothers and Others," 235.

27. Bassani, *The Gold-Rimmed Spectacles*, 24.

28. Ibid., 52.

29. Ibid., 51.

30. Ibid., 98.

31. Ibid., 122.

32. Ibid., 123.

33. Freud, *Civilization and Its Discontents*, 21:118–19.

34. Bassani, *The Gold-Rimmed Spectacles*, 124.

35. Ibid.

36. Ibid.

37. Eugene O'Neill, *Long Day's Journey into Night* (New Haven: Yale Univ. Press, 1989), 153–54.

38. Ibid., 153.

39. Ibid.

40. See Claudio Magris, *Lontano da dove: Joseph Roth e la tradizione ebraico-orientale* (Turin: Einaudi, 1971), 296–301.

41. Bassani, *The Gold-Rimmed Spectacles*, 72.

42. Levi Della Torre, *Mosaico*, 35.

43. Bassani, *Opere*, 313.

44. Bassani, *The Gold-Rimmed Spectacles*, 102–3.

45. Ibid., 102.

46. Ibid., 103.

47. Ibid., 142.

48. Ibid., 143.

49. Giorgio Bassani, *The Garden of the Finzi-Continis*, trans. William Weaver (San Diego: Harcourt Brace, 1977), 21.

50. Ibid., 22.

51. Ibid.

52. Ibid., 24.

53. Ibid.

54. Ibid., 25.

55. Ibid., 93.

56. Levi Della Torre, *Mosaico*, 45.

57. Bassani, *The Garden of the Finzi-Continis*, 20.

58. Ibid., 140.

59. Ibid., 140–41.

60. Ibid., 76.

61. Ibid., 116.

62. Jankélévitch, "Ressembler, dissembler," 44.

63. Bassani, *The Garden of the Finzi-Continis*, 200.

64. I am of course referring to Walter Benjamin's ninth thesis on the concept of history. See Walter Benjamin, *Selected Writings: 1938–1940*, 4:392–93.

65. Bassani, *The Garden of the Finzi-Continis*, 79.

66. Ibid.

67. Ibid., 71.

68. Ibid.

69. Walter Benjamin, "On Language," 1:73.

70. Bassani, *The Garden of the Finzi-Continis*, 104. This is the last stanza of Emily Dickinson's poem entitled "I died for beauty, but was scarce."

71. Bassani, *The Garden of the Finzi-Continis*, 126.

72. Benjamin, *Selected Writings*, 4:392–93.

73. Bassani, *The Garden of the Finzi-Continis*, 118.

74. Ibid.

75. Ibid., 99.

76. Ibid., 120.

77. Levi Della Torre, *Mosaico*, 42–43.

78. Bassani, *The Garden of the Finzi-Continis*, 3.

4. THE MODESTY OF STARBUCK: ON HYBRIDS, JUDAISM, AND ETHICS IN PRIMO LEVI

1. For this information on *The Search for Roots*, I'm indebted to Marco Belpoliti, "Le radici rovesciate," in Primo Levi, *La ricerca delle radici: Antologia personale* (Turin: Einaudi, 1981), vii–xviii.

2. See Levi's interview with Edoardo Fadini in Primo Levi, *The Voice of Memory: Interviews 1961–1987*, ed. Marco Belpoliti and Robert Gordon, trans. Robert Gordon (New York: New Press, 2001), 85: "I am amphibian . . . a centaur (I've even written stories about centaurs). It seems to me that the ambiguity of science fiction reflects my present destiny. I am split in two." In "Argon," Levi uses the figure of the centaur to describe the contrast inherent

to the human condition, for "man is a centaur, a tangle of flesh and mind, divine inspiration and dust" (Levi, *The Periodic Table*, 9). See also the short story entitled "Quaestio de Centauris," published in 1961 in the Italian journal *Il Mondo* and later in Levi's first collection of short stories, *Storie naturali* (Turin: Einaudi, 1966), 165–81.

3. After World War II, Levi's interest in several aspects of Jewish tradition and culture becomes evident from his many publications on the subject. Besides his three books on the Shoah—*Survival in Auschwitz* (1947), *The Truce* (1963), and *The Drowned and the Saved* (1986)—Levi wrote short stories, articles, and a novel inspired by Jewish history and themes. During his period of detainment in Auschwitz, Levi developed an interest in Eastern European Ashkenazi culture. Short stories such as "Our Seal," "The Cantor and the Barracks Chief," and "Lilìt," published in the Italian newspaper *La Stampa* and then, in 1981, in the volume *Lilìt e altri racconti* (Turin: Einaudi, 1981) (and published in English as *Moments of Reprieve*, trans. Ruth Feldman [New York: Summit Books, 1986]), are the results of this encounter. They are also the preparatory steps to the composition of *Se non ora, quando?* (Turin: Einaudi, 1982) (published in English as *If Not Now, When?* trans. William Weaver [New York: Summit Books, 1985]), Levi's novel about the Jewish resistance movement that was born out of his desire to show that the assertions that a Jewish resistance had never existed were unfounded. To write this novel, Levi undertook the study of Yiddish. In addition, in the first chapter of *The Periodic Table*, entitled "Argon," Levi wrote about the history and culture of Italian Jews in Piedmont. His long-standing interest in Jewish culture is also indicated by various references to Judaism in several poems published in the collection *At an Uncertain Hour* (1984). See, in particular, the poem entitled "Shemà." Levi also wrote a brief essay on the Schulchan Aruch entitled "Ritual and Laughter" (*Other People's Trades*, trans. Raymond Rosenthal [New York: Summit Books, 1989]) and, in 1983, translated Kafka's *The Trial*.

4. Quoted in Marco Belpoliti, *Primo Levi* (Milan: Mondadori, 1998), 70–71; interview with Raffaelle Manzini and Brunetto Salvarami in *Qol* 4, 1986.

5. Stefano Jesurum, *Essere ebrei in Italia* (Milan: Longanesi, 1987), 97. See also Levi, *The Drowned and the Saved*, 129.

6. Levi, *The Periodic Table*, 35.

7. For further reading on the relationship between Levi and Judaism, see Primo Levi, "Itinerario d'uno scrittore ebreo," in Levi, *Opere*, ed. Marco Belpoliti (Turin: Einaudi, 1997), 2:1213–29, as well as Levi, *The Voice of Memory*. H. Stuart Hughes, one of the first scholars who wrote extensively on the relationship between Judaism and contemporary Italian writers, dedicated the third chapter of his *Prisoners of Hope* to Primo Levi, 73–85; see also Paola Valabrega, "Primo Levi e la tradizione ebraico-orientale," *Studi Piemontesi* 11 (1982): 296–310, now in *Primo Levi: Un'antologia della critica*, ed. Ernesto Ferrero (Turin: Einaudi, 1997), 263–88; Stefano Levi Della Torre, "L'eredità di Primo Levi," *La rassegna mensile di Israel* (May–Dec. 1989): 191–204, now in Ferrero, *Primo Levi*, 245–62; Alberto Cavaglion, "Argon e la cultura ebraica piemontese," in *Primo Levi: Il presente del passato* ed. Cavaglion (Milan: Franco Angeli, 1991); David Meghnagi, "La vicenda ebraica: Primo Levi e la scrittura," in

Primo Levi: Il presente del passato, ed. Cavaglion, 152–61, now in Ferrero, *Primo Levi,* 289–99 , 152–61; Daniela Amsallem, "Le symbolisme du chien: Primo Levi et la littérature juive après la Shoah," *Chroniques italiennes, Université de la Sorbonne Nouvelle* (1993): 33–34; Amsallem, "Ebraismo, scienza e creazione letteraria: Primo Levi e i miti ebraici di 'Lilìt' e del Golem," in Carlà, De Angelis, and Ansallem, *L'ebraismo nella letteratura italiana*; Alberto Cavaglion, "La scelta di Gedeone: Appunti su Primo Levi e l'ebraismo," *Journal of the Institute of Romance Studies* 4 (1996): 187–98; and David Mendel, "Primo Levi and the Jews," 61–73, Joseph Sungolowsky, "The Jewishness of Primo Levi," 74–86, and Sergio Parussa, "A Hybridism of Sounds: Primo Levi between Judaism and Literature," 87–94, all in *The Legacy of Primo Levi* ed. Stanislao G. Pugliese (New York: Palgrave Macmillan, 2005). In the Italian journal *Ha Keillah,* there are several articles on Primo Levi and Judaism.

8. Levi, *The Search for Roots: A Personal Anthology,* trans. and ed. Peter Forbes (Chicago: Ivan R. Dee, 2002), 48.

9. Ibid., 214–15.

10. Levi Della Torre, *Mosaico,* 30.

11. Primo Levi, *The Monkey's Wrench,* trans. William Weaver (New York: Summit Books, 1986), 53.

12. Philip Roth, "A Conversation with Primo Levi," in Primo Levi, *Survival in Auschwitz,* trans. Stuart Woolf (New York: Summit Books, 1986), 178.

13. Ibid., 179.

14. Published in 1939 as *Terre des Hommes* (Earth of Men), the book is a memoir that recounts episodes of Saint-Exupéry's life as a pilot. The chapter's original title—"Naufraghi nel Sahara"—and its content recalls the experience of Auschwitz survivors that Levi recounts in *The Truce* (Antoine de Saint-Exupéry, *Wind, Sand, and Stars,* trans. L. Galantière [New York: Harcourt and Brace, 1949]; Primo Levi, *If This Is a Man, and The Truce,* trans. Stuart Woolf [New York: Cardinal, 1992]).

15. Levi, *The Search for Roots,* 118.

16. Robert Gordon, *Primo Levi's Ordinary Virtues: From Testimony to Ethics* (Oxford: Oxford Univ. Press, 2001), 25.

17. Primo Levi, *The Drowned and the Saved,* 75.

18. Ibid., 81–82.

19. Ibid., 85.

20. I adopt here the notion of collective memory as it has been described by Yosif H. Yerushalmi: "It may help to point out, however, that in repeatedly employing such terms as "collective memory" or "group memory" I do not have in mind some vaguely genetic endowment, not an innate psychic structure analogous to the Jungian archetypes. . . . It was the abiding merit of Maurice Halbwachs to have insisted to psychologists and philosophers alike that even individual memory is structured through social frameworks, and all the more that collective memory is not a metaphor but a social reality transmitted and sustained through the conscious efforts and institutions of the group" (*Zakhor,* xxxiv).

21. In Rav Dario Disegni's Italian translation of the *Tanakh*, the twenty-four books that form the Hebrew Bible, first published in 1960, the verb is rendered as *librarsi*. Disegni adds in a footnote to the text, "The Jewish root in the text precisely indicates the very light flight of the mother who barely brushes against her little ones in the nest." See *Bibbia ebraica: Pentateuco e Haftaroth,* ed. Rav Dario Disegni (Florence: Giuntina, 1995), 6.

22. Levi, *The Periodic Table,* 12.

23. Primo Levi, *Opere,* 2:525. Some lines of Levi's poem are paraphrases of the prayer that consists mainly of three portions: Deuteronomy 6:4–9, 11:13–21, and Numbers 15:37–41.

24. It is Levi himself who reminds us that remembering is also reading, that memory is deeply connected with the written text, when he mentions his father's passion for reading by means of humorous paraphrases of the passage in Deuteronomy 6:7 that commands memory: "My father was always reading three books simultaneously; he read 'when he sat at home, when he walked by the way, when he lay down and when he got up' (Deut. 6:7)" (Levi, *The Search for Roots,* xx). The passage in Deuteronomy, paraphrased by Levi, is "when thou sittest in thine house, and when thou walkest by the way, and when thou liest down, and when thou risest up."

25. Yerushalmi writes, "The biblical conception of history, where the continual oscillation of memory and forgetting is a major theme through all the narratives of historical events. Periodically Israel forgets the God of the Covenant and lapses into idolatry; subsequently it remembers and is reunited with him. The primary biblical imperative is to remember, not to forget" (*Freud's Moses,* 34).

26. For our discussion of Levi's reference to Genesis, I'm closely following Jacques Derrida's discussion of Yerushalmi's interpretation of Freud's Judaism in his *Freud's Moses: Judaism Terminable and Interminable,* in particular, Derrida's notion of archive and archive fever. Derrida writes that psychoanalysis is "a scientific project which . . . aspires to be a general science of the archive, of everything that can happen to the economy of memory and to its substrates, traces, documents, in their supposedly psychical or techno-prosthetic forms" (*Archive Fever: A Freudian Impression* [Chicago: Univ. of Chicago Press, 1995], 34). Later in the book he writes, "The question of the archive is not a question of the past. It is a question of the future, the question of the future itself, the question of a response, of a promise and of a responsibility for tomorrow. The archive, if we want to know what that will have meant, we will only know in times to come" (Derrida, *Archive Fever,* 36).

27. Levi, *The Drowned and the Saved,* 86.

28. Ibid., 87.

29. Yerushalmi, *Zakhor,* 117.

30. Born in Breslau in 1902, Anders fled Nazi Germany with his wife, Hannah Arendt, in 1933. They emigrated first to Paris and then, in 1936, to the United States. When Anders returned to Europe in 1950, he became one of the founders of the anti-nuclear movement.

31. Günther Anders et al., *Mein Judentum,* ed. Hans Jürgen Schultz (Stuttgart Berlin: Kreuz-Verlag, 1978), 74. See also "Zinc": "In order for the wheel to turn, for life to be lived, impurities are needed, and the impurities of impurities in the soil too, as is known, if it is to be fertile. Dissension, diversity, the grain of salt and mustard are needed: Fascism does not want them, forbids them, and that's why you're not a Fascist; it wants everybody to be the same, and you are not . . . I too am Jewish . . . I am the impurity that makes the zinc react. I am the grain of salt or mustard" (Levi, *The Periodic Table,* 34–35). The parable of the mustard seed as a messianic allegory of the heavenly kingdom can be found in Matthew 13:31 and in Mark 13:19.

32. Ibid., 63.

33. Primo Levi, *Survival in Auschwitz,* trans. Stuart Woolf (New York: Summit Books, 1986), 130.

34. Anders et al., *Mein Judentum,* 64.

35. Ibid., 65.

36. Isaiah 10:22: "For though thy people Israel be as the sand of the sea, [yet] a remnant of them shall return." See also Isaiah 37:32, "For out of Jerusalem shall go forth a remnant, and they that escape out of mount Zion," and Isaiah 46:3, "Hearken unto me, O house of Jacob, and all the remnant of the house of Israel, which are borne [by me] from the belly, which are carried from the womb."

37. Agamben, *The Time That Remains,* 45.

38. Anders, *Mein Judentum,* 76.

39. Ibid., 63.

40. Ibid., 65.

41. Levi, *Moments of Reprieve,* 45. In May 1965, Levi wrote poem dedicated to the figure of Lilith. The poem's English translation can be read in Levi, *Collected Poems: New Edition,* trans. Ruth Feldman and Brian Swann (London: Faber and Faber, 1992), 26.

42. Anders's critical theory of contemporary society, one should add, is also characterized by deep historical pessimism, a state of mind and a critical approach that is in contrast with Judaism and Jewish hope, and with the interpretation proposed in this essay. On more than one occasion, Anders said that one of our duties as human beings who live in a world haunted by nuclear annihilation is to live without hope. What happened in Hiroshima on August 6, 1945, had put an end to his messianic expectations for a kingdom of justice. Ahead of us, Anders wrote, there is no messianic kingdom to be founded, but an apocalypse without kingdom. After Hiroshima, he wrote, we are driven not towards a "not yet" but towards a "not anymore." In this belief, he thought that there was something profoundly un-Jewish, and he was not surprised that, among those who paid particular attention to his continuous warnings of the concrete possibility of a nuclear apocalypse, there were no Jews. Nonetheless, in his presence in Kyoto in 1958, in his conviction that one of our collective tasks is to work against the possibility of a global Hiroshima, and in hearing in his own words an echo of the words of the biblical prophets, there is the construction, perhaps an involuntary step contrary to his own historical pessimism, of a hope in the future.

43. Claude Eatherly and Günther Anders, *Burning Conscience: The Case of the Hiroshima Pilot, Claude Eatherly, Told in His Letters to Günther Anders*, ed. Bertrand Russell (London: Weidenfeld and Nicolson, 1961), 108.

44. Primo Levi has also written extensively on the relationship between humans and machines in terms of fortune and misfortune.

45. Eatherly and Anders,*Burning Conscience*, 108.

46. This methodological shift from memoir to fiction writing, or, as Cynthia Ozick would say, from the rights of history to the rights of imagination, will help to show how Levi's ethical Judaism can change writing. When fiction presents us with a set of raw and complex images to be interpreted, fiction can also be read as an attempt to recuperate, that is, to represent and perhaps understand by means of an aesthetic operation on language, a reality otherwise irretrievable and ultimately lost to memory ("The Rights of History and the Rights of Imagination," in *Quarrel and Quandary*, 103–19).

47. In Anders's use of the term *apparatus* to describe the machinery at work in our contemporary world, there may be a memory of Kafka.

48. Frank Kafka, *The Trial*, trans. Richard Stokes (London: Hesperus Press, 2005), 210. Kafka began to write *The Trial* in 1914. In the same year, he composed *In the Penal Colony*. Unlike the novella, which was published in 1919, the novel was published only posthumously in 1925.

49. Franz Kafka, *Kafka's the Metamorphosis and Other Writings*, ed. Helmuth Kiesel, trans. by Volkmar Sander and Daniel Thersen (New York: Continuum, 2002), 110.

50. Elias Canetti, *Kafka's Other Trial: The Letters to Felice*, trans. Christopher Middleton (New York: Schocken Books, 1974).

51. Giulio Einaudi also proposed *Lord Jim* to Italo Calvino and *Madame Bovary* to Natalia Ginzburg. On Levi's translation of Kafka, see also Miriam Anissimow's interview with the Italian Germanist Cesare Cases: "Levi was a basically optimistic man. . . . Kafka's pessimism was totally foreign to him. . . . Kafka is enigmatic and Primo was a philosopher of the Enlightenment, a positivist, a man of science. . . . Kafka was not for him. I'll give you an example: in the opening line of *The Trial*, Joseph K wakes up and notices that Anna, the servant, hasn't brought his breakfast yet. Kafka writes: '*Das war noch niemals geschehen.*' Primo Levi translated it into Italian as: 'It was the first time it had happened.' Which means that he still had faith in the continuity of time, whereas Kafka wants to indicate a break after which time no longer exists. Levi almost got the meaning wrong, and there are many other instances in his translation" (Anissimov, *Primo Levi: Tragedy of an Optimist*, trans. Steve Cox [London: Aurum Press, 1998], 357).

52. The interview with Luciano Genta, "Primo Levi: Così ho rivissuto 'Il processo' di Kafka," was originally published in *Tuttolibri*, the cultural supplement of the Italian newspaper *La Stampa*, on April 9, 1983. See also "Tradurre Kafka," in Primo Levi, *Racconti e saggi* (Turin: Editrice La Stampa, 1986), 111–13; now in Levi, *Opere*, 2:939–41. Levi's essay can be read in English translation in Primo Levi, *The Mirror Maker*, trans. Raymond Rosenthal (New York: Schocken Books, 1989), 106–9.

53. Levi, *The Mirror Maker*, 109.

54. Giorgio Agamben, *The Assistants*, in *Profanations*, trans. Jeff Fort (New York: Zone Books, 2007), 29–35.

55. Levi, *The Search for Roots*, viii.

56. In the chapter of *The Drowned and the Saved* entitled "The Intellectual in Auschwitz," Levi writes on the cliché of love and death: "The intellectual [in Auschwitz] has drawn from his reading an odorless, ornate and literary image of death. For us, in Italy, death is the second term of the binomial 'love and death'; it is Laura's, Ermengarda's and Clorinda's tender transfiguration; it is the sacrifice of the soldier in battle ('who for his country dies has lived greatly'); it is 'a beautiful death honors all of life.' This boundless archive of defensive and thaumaturgic formulations in Auschwitz (and also for that matter today in any hospital) was short lived: *Death in Auschwitz* was trivial, bureaucratic, and an everyday affair. It was not commented on, it was not 'comforted by tears'" (Levi, *The Drowned and the Saved*, 147–48).

57. Levi, *Other People's Trades*, 149–50.

58. Ibid., 92–96.

59. Ibid., 170.

60. See Giorgio Agamben, *Remnants of Auschwitz: The Witness and the Archive* (New York: Zone Books, 1999), 13: "As we shall see, almost none of the ethical principles of our age believed it could recognize as valid has stood the decisive test of an *Ethics more Auschwitz demonstrata*."

61. Tony Kushner, *Thinking about the Longstanding Problems of Virtue and Happiness: Essays, a Play, Two Poems, and a Prayer* (New York: Theater Communications Group, 1995), 109.

62. I'm indebted for this quote, as well as for the following one from Leviticus, to Anthony Hecht, "St. Paul's Epistle to the Galatians" in *Melodies Unheard: Essays on the Mystery of Poetry* (Baltimore: Johns Hopkins Univ. Press, 2003), 238–51.

63. Freud, *Civilization and Its Discontents*, 21:120.

64. For Paul's repudiation of the law of Moses, see Galatians 5:6: "For in Jesus Christ neither circumcision availeth any thing, nor uncircumcision; but faith which worketh by love."

65. Emmanuel Levinas, *Beyond the Verse: Talmudic Readings and Lectures*, trans. Gary D. Mole (Bloomington: Indiana Univ. Press, 1994), 61.

66. Herman Melville, *Moby-Dick or The Whale* (Evanston, Ill.: Northwestern Univ. Press, 2001), chapter 109.

EPILOGUE

1. Arnaldo Momigliano, *Saggezza straniera: l'ellenismo e le altre culture* (Turin: Einaudi, 1980), 159–60.

Bibliography

Acocella, Joan Ross. *Twenty-Eight Artists and Two Saints: Essays*. New York: Pantheon Books, 2007.

Agamben, Giorgio. *Genius*. In *Profanations*. Translated by Jeff Fort. New York: Zone Books, 2007, 9–18. Originally published as *Genius*. Rome: Nottetempo, 2004.

———. *The Assistants*. In *Profanations*. Translated by Jeff Fort. New York: Zone Books, 2007, 29–35. Originally published as *Il giorno del giudizio*. Rome: Nottetempo, 2004.

———. *Remnants of Auschwitz: The Witness and the Archive*. New York: Zone Books, 1999.

———. *The Time That Remains: A Commentary on the Letter to the Romans*. Translated by Patricia Dailey. Stanford: Stanford Univ. Press, 2005.

Almansi, Federico. *Poesie (1938–1946)*. Florence: Fussi, 1948.

Améry, Jean. *At the Mind's Limits: Contemplations by a Survivor on Auschwitz and Its Realities*. Translated by Sidney Rosenfeld and Stella P. Rosenfeld. Bloomington: Indiana Univ. Press, 1980.

Amsallem, Daniela. "Le symbolisme du chien: Primo Levi et la littérature juive après la Shoah," *Chroniques italiennes, Université de la Sorbonne Nouvelle* (1993): 33–34.

Anders, Günther, et al. *Mein Judentum*. Edited by Hans Jürgen Schultz. Stuttgart Berlin: Kreuz-Verlag, 1978.

Anissimov, Miriam. *Primo Levi: Tragedy of an Optimist*. Translated by Steve Cox. London: Aurum Press, 1998.

Appelfeld, Aharon. *Beyond Despair*. New York: Fromm International, 1994.

Arian Levi, Giorgina, and Giulio Disegni. *Fuori dal ghetto: Il 1848 degli ebrei*. Preface by Guido Neppi Modona. Rome: Editori Riuniti, 1998.

Aristotle. *Politics*. Translated and edited by C. D. C. Reeve. Indianapolis: Hackett, 1998.

Auden, Wystan H. "Brothers and Others." *The Dyer's Hand and Other Essays*. London: Faber and Faber, 1963.

Auerbach, Eric. *Mimesis: The Representation of Reality in Western Literature.* Translated by Willard R. Trask. Princeton, N.J.: Princeton Univ. Press, 2003.

Baeck, Leo. *Judaism and Christianity: Essays.* Translated by Walter Kaufmann. Philadelphia: Jewish Publication Society of America, 1958.

Baldi, Nora. *Il paradiso di Saba.* Milan: Mondadori, 1958.

Barthes, Roland. "Historical Discourse." In *Introduction to Structuralism,* ed. Michael Lane, 145–55. New York: Basic Books, 1970.

Bassani, Giorgio. *The Garden of the Finzi-Continis.* Translated by William Weaver. San Diego: Harcourt Brace, 1977.

———. *Gli occhiali d'oro.* Milan: Mondadori, 1958.

———. *The Gold-Rimmed Spectacles.* Translated by Isabel Quigly. New York: Atheneum, 1960.

———. *Opere.* Edited by R. Cotroneo. Milan: Mondadori, 1998.

Belpoliti, Marco, ed. *Primo Levi.* Milan: Marcos y Marcos, 1997.

———. *Primo Levi.* Milan: Mondadori, 1998.

Benjamin, Walter. "On Language as Such and On the Language of Man." In Benjamin, *Selected Writings, 1913–1926.* Edited by Marcus Bullock and Michael W. Jennings, vol. 1. Cambridge, Mass.: Belknap Press of HUP, 1996.

———. *Selected Writings.* Edited by Marcus Bullock and Michael W. Jennings, 4 vols. Cambridge, Mass.: Harvard Univ. Press, 1996.

Bonfil, Robert. *Jewish Life in Renaissance Italy.* Translated by Anthony Oldcorn. Berkeley: Univ. of California Press, 1994.

Boswell, John. *Christianity, Social Tolerance, and Homosexuality: Gay People in Western Europe from the Beginning of the Christian Era to the Fourteenth Century.* Chicago: Univ. of Chicago Press, 1980.

Boyarin, Daniel. "*Goyim Naches,* or, Modernity and the Manliness of the *Mentsh.*" In *Modernity, Culture, and "the Jew,"* ed. Bryan Cheyette and Laura Marcus, 63–87. Cambridge, UK: Polity Press, 1998.

———. *Unheroic Conduct: The Rise of Heterosexuality and the Creation of the Jewish Man.* Berkeley: Univ. of California Press, 1997.

Boyers, Peg. "An Interview with Natalia Ginzburg." In *Natalia Ginzburg: A Voice of the Twentieth Century.* Edited by Angela M. Jeannet and Giuliana Sanguinetti Katz. Toronto: Univ. of Toronto Press, 2000, 18–19. The interview was previously published in *Salmagundi* 96 (1992): 130–56.

Bullock, Alan. *Natalia Ginzburg: Human Relationship in a Changing World.* Oxford: Berg, 1991.

Calimani, Dario. "Saba e la capra semita." In *Appartenenza e differenza: Ebrei d'Italia e letteratura.* Edited by Juliette Hassine, Jacques Misan-Montefiore, and Sandra Debenedetti Stow. Florence: Giuntina, 1998.

Calvino, Italo. "Natalia Ginzburg o la possibilità del romanzo borghese." *L'Europa letteraria,* June–Aug. 1961, 134.

Canetti, Elias. *Kafka's Other Trial: The Letters to Felice.* Translated by Christopher Middleton. New York: Schocken Books, 1974.

Carlà, Marisa, Lucia De Angelis, and Daniela Ansallem, eds. *L'ebraismo nella letteratura italiana del Novecento.* Palermo: Palumbo, 1995.

Carmi, T., ed. *The Penguin Book of Hebrew Verse.* New York: Penguin, 1981.

Cary, Joseph. *Three Modern Italian Poets: Saba, Ungaretti, Montale.* New York: New York Univ. Press; London: London Univ. Press, 1969.

Cassuto, Umberto. *Dante e Manoello.* Florence: Israel, 5682 [1921].

Cavaglion, Alberto, ed. *Ebrei senza saperlo.* Naples: L'ancora del mediterraneo, 2002.

———. *La filosofia del pressappoco: Weininger, sesso, carattere e la cultura del Novecento.* Naples: L'ancora del Mediterraneo, 2001.

———. "La scelta di Gedeone: Appunti su Primo Levi e l'ebraismo." *Journal of the Institute of Romance Studies* 4 (1996): 187–98.

———. *Primo Levi: Il presente del passato.* Milan: Franco Angeli, 1991.

Cicioni, Mirna. "Insiders and Outsiders: Discourses of Oppression in Giorgio Bassani's *Gli occhiali d'oro.*" *Italian Studies* 41 (1986): 101–15.

———. *Primo Levi: Bridges of Knowledge.* Oxford: Berg, 1995.

Contini, Gianfranco. *Poeti del Duecento.* 2 vols. Milan: Ricciardi, 1960.

———. "Preliminari sulla lingua del Petrarca." Preface to Francesco Petrarca, *Canzoniere.* Turin: Einaudi, 1964.

Curiel, Riccardo. "Un'autobiografia senza protagonista." *Rassegna mensile di Israel* (July–Aug. 1963): 346 48.

David, Michel. *Letteratura e psicoanalisi.* Milan: Mursia, 1967.

———. *La psicoanalisi nella cultura italiana.* Turin: Boringhieri, 1966.

———. *La psicoanalisi nella cultura italiana.* Turin: Bollati Boringhieri, 1990.

De Angelis, Luca. *Qualcosa di più intimo: Aspetti della cultura ebraica del Novecento italiano: Da Svevo a Bassani.* Preface by Alberto Cavaglion. Florence: Giuntina, 2006.

Debenedetti, Giacomo. *Intermezzo.* Milan: Mondadori, 1963.

———. *October 16, 1943: Eight Jews.* Translated by Estelle Gilson with a preface by Alberto Moravia. Notre Dame, Ind.: Univ. of Notre Dame Press, 2001.

Del Monte, Crescenzo. *Sonetti giudaico-romaneschi, sonnetti romaneschi, prose e versioni.* Edited by Micaela Procaccia and Marcello Teodonio. Florence: Giuntina, 2008.

Derrida, Jacques. *Archive Fever: A Freudian Impression.* Chicago: Univ. of Chicago Press, 1995.

DiNapoli, Thomas P., ed. *The Italian Jewish Experience.* Stony Brook, N.Y.: Forum Italicum, 2000.

Disegni, Rav Dario, ed. *Bibbia ebraica: Pentateuco e Haftaroth.* Florence: Giuntina, 1995.

Eatherly, Claude, and Günther Anders. *Burning Conscience: The Case of the Hiroshima Pilot, Claude Eatherly, Told in His Letters to Günther Anders.* Edited by Bertrand Russell. London: Weidenfeld and Nicolson, 1961.

Felman, Shoshana, and Laub Dori. *Testimony: Crises of Witnessing in Literature, Psychoanalysis, and History.* New York: Routledge, 1992.

Ferrero, Ernesto, ed. *Primo Levi: Un'antologia della critica.* Turin: Einaudi, 1997.

Fiedler, Leslie. *Fiedler on the Roof: Essays on Literature and Jewish Identity.* Boston: David R. Godine, 1991.

Foa, Vittorio. *Il Cavallo e la Torre: Riflessioni su una vita.* Turin: Einaudi, 1991.

Folena, Gianfranco, ed. *Tre narratori: Calvino, Primo Levi, Pavese.* Padova (Padua): Liviana, 1989.

Fontanella, Luigi. "Natalia Ginzburg between Fiction and Memory: A Reading of *Le voci della sera* and *Lessico famigliare.*" In *Natalia Ginzburg: A Voice of the Twentieth Century.* Edited by Angela M. Jeannet and Giuliana Sanguinetti Katz. Toronto: Univ. of Toronto Press, 2000.

Freud, Sigmund. *The Standard Edition of the Complete Psychological Works of Sigmund Freud.* Translated and edited by James Strachey, 24 vols. London: Hogarth Press, 1953–1974.

Gilman, Sander. *The Jew's Body.* New York: Routledge, 1991.

Ginzburg, Natalia. *Cinque romanzi brevi.* Turin: Einaudi, 1964.

———. *The City and the House.* Translated by Dick Davis. New York: Arcade, 1989.

———. *Dear Michael: A Novel.* Translated by Sheila Cudahy. London: Owen, 1975.

———. "È davvero una servitù? Essere donna." *La Stampa,* April 15, 1973.

———. *The Family and Borghesia.* Translated by Beryl Stockman. Manchester: Carcanet, 1988.

———. "Fra guerra e razzismo" (review of Primo Levi's "Argon,"), *Corriere della Sera*, May 25, 1975. Reprinted in *Primo Levi*, ed. Marco Belpoliti (Milan: Marcos y Marcos, 1998).

———. *It's Hard to Talk about Yourself*. Edited by Cesare Garboli and Lisa Ginzburg. Translated by Louise Quirke. Chicago: Univ. of Chicago Press, 2003.

———. *Lessico famigliare*. Introduction by Cesare Garboli. Turin: Einaudi, 1999.

———. *The Little Virtues*. Translated by Dick Davis. Manchester: Carcanet, 1985.

———. *Never Must You Ask Me*. Translated by Isabel Quigly. London: Joseph, 1973.

———. *Non possiamo saperlo: Saggi 1973–1990*. Edited by Domenico Scarpa. Turin: Einaudi, 2001.

———. *Opere: Raccolte e ordinate dall'autore*. 2 vols. Edited by Cesare Garboli. Milan: Mondadori, 1987.

———. *A Place to Live and Other Selected Essays of Natalia Ginzburg*. Translated by Lynne Sharon Schwartz. New York: Seven Stories Press, 2002.

———. "Se vien meno la memoria." *Rinascita*, no. 16 (May 27, 1990).

———. *The Things We Used to Say*. Translated by Judith Woolf. Manchester: Carcanet, 1997.

———. *Valentino and Sagittarius: Two Novellas*. Translated by Avril Bardoni. Manchester: Carcanet, 1987.

Gordon, Robert. *Primo Levi's Ordinary Virtues: From Testimony to Ethics*. Oxford: Oxford Univ. Press, 2001.

Gunzberg, Lynn M. *Strangers at Home: Jews in the Italian Literary Imagination*. Berkeley: Univ. of California Press, 1992.

Harrowitz, Nancy, and Barbara Hyams, eds. *Jews and Gender: Responses to Otto Weininger*. Philadelphia: Temple Univ. Press, 1995.

Hartman, Geoffrey H. *The Longest Shadow: In the Aftermath of the Holocaust*. Bloomington: Indiana Univ. Press, 1996.

———, ed. *Holocaust Remembrance: The Shapes of Memory*. Oxford: Blackwell, 1994.

Hawthorne, Nathaniel. *Selected Tales and Sketches*. Edited by Michael J. Colacurcio. New York: Penguin, 1987.

Hecht, Anthony. "St. Paul's Epistle to the Galatians." In *Melodies Unheard: Essays on the Mystery of Poetry*. Baltimore: Johns Hopkins Univ. Press, 2003.

Horkheimer, Max, and Theodor W. Adorno. *Dialectic of Enlightenment: Philosophical Fragments.* Edited by Gunzelin Schmid Noerr. Translated by Edmund Jephcott. Stanford: Stanford Univ. Press, 2002.

Hughes, Henry Stuart. *Prisoners of Hope: The Silver Age of the Italian Jews, 1924–1974.* Cambridge, Mass.: Harvard Univ. Press, 1983.

Jabès, Edmond. *The Book of Questions.* Translated by Rosmarie Waldrop. Middletown, Conn.: Wesleyan Univ. Press, 1976.

Jankélévitch, Vladimir. "Ressembler, dissembler." In *Sources,* 37–121. Paris: Seuil, 1984.

Jeannet, Angela M. "Natalia Ginzburg: Making a Story Out of History." In *Natalia Ginzburg: A Voice of the Twentieth Century.* Edited by Angela M. Jeannet and Giuliana Sanguinetti Katz. Toronto: Univ. of Toronto Press, 2000.

Jeannet, Angela M., and Giuliana Sanguinetti Katz, eds. *Natalia Ginzburg: A Voice of the Twentieth Century.* Toronto: Univ. of Toronto Press, 2000.

Jesurum, Stefano. *Essere ebrei in Italia.* Milan: Longanesi, 1987.

Kafka, Franz. *Kafka's the Metamorphosis and Other Writings.* Edited by Helmuth Kiesel. Translated by Volkmar Sander and Daniel Thersen. New York: Continuum, 2002.

———. *Letters to Milena.* Edited and translated by Philip Boehm. New York: Schocken Books, 1990.

———. *The Trial.* Translated by Richard Stokes. London: Hesperus Press, 2005.

Kertzer, David. *The Kidnapping of Edgardo Mortara.* New York: Vintage Books, 1998.

———. *The Popes against the Jews: The Vatican Role in the Rise of Modern Anti-Semitism.* New York: Alfred A. Knopf, 2001.

Kushner, Tony. *Thinking about the Longstanding Problems of Virtue and Happiness: Essays, a Play, Two Poems, and a Prayer.* New York: Theater Communications Group, 1995.

Lavagetto, Mario. *La gallina di Saba.* Turin: Einaudi, 1989.

Levi, Primo. *Collected Poems: New Edition.* Translated by Ruth Feldman and Brian Swann. London: Faber and Faber, 1992.

———. *The Drowned and the Saved.* Translated by Raymond Rosenthal. New York: Summit Books, 1988.

———. *If Not Now, When?* Translated by William Weaver. New York: Summit Books, 1985.

———. *If This Is a Man, and The Truce.* Translated by Stuart Woolf. New York: Cardinal, 1992.

———. *La ricerca delle radici: Antologia personale.* Turin: Einaudi, 1981.

———. *Lilìt e altri racconti.* Turin: Einaudi, 1981.

———. *The Mirror Maker.* Translated by Raymond Rosenthal. New York: Schocken Books, 1989.

———. *Moments of Reprieve.* Translated by Ruth Feldman. New York: Summit Books, 1986.

———. *The Monkey's Wrench.* Translated by William Weaver. New York: Summit Books, 1986.

———. *Opere,* 2 vols. Edited by Marco Belpoliti. Turin: Einaudi, 1997.

———. *Other People's Trades.* Translated by Raymond Rosenthal. New York: Summit Books, 1989.

———. *The Periodic Table.* Translated by Raymond Rosenthal. New York: Schocken Books, 1984.

———. *Racconti e saggi.* Turin: Editrice *La Stampa,* 1986.

———. *The Search for Roots: A Personal Anthology.* Translated by and edited by Peter Forbes. Chicago: Ivan R. Dee, 2002.

———. *Storie naturali.* Turin: Einaudi, 1966.

———. *Survival in Auschwitz.* Translated by Stuart Woolf. New York: Summit Books, 1986.

———. *The Voice of Memory: Interviews 1961–1987.* Edited by Marco Belpoliti and Robert Gordon. Translated by Robert Gordon. New York: New Press, 2001.

Levi Della Torre, Stefano. *Mosaico: Attualità e inattualità degli ebrei.* Turin: Rosenberg and Sellier, 1994.

———. *Zone di turbolenza: Intrecci, somiglianze, conflitti.* Milan: Feltrinelli, 2003.

Levinas, Emmanuel. *Beyond the Verse: Talmudic Readings and Lectures.* Translated by Gary D. Mole. Bloomington: Indiana Univ. Press, 1994.

Lilla, Mark. "Slouching towards Athens." *New York Review of Books,* June 23, 2005, 46–48.

Magris, Claudio. *Lontano da dove: Joseph Roth e la tradizione ebraico-orientale.* Turin: Einaudi, 1971.

Marcovecchio, Aldo. "Saba e il 'celeste scolaro.'" *Il Giornale,* Nov. 10, 1985.

Mattioni, Stelio. *Storia di Umberto Saba.* Milan: Camunia, 1989.

Mauro, Walter. "Walter Mauro parla con Natalia Ginzburg." In *Natalia Ginzburg: La narratrice e i suoi testi.* Edited by Walter Mauro et al. Rome: La Nuova Italia Scientifica, 1986.

Mauro, Walter, et al. *Natalia Ginzburg: La narratrice e i suoi testi.* Rome: La Nuova Italia Scientifica, 1986.

Meier, Christian. *From Athens to Auschwitz: The Uses of History.* Cambridge, Mass.: Harvard Univ. Press, 2005.

Melville, Herman. *Moby-Dick or The Whale.* Evanston, Ill.: Northwestern Univ. Press, 2001.

Milano, Attilio. *Storia degli ebrei in Italia.* Turin: Einaudi, 1963.

Milano, Paolo. "Una famiglia come romanzo." *L'espresso.* Apr. 14, 1963.

Momigliano, Arnaldo. *Alien Wisdom: The Limits of Hellenization.* Cambridge: Cambridge Univ. Press, 1975.

———. *Essays on Ancient and Modern Judaism.* Edited and with an introduction by Silvia Berti. Chicago: Univ. of Chicago Press, 1994.

———. *Saggezza straniera: l'ellenismo e le altre culture* (Turin: Einaudi, 1980), 159–60.

Montale, Eugenio. *New Poems: A Selection from "Satura" and "Diario del '71 e del '71."* Translated by G. Singh. New York: New Directions, 1976.

Neher, André. *The Exile of the Word: From the Silence of the Bible to the Silence of Auschwitz.* Translated by David Maisel. Philadelphia: Jewish Publication Society of America, 5741 [1981].

Nieger, Ada. *Bassani e il mondo ebraico.* Naples: Loffredo, 1983.

Nietzsche, Friedrich. *Ecce Homo and The Antichrist.* Translated by Thomas Wayne. New York: Algora, 2004.

Nirenstein, Fiamma. "Il dovere dell'identità." Fondazione Magna Carta, Roma. Dec. 17, 2005. http://www.magna-carta.it/indice.asp (accessed Dec. 17, 2005).

O'Neill, Eugene. *Long Day's Journey into Night.* New Haven: Yale Univ. Press, 1989.

Ozick, Cynthia. *Quarrel and Quandary.* New York: Knopf, 2000.

Pasolini, Pier Paolo. "La storia di Bassani scrittore cominciò con un dubbio: F o Ferrara?" In Pier Paolo Pasolini, *Saggi sulla letteratura e sull'arte,* 2:1990–94. Edited by Walter Siti and Silvia De Laude. 2 vols. Milan: Mondadori, 1999.

Patruno, Nicholas. *Understanding Primo Levi.* Columbia: Univ. of Southern Carolina, 1995.

Pflug, Maja. *Natalia Ginzburg, arditamente timida: Una biografia.* Translated from the German by Barbara Griffini. Milan: La tartaruga, 1997.

Popper, Karl. *The Open Society and Its Enemies.* New York: Harper, 1962.

Proust, Marcel. *Remembrance of Things Past*. Vol. 1, *Swann's Way*. Translated by C. K. Scott Moncrieff. New York: Modern Library, 1956.

Pugliese, Stanislao G., ed. *The Legacy of Primo Levi*. New York: Palgrave Macmillan, 2005.

———. *The Most Ancient of Minorities: The Jews of Italy*. Westport, Conn.: Greenwood, 2002.

Quarsiti, Maria Luisa. *Natalia Ginzburg: Bibliografia 1934–1996*. Florence: Giunti, 1996.

Quinzio, Sergio. *Radici ebraiche del moderno*. Milan: Adelphi, 1990.

Roditi, Edouard. "The Great Tradition of Italian-Jewish Literature." *Midstream: A Monthly Jewish Review* (November 1984): 53–55.

Romano, Immanuel. *L'Inferno e il Paradiso*. Edited by Giorgio Battistoni. Translated by Emanule Weiss Levi. Preface by Amos Luzzatto. Florence: Giuntina, 2000.

———. *Mahbereth Prima (Il destino)*. Edited by Stefano Fumagalli and M. Tiziana Mayer. Milan: Aquilegia, 2002.

———. *Tophet and Eden (Hell and Paradise): In Imitation of Dante's "Inferno and Paradiso."* Edited and translated by Hermann Gollancz. London: London Univ. Press, 1921.

Roth, Cecil. *The History of the Jews of Italy*. Philadelphia: Jewish Publication Society of America, 5706 [1946].

Ruderman, David, ed. *Essential Papers on Jewish Culture in Renaissance and Baroque Italy*. New York: New York Univ. Press, 1992.

Saba, Umberto. *Atroce paese che amo: Lettere famigliari (1945–1953)*. Edited by Gianfranca Lavezzi and Rossana Saccani. Milan: Bompiani, 1987.

———. *Ernesto*. Translated by Mark Thompson. New York: Carcanet, 1987.

———. *History and Chronicle of the Songbook*. Translated by Stephen Sartarelli. Riverdale-on-Hudson, N.Y.: Sheep Meadow Press, 1998.

———. *La spada d'amore: Lettere scelte 1902–1957*. Edited by Aldo Marcovecchio and introduced by Giovanni Giudici. Milan: Mondadori, 1983.

———. *Lettere sulla psicoanalisi: Carteggio con Joachim Fliescher 1946–1949*. Edited by Arrigo Stara. Milan: SE, 1991.

———. Preface to Federico Almansi, *Poesie (1938–1946)*. Florence: Fussi, 1948.

———. *Songbook: Selected Poems from the "Canzoniere" of Umberto Saba*. Translated by Stephen Sartarelli. Riverdale-on-Hudson, N.Y.: Sheep Meadow Press, 1998.

————. *The Stories and Recollections of Umberto Saba*. Translated by Estelle Gilson. Riverdale-on-Hudson, N.Y.: Sheep Meadow Press, 1993.

————. *Tutte le poesie*. Edited by Arrigo Stara. Introduction by Mario Lavagetto. Milan: Mondadori, 1988.

————. *Tutte le prose*. Edited by Arrigo Stara. Introduction by Mario Lavagetto. Milan: Mondadori, 2001.

————. *Umberto Saba: An Anthology of His Poetry and Criticism*. Translated by Robert Harrison. Troy, Mich.: International Book Publishers, 1986.

Saba, Umberto, and Pierantonio Quarantotti Gambini. *Il vecchio e il giovane: Carteggio 1930–1957*. Edited by Linuccia Saba. Milan: Mondadori, 1965.

Saint-Exupéry, Antoine de. *Wind, Sand, and Stars*. Translated by L. Galantière. New York: Harcourt and Brace, 1949.

Sanvitale, Francesca. "I temi della narrativa di Natalia Ginzburg: Uno specchio della società italiana," in *Natalia Ginzburg: La narratrice e i suoi testi*, ed. Walter Mauro et al. (Rome: La Nuova Italia Scientifica, 1986), 24.

Scarpa, Domenico. *Cronistoria di "Lessico famigliare."* Appendix to *Lessico famigliare*, by Natalia Ginzburg, 247–50. Introduction by Cesare Garboli. Turin: Einaudi, 1999.

Sereni, Clara. *Keeping House: A Novel in Recipes*. Translated by Giovanni Miceli Jeffries and Susan Briziarelli. Albany: State University of New York Press, 2005.

Shakespeare, William. *The Merchant of Venice*. Edited by M. M. Mahood. Cambridge: Cambridge Univ. Press, 2003.

Sodi, Risa B. *A Dante of Our Time: Primo Levi and Auschwitz*. New York: P. Lang, 1990.

Sontag, Susan. *Illness as Metaphor*. New York: Farrar, Straus, and Giroux, 1978.

Sophocles. *Philoctetes*. Edited by R. G. Ussher. Warminster, UK: Aris and Phillips, 1990.

Steiner, George. *No Passion Spent: Essays, 1978–1995*. New Haven: Yale Univ. Press, 1996.

Stille, Alexander. *Benevolence and Betrayal: Five Italian Jewish Families under Fascism*. New York: Summit Books, 1991.

Thomson, Ian. *Primo Levi: A Life*. New York: Metropolitan Books, 2003.

Ward, David. "Natalia Ginzburg's Early Writings in *L'Italia libera*," in *Natalia Ginzburg: A Voice of the Twentieth Century*. Edited by Angela M. Jeannet and Giuliana Sanguinetti Katz. Toronto: Univ. of Toronto Press, 2000.

Weininger, Otto. *Sex and Character: An Investigation on Fundamental Principles.* Edited by Daniel Steuer and Laura Marcus. Bloomington: Indiana Univ. Press, 2005.

Wirth-Nesher, Hana, ed. *What Is Jewish Literature?* Philadelphia: Jewish Publication Society, 1994.

Yerushalmi, Yosif Hayim. *Freud's Moses: Judaism Terminable and Interminable.* New Haven: Yale Univ. Press, 1991.

———. *Zakhor: Jewish History and Jewish Memory.* Introduction by Harold Bloom. Seattle: Univ. of Washington Press, 1982.

Young, James E. *Writing and Rewriting the Holocaust: Narrative and the Consequences of Interpretation.* Bloomington: Indiana Univ. Press, 1988.

Zuccotti, Susan. *The Italians and the Holocaust: Persecution, Rescue, and Survival.* Introduction by Furio Colombo. Lincoln: Univ. of Nebraska Press, 1996.

———. *Under His Very Windows: The Vatican and the Holocaust.* New Haven: Yale Univ. Press, 2000.

Index